Elephants In The Sunset

Random Jaunts Around Africa

By

Geoffrey Leo

ISBN: 9798488425231

Also by the author:

Laughter On The Bus, Random Jaunts Around The Americas

Sunshine On The Water, Random Jaunts Around Asia

Acknowledgements:

I would like to thank all of the people and organisations who have helped and guided me safely and mostly soundly to and from all of the destinations found in this book. A special thank you must go to Linzi Cooke, who has edited and guided my writing throughout. It was she who suggested "Fishy Faeces" to be the title of a heavy metal group.

As always, all profits from this publication will go to Compton Care Wolverhampton's excellent centre for palliative care.

This book is dedicated to:

Daniella, Adam, Natalie and Kelsey
The bringers of grandchildren

And in Loving Memory of

Edna May Leo (nee Wythe)
1928 - 2013

Alan William Leo
1947 -2017

John Henry Leo
1959 - 2020

Contents

Introduction

Africa, the dark continent, as it was known well into the last century.

We now know this is no longer the case.

There are so many Africas. Africans themselves see it as one land, a horse's head (revolve your atlas to the left). They are proud of this land and its diverse peoples, cultures, landscapes and histories. The borders and different countries were artificially created during the European Scramble for Africa in the age of New Imperialism, brought to a halt by the Great War. Borders split tribes, brought others into conflict and rarely took into account the natural evolution, created over millennia, of the people and their land.

For outside observers, it's easy to look at Africa and see one great divide. In the north there are the Arab countries. Then comes the Sahara Desert, the size of the USA. And south of this, what we simplistically refer to as sub-Saharan Africa: Black Africa.

In all there are 58 countries, amassing a population in excess of 1.3 billion. As well as the Sahara, the largest desert in the world, and the Namib, the oldest, there is the longest river, The Nile, from which sprang the Egyptians, the first great civilisation. Out of the Great Rift Valley homo sapiens evolved to migrate and conquer the world. The forests and savannahs are home to great populations of mammals, from the alpha predators of lion, leopard and cheetah to the giant herbivores, elephant, rhino and hippo. There are sweeping herds of antelope, gazelle, wildebeast and giraffe, and the primates: monkeys and ape, baboon, chimpanzee and gorilla. Its highest mountain, Kilimanjaro takes you from the equator to the Arctic in 19,000 feet. The eastern coast has the Indian Ocean with its great coral reefs; to the west the hot and steamy Atlantic; and in the north the Mediterranean, the very cradle of civilisation.

I am an explorer, an adventurer, following in the footsteps of the greats, Burton, Livingstone and Stanley, Palin and Fiennes, Lumley, Levinson Wood and Ranganathan. In my mind my mission is to boldly go, to discover people and places, flora and fauna, and experience adrenalin-fuelled, swashbuckling adventure. But to my family I am simply a hapless tourist, a teacher with his head stuck in the clouds, a fantasist, gallivanting abroad on holiday.

Be that as it may, my misadventures have taken me to the Americas; North, South and Central, to Asia; the Levant, the Orient and beyond. There has been Laughter On The Bus and Sunshine On The Water. Now I am in Africa, seeking Elephants In The Sunset.

Here goes.

Chapter One

Morocco

The Storks of Marrakesh

Who wouldn't want to travel on the Marrakesh Express, taking you to Marrakesh. Surely you'd have to find a gin joint in Casablanca and ask Sam to play As Time Goes By. And trek into the Atlas mountains, to live with the Berbers.

This jaunt took place in the olden days, before booking.com or even Ask Jeeves. I would have to study a Rough Guide and telephone long distance to speak to actual people in order to secure rooms or book tickets. And I did it all in French. Kaz was well impressed.

Morocco stands at the north west corner of Africa and has the distinction (with France and Spain) of being one of only three countries to have coastlines on both the Mediterranean and the Atlantic. Officially a Kingdom, its capital is Rabat, my first port of call was Casablanca. It should have been a mere four hours, but before Easyjet and Ryanair made European citybreaks a middle class weekend pastime, Morocco wasn't really on the tourist map. Still 21st century though.

The first leg was a midnight express bus from Wolverhampton on a Friday night. I had to wait 25 freezing minutes as the pubs and clubs emptied. It was a little threatening. I slept till Heathrow, faced an interminable check-in behind a 'large' family, endured a fire alarm mini-evacuation, then flew to Brussels. From Brussels to Casablanca was indeed four hours. I arrived at 1pm, realised the next train into Cas wasn't until 3, so took an expensive taxi the 30 miles to the Hotel du Centre. The journey was a revelation as we passed green meadows full of orange, yellow and purple flowers with families picnicking in woodland glades. Didn't seem very deserty.

Casablanca

I was deposited at the hotel, which was a little dated and dingy, but adequate, even if it did have the smallest and possibly oldest lift in the world.

You can smell Africa. In the cities and villages, jungles and plains, beaches and deserts, Africa has a distinctive odour. It is almost impossible to put a finger on it, but there will be the faintest scent of woodsmoke, mixed with elephant dung, possibly cinnamon or nutmeg and topped off with a hint of freshly mown grass.

I took myself into the city, walking through the Medina, the ancient market place, past the derelict cathedral and onto palm-lined boulevards. I stopped at a cafe on the Place Mohammed V and watched the crowds pass by. The roads were busy if not choked and there was a mix of private and commercial vehicles. Pigeons vied for attention with the mint-tea vendors. For Africa things seemed relaxed, perhaps the French influence.

I commandeered a petit-taxi for the short journey to the Mosquée Hassan II, which was absolutely wonderful. I couldn't enter, - a guard asked "Vous n'êtes pas Musselman?" - but wandered around the courtyards and perimeter. It was built on a short promontory and, therefore rises out of the sea. It is the second biggest Mosque on the continent, and its squared minaret is the second highest in the world. The place is beautiful, with marble and tile facades all decorated in the most intricate blue and green geometric patterns.

I walked back through the Medina and a realisation struck me. Here were a variety of narrow souks, each specialising in food, or carpets, or metalwork, or shoes, or whatever. On the outside and around the edges, unofficial traders simply throw down a piece of cardboard upon which to display their wares. The Medina is a hill, and I understood. This hill had evolved from all the detritus of history; rubbish and leavings gradually being trodden in over the centuries and becoming part of the whole.

I returned to the hotel and slept. Awake at eight, I found a bar for beers and poulet-frites. This had been quite a day. Since Brussels, I'd not spoken a word of English nor seen another European face, and I had managed to ward off various accostings with a confident French defence. The only disconcerting moment was when a child beggar wrapped herself around me. Prising her off my leg was no mean feat.

I had discovered this was not a city to visit expecting to relive the Casablanca film experience. There were no gin joints; this was no wartime neutral city in which unprincipled but well-meaning French, British, American and German parties uneasily circled in a cold war style spy romance. And no-one sings As Time Goes By. This is a modern Arab-Muslim city, wealthy for Africa, and very confident in its own skin. Rick and Louis might have struck up a beautiful friendship, but their like and the likes of Sam and Ilse and Victor had left many decades before.

I awoke to a glorious sunny day. It was over 20 degrees but watching the local populace scurrying to work from a couple of floors above, they were all in heavy coats. At least no hats, scarves and gloves. I breakfasted en francais, that is to say, coffee and croissants, baguette and jam.

I resolved to walk, once again to the Mosquée. Yesterday the tide had been out, now it was up and the sound of breaking waves added to the majesty of the whole place. The Mosquée dwarfs St Peter's in Rome, but its position out on the ocean gives it a special appeal. And still I couldn't go in. I was one of about only 50 people in an area the size of what, four football fields?

After a while I stepped back, across the coast road, to take in the whole building, and I could see the religious power. Here was the greatest work? that man could achieve to worship their God, but even this paled compared to God's nature that surrounded it. Perfect peace and solitude, another of His gifts

I walked said coast road towards the suburb of Ain Diab as it became a corniche above the beaches. There were beach clubs, which were either in serious disrepair or totally derelict, quite sad. I know this was the end of the season, but these seemed to reflect a serious downturn in fortunes. I found two open; one was private, but the Club Italienne allowed me to swim and sunbathe provided I took lunch there. This was a very acceptable pasta in gorgonzola cream, with drinks. It was almost like being on holiday. Already someone tried to sell me a tee-shirt.

I had booked an evening bus to Essaouira so made my way back into town. Foolishly I then made the mistake that all British travellers, however experienced, will occasionally commit. I came down the steps of a posh hotel, having used its amenities, spotted a petit-taxi to my right, hurried across the path, hailed it then headed across the road. At the last moment I glanced left to see two cars and a motorbike bearing down on me. I took a step back as they rushed past. One second later, and splat.

At 5pm I was seated at the Cafe de France, just off the Medina, next to the clock tower. It was Sunday evening and there was a hubbub of traffic about me, both vehicular and pedestrian, There was a cacophony of whistling and hooting. The bus arrived and I took myself upstairs to sit at the front, the best seat, above the driver. Soon out of Casablanca, we headed south, verdant and fertile land on both sides and occasionally the Atlantic Ocean to our right. It was a single carriageway road, but we made good progress. At 6:30 there was the most amazing sunset, red sky all around, but with the night came a new phenomenon.

Headlights on, the bus careered down the centre of the road. Occasionally there would be headlights from the other direction, lorry, car or bus, and they were doing the same, hurtling up the middle of the road. And it was only at the last second that we both swerved to the right. From my position on high, the manoeuvre was quite disconcerting. After this afternoon's little lapse of concentration, I was glad I wasn't driving.

Essaouira

The Mumtaz Express was six hours, not the 4½ I was promised and we arrived at well past eleven. The town appeared shut. The hotel was most definitely locked up for the night, but I managed to wake the night porter who led me to my room. This was a dank affair in the basement, with no window, and with toilet and shower actually in the room. It begged the question; was I in a room with en suite, or a toilet with a bed? I managed to find a bar and had a couple of beers. But this is a town popular with the cerf-volants, sail boarders. When a couple of young drunks became a little too friendly, I made my way back to the hotel where thankfully the night porter came quickly to my rescue.

I slept well and late before falling into a cold shower. Breakfast however was superb, then I made my way to the ramparts.

Essaouira is a walled port on the Atlantic, built by the Portuguese, hence a reminder of Galle, my favourite town of Sri Lanka. The views from the ramparts were très panoramique. Below ran the narrow souks which were very Arab and full of merchants. I had previously noted that beyond the walled town, the architecture was French colonial, such a mix of peoples. In the souks the shops were all narrow and crammed with goods. Sometimes it was difficult to see the shopkeeper, seated camouflaged amongst his wares. I was most impressed with the ateliers, workshops where craftsmen made their goods in tiny spaces, displayed outside. The patisseries similarly.

I wandered the sometimes crowded alleyways, but there was no hassle, this was a very relaxed place, possibly a hangover from its reputation as a hippy paradise in the 1960's. Returning to the ramparts above I wandered to the port with its colourful fishing boats, watched some fish butchery, was deposited on from a great height by a generous gull, and took lunch on a terrasse overlooking the ocean. It was warm but breezy, and I decided I'd return to this very spot for the sunset. It was easy to see why they call this place La Perle du Maroq.

Lunch was a tagine de cervettes, a little like a prawn balti, with a baguette. Below the ramparts, the ocean crashed onto the rocks, so I headed for the beach, a huge semicircle of soft sand washed by the lagoon, above which the surf boarders fly.

Whilst paddling I became aware I had been joined by a camel splashing beside me. She was accompanied by Yousuf, a young Berber dressed in a blue djellaba and turban. He assured me a trip on his camel usually cost 250 dirham, but for me, as I was alone, he would charge only 50dm, about £3. Well, why not? Touristy, I know, and camels are not comfortable, but it would pass the time.

It proved a superb trip. Yousuf took me all along the wide sweep of beach passed the Berber village to the ruined castle at the southern end, and back. So impressed was I, I gave Yousuf an extra 20 dm's, to treat his camel.

I returned to the hotel and tried to change my dank, dismal, unlockable room. "Oh, if only you had asked this morning, Monsieur Leo, but now all rooms are full." I'm English, I didn't complain.

I bought a couple of small bottles of cold beer to help me watch the sunset, the antics of two herons and a platoon of red-footed sandpipers running in and out of the surf comically in unison.

In a shed next to the port, a fish auction was taking place. I watched and listened for a while, fascinated by the goings on, but hadn't the foggiest who was bidding how much for what catch, nor when the gavel fell, but once more, it passed the time.

Evenings for the solo traveller can be a difficult time. Last night I spent it on a bus, and I have a bus booked for 4 pm tomorrow, but what to do now? Well, first to dine. And I dined superbly on a fresh fish, cooked at a gaslit stall where I sat on the attached bench, overlooking the ocean. The fish, called a poigeot royale was a sea bream, and was grilled spatchcock style.

Later I met an Irish couple, here for the surfing who didn't even know that Morocco had a Casablanca ("What, like in the fillum?"), and an English couple who warned me off Marrakesh. "Too much hassle," they complained. "They'll target you being on your own." Charming.

One thing that always amazes people I meet is my full itinerary. After all, I've done both Cas and Essaouira, and I'm off to Marrakesh tomorrow, yet I've been away only half a week. What amazes me, is how little other travellers do. I remember David who had spent three months of his gap year and had yet to leave Panama, and Andrew who had been in Cairo a whole week without seeing the pyramids. "Going tomorrow," he always promised.

Perhaps it's me, do I just skim places and only receive a flavour of the history and culture? This reminded me of the speed reader I once met. "Did War and Peace in an afternoon," she boasted, "It's about Russia!"

I woke and checked out of my toilet bedroom and had a few hours to kill in Essaouira before my late afternoon bus up to Marrakesh. I retraced my steps through the souks of the walled town, spending some time admiring the architecture of the various arches and little squares, especially enjoying the ancient beautifully carved heavy wooden doors and window shutters, sometimes natural, more often a sky blue to set off the gleaming, whitewashed walls. I browsed the shops awhile then climbed the stone steps to return to my preferred position, the ramparts and battlements overlooking the Atlantic, with rollers crashing onto the rocks beneath.

I took a long lunch at my favourite fish stall, a fried John Dory, delicious, and left Essaouira. Did I have regrets leaving such a Pearl? Of course. But I had done everything I wanted. It will always have a special place in my memory, but my itchy feet mean I have to move on. I couldn't have spent another night in the toilet room, nor anywhere else. When it is time to go, go.

Marrakesh

The bus took me east, climbing all the time as the verdant landscape gradually evolved into a rocky, scrubby terrain. We passed several villages with little white and grey adobe houses centred around a village square, shop and mosque. A few well-placed, scrawny, ancient acacia trees provided the essential shade. As we climbed and the rocks and earth grew redder, so did the houses.

I arrived in Marrakesh and a petit-taxi took me to my hotel. The Atlas promised to be just a few steps from the Fnaa. It was already night, and after checking into a comfortable room I took my first steps towards the Place of the Dead (probably an ancient execution site).

The Djemaa-el-Fnaa is simply a town square, perhaps a little bigger than a rugby pitch, surrounded on two sides by the walls of the old Medina, on top of which are overlooking restaurants. On the third side is the Koutoubia mosque with its impressive square minaret, then opening onto the new town from which I now entered. In Britain enlightened town planners would have built on it in the 1960's. Luckily the good Berbers of Marrakesh have preserved their history, now a major tourist attraction, which hasn't lost its centuries-old purpose.

I'll try to explain.

It was already dark and smoke and steam was rising from the food stalls. It hung in a pall, seeming to smother the place. But they were mainly on the periphery. Also patrolling around the outside were brightly dressed water sellers, carrying their tanks and brass cups, magnificent in their wide brimmed hats and flamboyantly bejewelled red djellabas. There was the occasional snake charmer, or juggler, or acrobatic troupe, but these were for the tourists. Berbers from the mountains sat cross-legged on flattened bits of cardboard, displaying their simple wares; cigarettes, tissues, cans of pop, perhaps, their Nokias displayed proudly beside them.

It was when I sidled behind them, onto the heart of the Fnaa, that I discovered the real magic. A small crowd had gathered around an old man. He was wizened and mostly bald, thin to the point of skinny, with perhaps three or fewer teeth, wearing a shabby cloak, and he walked with a stick. But this was more of a prop as he gesticulated wildly, prodding it at various members of his audience as his tale unfolded. He didn't need to shout; the assembled Moroccans listened intently, murmuring responses, nodding or shaking their heads at the appropriate junctures.

Here was the storyteller. This is the purpose of the Fnaa. Local people from the towns and villages, the coast or mountains make their pilgrimages to listen to the tales of the elders, the tales of their history, the tales their ancestors told, and the tales they will in turn tell to their children. The Fnaa is there to keep Berber history alive. Yes, there is an occasional tourist, like me, mingling with the crowds, with absolutely no idea what story is being told, but appreciating the telling. And he is not alone, this storyteller, there are more, dotted across the Fnaa, weaving their tales for posterity. I felt very privileged, and I must say, very safe indeed. There was no hassle in this very natural scene. Tourists weren't just tolerated; I had the feeling the locals were proud to show off their culture, proud to show how they celebrated the preservation of their chronicles.

I wandered for a while, taking all this in. There were comic acts as well; in one corner I found a troupe of actors performing slapstick in drag, then young male and female dancers whirling dervishly to pipe music.

I stopped at a stall and seated myself on the bench. "Could I have a special coke?" I asked tentatively.

"Oui, monsieur, blanc ou rouge?"

The stallholder poured me a plastic cup of red wine from a small barrel he kept beneath the counter. I had been advised of this little exercise in subterfuge, which is mainly used during the fast of Ramadan. Very useful.

I dined at the same stall, a dish of succulent fried white fish on the bone, a triangular bone. "Qu'est-ce que c'est?" I asked querulously. "Conga," came the reply.

I spent the rest of the night wandering around and taking in the sights and sounds of one of the most vibrant places in the world (and this happens every night), stopping only for the occasional special coke.I can't recall what time I took myself off to bed, but nothing had ceased, apart from my stamina.

My next experience of the Fnaa was quite surreal. I woke and breakfasted well on honeyed pancakes before eagerly going out to experience Marrakesh in the daytime. I strode to the Fnaa, and the first strange thing was the traffic. Vehicles were zooming around the Fnaa as if it was some huge traffic island (apparently the road is closed at 2pm). Once I eventually crossed onto the square I was shocked and amazed. It was empty. Everything, all the stalls, all the people had vanished. The place was just one huge vacuum. Where were all the stalls, how had they been removed, where were the people? And almost equally strange, after a gathering like that of the previous evening anywhere else in the world, the place would be full of litter, but no, it was clean. A very slight mound of impacted black earth. Empty, save for a few people like myself, wandering around and blinking in the bright sunshine, arms wide asking the same question. Where did it all go?

Some minutes later I had composed myself and resolved to find my way around Marrakesh's many other sites of interest. I began with the Koutoubia, circling the impressive minaret before heading through the narrow souks for the El Badi Palace.

There was one wonderful moment when I was sure I glimpsed a stork flying above in the small patch of sky I could see. A beautiful black and white bird with a huge wingspan, long legs and an impressive beak. A few yards further on and I saw a stork sitting on its nest atop an archway. I had to stop for the photo opportunity. Another few yards and there was a nest with two storks. Remarkable, another photo. Then I had to stop to admire two nests.

Eventually I reached the entrance to the palace and paid to go in. It must have been very impressive in its heyday, but now it was a sad ruin. I wandered the various courtyards and living quarters, sadly now just shells with orange trees and shrubbery growing amongst piles of stones. There were storks flying above, so for a moment I loved the peace and tranquillity of a grand palace returning to nature.

The El Badi had been the jewel in the crown of the Saadian dynasty in the 1600's, but fell into disuse, with its treasures and even building materials plundered for other projects, after the death of Sultan Al-Mansur.

I was reflecting on the sadness of the ruin as I climbed the stairs to the top of the surrounding walls where I was greeted by the most incredible sight. In the distance reflecting against the blue sky were the snow-capped peaks of the Atlas mountains, but here, on top of these perimeter walls were hundreds of stork nests. Birds flew in with building materials, and out to find more, others sat on their nests awaiting a partner, and in some of the nests sat both partners joyously clacking each other's beaks in a display of loyalty to one another. The Storks of Marrakesh. And to think, a little while earlier I had been excited to glimpse just the one.

I returned to the orange blossom for a while and continued my tour of the place grounds before coming back to the storks and their mountains, even brighter now with the sun higher.

It is impossible to see Moorish architecture without comparing to the Generalife in Spain's Granada, wonderfully preserved, especially the water gardens. That was why I found El Badi such a sad place. Sadder still were the Saadian tombs I visited next, but at least these were well preserved and a fair representation of the beauty of Moorish architecture and their interior designs.

I left the Saadian history to walk back into the pink city and was stopped by an English couple, the wife saying how the tombs were "Quaite lyavely!"

"How do we get to the Royal Palace?" asked the flustered husband.

"You'll have to marry a princess," I quipped, which amused his wife more than him.

I took lunch before visiting the 5 star hotel La Mamounia. This was Winston Churchill's chosen accommodation on many holidays in Marrakesh. It was to Marrakesh that he brought an ailing President Roosevelt after the Casablanca summit to decide how to defeat the Nazis in 1943. They both enjoyed the sunsets over the Atlas mountains, FDR declaring that he felt like a Sultan. He died before the war ended.

The hotel was sumptuous, and I enjoyed wandering the manicured gardens. There were birds and flowers and colours galore. Fish swam among the cascades and fountains of the water features, and I was sure I could hear the hoots and whistles of frogs amongst the tranquillity.

Feeling suitably relaxed I took a petit-taxi to the Jardin Majorelle, famously refurbished by Yves St Lauren. The gardens seemed smaller and more tightly planned than La Mamounia, and the avenues felt like a maze. Hence it was dark and sombre, not helped by the recent downpour a rogue cloud delivered. The rain appeared to have enhanced the floral aromas. This was a perfumed garden. Water features, blue mosaics, perfect symmetry and a museum of modern art, what could be better?

I had a sudden revelation, I was in the desert, doing gardens. Marrakesh is a remarkable oasis.

Eventually, quite wearily I returned to the hotel noting that even in late afternoon the Fnaa was still empty save for a few performing monkeys, a couple of snake charmers, some tourists (hence the monkeys and snakes) and the flamboyant water sellers.

I dozed until dusk, dreaming of storks, and returned to the Fnaa and was again astounded. It was packed with gaslit stalls, smoke rising into the air. The storytellers, acrobats, dance troupes had all returned, and so had the voyeurs and tourists. Where they had all come from, and how they had set up so quickly remained a mystery, but the evening entertainment was in full swing.

Again I thoroughly enjoyed listening in to the storytellers. I hadn't the foggiest what tales they were telling; for all I knew they could have been smutty jokes. I ate scrawny, tough fried chicken - should have kept to the eel - then crept home for an early night. Tomorrow I'm trekking in the High Atlas.

Tighze

Ibrahim was waiting in reception as I checked out. "Je reviendrai en quatre jours," I reminded the clerk who wished me 'bon chance', and we were away.

Hazel was already seated on the minibus as I entered and made a brief introduction. Ibrahim drove us to two more hotels where we picked up twin sisters Hannah and Kate, and married couple Derek and Chris, then we were out of Marrakesh on the main road to Ouzouarzet. After a couple of hours we turned left and started the inexorable climb into the mountains. It was spectacular and hairy, if slow going, winding up and up and up, and we eventually stopped for lunch in a tent outside the run-down fortress, the Kasbah of Telouet. "From here we are walking," explained Ibrahim.

Well-fed on a tagine of chicken, cous-cous and apricots, we stretched off, tightened our boots, checked water, hat, sunglasses and sunscreen, hauled on our back packs, and began the trek, single file, behind our leader, into the Atlas Mountains.

Toubkal at nearly 14,000 feet is the highest mountain in North Africa, but we wouldn't be attempting anything quite so ambitious. We'd have needed crampons, ropes and carabiners and all that paraphernalia. No, this expedition was a simple hike in the foothills, no higher than 2,500 metres (8,000 feet) and no more than 15 miles a day, in three big loops from our base camp, which we reached in 90 minutes. The Gite d'Etape (literally 'stopover') was very simple accommodation in the tiny village of Tighza.

On the trek up I'd been chatting with Derek and Chris, who were quite the celebrities. They were retired Brummies living in a static caravan near Aberystwyth where Derek supplemented his pension working as the camp odd job man; mowing and strimming, that sort of thing (he wasn't that camp, boom boom!).

They spent their time applying to go on television game shows. Chris had already been knocked out of the Chase by chaser Anne Hegarty having amassed only £3,000 in the cash builder. They had both appeared on Noel Edmunds' Deal or No Deal, sparring with the Banker and opening a box with a blue amount (below £1,000). They were most proud, however of their appearance on BBC's Bargain Hunt where everything they bought made a loss at auction, even their bonus buy.

As a group we started talking about the nature of celebrity, so many so-called Z listers appearing on reality shows like I'm a Celebrity Get Me Out Of Here.

Helen, the twins and I declared that we didn't think we had ever met any celebrities.

Then later, in my cell bed I began going over my history and realised I'd met a few. I told the gang some of my findings the next day on our trek.

As a boy scout I was featured in the Express and Star washing John Hanson's Rolls Royce. The famous British tenor was in Wolverhampton playing the Red Shadow from The Desert Song at the town's Grand Theatre.

Fast forward and my first wife, Sue, was Midlands Nurse of the Year, and came second in the national final. She was featured on Central television (ATV then?) and we met people like Bob Warman, Frank Ifield and Jean Morton. Dame Anna Neagle presented her with her prize.

My second wife. Giuseppina (Jo) - her brother, Giorgio, had been the guitarist with the 1960's pop/comic group, Freddie and the Dreamers. Every night on stage, Freddie pulled his trousers down.

(Chris interrupted, she was the niece of Slade drummer Don Powell. Impressive.)

I'd met Derek Dougan and Linford Christie, and knew most of the Wolves team of the 1970/80's, when I had been a coach working with John Barnwell, even tangling with big Ron Atkinson.

In the 1980's I had made several appearances on local Radio as spokesperson for a Birmingham College.

My father, bless his soul, had invented the Screw Ball, the plastic cone filled with soft ice cream, with a bonus bubbly in the bottom. For me that puts him on a par with Percy Shaw (cat's eyes) and James Dyson.

I used to tell my classes (and sometimes they would listen) that although I had played football, golf and rugby for all of my adult life, I had never been invited onto Question Of Sport, never even featured on the Picture Board. I had, I assured them, once been a Mystery Guest disguised as Santa, but neither team recognised me. Some bought it.

And then my Pièce de Résistance, a story I would tell new recruits at my rugby club.

We invited Prince Charles to present end of season prizes and awards to our colts in 1995. When he arrived, he was wearing a dead animal on his head. When I asked why, he told me he had had an audience with the Queen, that very morning.

"Where are you going today, Charles?" she had asked

"I told her, to Willenhall Rugby Club which is in Essington, Staffordshire, up Hobnock Road, off Bognop Road. That's when she told me."

"Told you what?"

"Wear the Fox Hat."

Helen mentioned that once on holiday to Barbados, she had met Glenn Hugill, then actor on Coronation Street who went on to become the Banker on Deal Or No Deal, and the conversation had come full circle.

The village of Tighza was tiny, no more than a scattering of mud-brick outhouses, with children playing and a few chickens scratching about in the dirt alongside the family mule. The mule was without doubt the main beast of burden in these hills.

The Gite at the top of the hill was no grander. Built on two levels, the sleeping quarters were below, with a communal mess and eating area above.

A large sign announced "Alcohol Interdit" as we were welcomed. My room was a windowless cell, no more than eight feet square, with a thin mattress laid out on the concrete floor. Toilets and showers down the corridor to the rear.

As I lowered my rucksack, unpacked and laid out my sleeping bag, I felt relieved I had secreted away a quarter bottle of Teachers (what else). Now I faced a dilemma. Did I share the whisky with my colleagues and become a camp hero, but risk having nothing left for our other two nights in the Gite, or do I keep it to myself like the tight git I have the reputation for being. Why should I be penalised because I had the foresight to be prepared?

Thus it was that evening we were seated on the lower terrace, looking down the valley as the sun set due west, drinking through straws the radio-active coloured orange Fanta from multi-recycled scratched bottles found all over Africa. There were a variety of old plastic, wooden, or metal chairs from which to choose, all in various states of brokenness. This place wasn't created for comfort.

We were chatting about previous trekking experiences. I mentioned my Asian experiences, where I had followed in the footsteps of greats like Moses, Lawrence of Arabia, Alexander the Great and Jeremy Clarkson. Helen was saying she'd also experienced the Annapurna Trail. The twins, who were quite self-centred giggled about their times rambling the Peak District. Chris and Derek confessed to enjoying rambling, but not the thought of climbing anything strenuous. Today's uphill struggle from the Kasbah had been as arduous as they would want. Ibrahim assured everybody there would be nothing too energetic ahead.

With the sun gone and the sky darkening I judged the group were ready for the story of my accidental groping of Judy. We were climbing the Cerro Negro in Nicaragua, a very young volcano, and I had stumbled over a volcanic cannon ball. Trying to find a foothold I trod on another round bomb with my secure foot. Judy was nearby and reached to steady me at the same time as I reached for something to save me. I managed to grab hold of her and and she caught me before I could fall. It was only as I was thanking her profusely that I realised I had a firm grip of her left breast. She smiled sweetly and said, "You can let go now". I looked at my hand, exclaimed in horror and released. Judy was very good about the whole matter.

We wondered whether the stories told by the old men on the Fnaa were of similar ilk.

The laughter was subsiding as I noticed a light in the sky. Venus, the evening star had appeared, and with the Earth continuing to turn east, she was gradually moving down towards the horizon.

"We've seen the sun set," I said, "in a few minutes Venus, being in the same Solar System will set in the same place." We continued to watch as the planet slowly sank beneath the horizon. Venus set

"Quickly!" I thought and shouted at the same time. "Let's run up the stairs."

I upped and went immediately, the others a little slower and slightly confused behind me. But I had been correct. When we reached the second storey terrace, the tiny bright light in the sky that had been Venus could still be seen. We had the great fortune to see it set for a second time.

We ate, more chicken stew with cous-cous, and crept off to our cells. After a few glugs from my secret bottle I was away, two inch mattress, cold concrete floor, sense of guilt, and celebrity thoughts and all.

Three days we trekked the Atlas. Wonderful walks where we experienced rivers and lakes, valleys and dales, and picnicked and snoozed and sun-bathed in sheltered glades with babbling brooks and gentle cascades. We had the most wondrous views of distant snow- capped mountains atop terraced slopes, and in the foreground the pinks and greens and reds of a boulder strewn shrubby landscape. Glorious weather and total peace and serenity in the land of the Berber. We'd laughed and told and retold stories and anecdotes of our experiences. We even discussed politics and pedagogy, religion and sport, society and culture. But there was something missing. Something we asked Ibrahim, for which he could find no answer.

Where was the wildlife? Apart from mules and fowl and goats, we'd seen nothing. These are the mountains that separate the Sahara from the Mediterranean, and we expected Barbary apes, like on Gibraltar, (really macaque monkeys), antelope and gazelle, leopard and badgers, ibis and eagle, perhaps the elusive Barbary Lion (what a wonderful thought, but the last one was shot in 1942). There had been nothing exotic, only a few rodents and crows. Well much of it might be nocturnal, but not all.

It was our only disappointment.

At the end of our second trek we had visited a village house. A very simple affair of red mud walls, rooms separated by ragged curtains, earth floors covered in threadbare carpets and limp cushions. There were small windows and low ceilings, mostly designed to keep the heat out, but with an awareness that winters at this altitude can be icy and cold.

Mama had prepared a simple meal of flat breads and oily dips and dates, with mint tea. We sat and dipped and ate, making appreciative noises, with her and her husband whilst their two small, ragamuffin children watched and giggled nervously. It was delicious, but there was something else, something ancient, even biblical. The simple process of breaking and sharing bread is a ritual that brings humanity together spiritually. We didn't share a language, except one with nods and smiles and laughter, and mutual respect. It was a special moment.

On our last night in the gite I experienced a bout of night najjers. This is an affliction with which I occasionally suffer, usually at altitude.

My journal entry read:

"04:28. Then the night najjers came. A dream turns into a nightmare and the characters morph into grotesque cartoon creatures with huge mouths and teeth which eat at the elements of your life, casting doubts and creating fears...Vampires of the Soul. I'm scared to turn on the light to take a sip of water, the concrete that surrounds me has become liquid and will swallow me should I stray from this mattress. 90 minutes away from get-up, I'm trapped in a pitch black cell with persistent nagging and torment which can drive you into insanity. Is it the price of sobriety or the consequences of guilt?"

Leaving the Gite d'Etape we walked back down to the Kasbah. Helen told me about her father. He had recently celebrated his 100th birthday, and he still played golf, the occasional 9 holes at Grasshoppers Rugby Club in Middlesex. I'd once been there, for a liquid lunch en route to Twickers. Now there's a target to aim for.

Remarkably it had snowed on the lower slopes, and there were drifts of ice to walk through.

I caught up on some much needed sleep as we drove back to Marrakesh. The seven of us agreed to meet up that evening in Ibrahim's favourite restaurant. In the meantime I had two more quests to undertake in Marrakesh.

In the early afternoon I left the hotel and crossed the Fnaa, empty save for a few tourists, walked past the Koutoubia and eventually encountered a long clay brick wall. The sun beat down from a perfect blue sky as beyond this wall I found the entrance to the Menara Gardens. These ancient gardens feature a huge central pool which reflect perfectly the surrounding fauna, the Atlas mountains and most spectacularly a Saadian pavilion. These are a lot less formal than the Majorelle, or Mamoudia, and feel more natural. I strolled and relaxed amongst the olive groves, orange orchards and cypresses. There were several families picnicking. With their woven baskets, cotton table cloths and seated attitudes, it could have been a scene from Enid Blyton.

Having enjoyed Menara I strolled back into the pink city and took one last look at El Badi Palace. Les Cigognes de Marrakesh. To see the storks again, flying to and fro, landing elegantly with wings flapping back into their huge nests of higgledy-piggledy twigs, and greeting their partners with exaggerated sword play clacks of their fine beaks. Wonderful.

They are, of course, revered here. Legend has it that an ancient Imam in black and white robes found himself drunk on wine and climbed the Koutoubia Minaret to make a nonsense of the Adhan call to prayer. An unforgiving God turned him into a stork. Berbers believe all storks are transformed humans, and in the city of Marrakesh the offence of disturbing a stork carries a three month prison sentence. I had no intention of disturbing this spectacular scene. Why haven't people always looked upon our wildlife with gracious appreciation instead of seeking to destroy it?

I returned to the city and had a haircut. Quite an experience, especially when with a finishing flourish my barber set fire to tissues which instantly incinerated the hairs from my ears.

I crossed the empty Fnaa back to my hotel, showered and readied myself, and returned to the Fnaa, now full, busy and smoky. I still didn't know how they did it.

The restaurant Ibrahim had chosen was one overlooking the Fnaa from the south eastern corner. I'd have preferred to eat at one of the stalls, but Ibrahim claimed they were dodgy. Not my experience. My trekking partners were waiting with him to greet me, and together we climbed the stairs.

What followed was awful. A waiter showed us to our table and explained there was a self-service buffet. From our table there was a definite smell of sewage, or at least bad drains. We asked to be reallocated, but the waiter shrugged saying this was the only table available. "Let's go back to the Fnaa," I ventured, but no, everyone was willing to put up with it.

"Ok, drinks. Six cold beers please?"

"Sorry, no alcohol"

"I'll have a special coke then," I winked.

"Only Coca here. Special coke downstairs on the Fnaa."

So we ordered Fantas and Cokes which came in dirty bottles with straws which might not necessarily have been single use.

The food was bland, with chewy meat, soggy rice, then dried up desserts. Even the coffee was only lukewarm.

And then came the bill. Helen divided it by six (we paid for Ibrahim, possibly why hc'd chosen this overpriced establishment) and then suggested 50 Dirhams each for a tip.

I was incensed. "Tip!" I exclaimed. "Tip!" I repeated with incredulity. "We been plonked here, next to a smelly toilet, had to help ourselves to garbage and experienced a total lack of service. Why on earth should we be expected to leave a tip?" Maybe my rant was a build up of frustrations caused by the Gite and lack of sleep. But I'm one of those people, I'm British, who believe that tipping, as the New Zealanders put it, is for wankers.

I think we fell out, and for the rest of the evening as we enjoyed the delights of the dancers, acrobats and storytellers on the Fnaa, I felt a little ostracised. In the end we exchanged frosty farewells. I did exchange email addresses with Chris and Derek, however. They've applied for Tipping Point.

The Question of Tipping

"Nothing appears to create more angst amongst customers than "What tip should I leave?" (apart from climate change, environmental damage and ecosystem destruction). But it is an issue, and can tie people up in knots. I am of the school that believes people like restaurant workers should be paid a living wage by their employers, and only receive extra rewards if their service goes beyond normal expectations. But if you live in America or Canada and you wish ever to be welcomed back into restaurants, diners, hairdressers, or any establishment providing a personal service, then it is the done thing always to leave a generous tip. There are books and articles written about what constitutes the correct level of tipping under a variety of circumstances. These also ask questions like Why do we tip taxi drivers but not bus drivers, Why waiters but not shop assistants, Why barbers and not dentists. Many people in "tipping" countries have to carry ready reckoners to work out their gratuity obligation. One of the problems Americans also face is that prices quoted are never those you pay, as taxes have to be added. Nightmare.

Don't get me wrong, I am quite happy to pay for a £39.50 meal with two £20 notes, and generously leave before change can be provided. Similarly if change in a shop comes to a few pence it is quite reasonable these days to simply nod towards the charity box. And it is also reasonable for a box marked "Gratuities" be left on the counter for your discretion. But when hotel porters hold their hands out for said gratuities, when their colleagues on the desk or in the kitchens will receive no share, then that is wrong. Similarly I absolutely abhor when I've seen Americans stuffing dollar bills into a waiter's top pocket, how horribly patronising. And then waiters actually chase you down the street, "Oi, what about a tip?", "OK, don't eat yellow snow or (in one case) don't spill the red wine" then it has become out of hand.

It is no wonder the practice of tipping has been outlawed in Japan and is similarly frowned upon in civilised countries like Australia and New Zealand.

I think there is also a problem when some establishments automatically add a gratuity to their bill. Are you within your rights to take that 10% off? Of course you are, but many people don't, and those who are less observant, or more tolerant are the ones the management are aiming this racket at. To my mind the practice is the height of impertinence.

Of course, different countries around the world have different norms meaning the international traveller needs to conduct relevant research prior to their visit, and act accordingly, as the locals.

Finally there is the consideration of the service that is actually performed in many countries, especially the aforementioned US of A. Apparently whenever a customer enters an establishment, immediately leaping to your side is the most sincere person hoping you are having a good day, are in perfect health, and declaring their deepest desire to help you with your deliberations. For some this epitomises the phrase "good customer service" whereas others might treat this instant best friend with the cynicism it deserves. I know I certainly do."

The Marrakesh Express

The next morning I was up at dawn to check out. I walked to the centre of a deserted Fnaa, did a full 360 and with jazz hands declared in my best Max Bygraves voice, "I wanna tell you a story!" Only a cat looked up.

I then hoisted my backpack and walked to the railway station. Ok, I was doing it the wrong way round, but today, wouldn't you know I'm riding on the Marrakesh (to Casablanca) Express. All aboard the train.

I was alone in a six-seater compartment in a 1950's carriage, hauled by a diesel locomotive. The romance doesn't include a steam engine, but save for the landscape this could be the Hogwart's Express.

And the landscape. Leaving the pink city of Marrakesh, we were soon into the pink desert. Mountains to my right. In the foreground was a scrubby and rocky terrain with many palm trees and the occasional olive grove. I could see the heat shimmer off the rocks as we sped beneath clear Moroccan skies to Casablanca. Three hours later we passed through the shanty town outskirts I'd not previously seen, a reminder we were in Africa.

There was a connection direct to the airport so all that was left was to rid myself of my remaining Dirhams. I had three 100 notes, two 20's and a ten. In the souvenir shop I noticed all of the prices were in Euros, so I asked the man at the till how much I had. He took the notes from me, and shuffled them around a couple of times, then he punched several figures into his calculator and wrote down the figure displayed on his screen. Finally he proudly announced:

"You have 350 Dirhams, Monsieur"

I concluded my shopping, flew to Brussels, then Heathrow and boarded the National Express to Wolverhampton, arriving at midnight again. I was in work for 8:30.

"Been anywhere nice?" asked Terri.

"Morocco." I answered.

"Oh, gallivanting again."

Chapter Two

Tunisia and Ancient Carthage

The northern most country of Africa is Tunisia. Cape Angela extends into the Mediterranean, while the southern extreme is considered the gateway to the Sahara Desert. On either side Tunisia borders Algeria and Libya, two countries sadly closed off to the casual visitor. No chance of gallivanting there.

I was happy to visit Tunisia, another French speaking country of north Africa, and home to the Carthaginians, an ancient civilisation which rivalled the Roman Empire. Hannibal, their most famous son, crossed the sea, the Pyrenees and the Alps with an army of elephants to defeat Rome. More of which later

Tunisia is now home to some pretty awful coastal resorts, full of hastily built mock-arabic hotels and fake medinas. Hammamet, Sousse and Port El Kantaoui are on the east coast, a short ride from the airport, and I stayed in the latter with Kaz. We were disappointed with the littered beaches, the sales pressure of the street traders, and the child beggars. I felt sorry for the children. One little group told us that if they didn't return home with their targetted income, they would be beaten. Mind you, another urchin tried to unzip my bumbag and steal its contents whilst his elder brother distracted us. I had a little less sympathy for these.

However, for a few days we enjoyed the sunshine and the pool, watched martins swooping to and from their nests on the balconies, and admired the tennis played at a remarkably high standard as the evenings cooled. We paraglided from the beach to an amazing height with other parachutes appearing as tiny bubbles beneath us. A highlight was horse riding along the beach at dawn, our steeds taking us into the sea up to their necks.

We took a day trip dolphin cruise. I neglected to mention to our fellow dolphin watchers that when it came to safaris, I was a Jonah, and sure enough we saw no dolphins. We even took advantage of the captain's guarantee "if we see no dolphins you can have another cruise tomorrow, free of charge". Sure enough the cetaceans remained hidden from view. No such assurance for a third trip, so I positioned myself on the beach to interrogate the returning passengers of that third day.

"Ha, so you didn't see any dolphins then!" I gloated

"Oh Ja. ve saw several schools, und sehr spectacular, for sure," confirmed a German family.

Why always me? I contemplated that evening, the fruitless dolphin and whale trips I had experienced. From Kenya's Diani Beach, great snorkelling and coral reefs and giant land crabs, but no dolphins. From Castletownshend in Ireland, near the Lusitania's sinking, famous for fin whales and minkes. We saw nothing but gannets, seals and mackerel. Nothing off Mexico's Yucatan peninsular at Tulum. At Florida's Keys I saw one manatee, but off Barbados' west coast in a catamaran, another blank. Newquay in mid Wales, we saw them in the harbour, but not on the boat trip.

I had finished with the beach and it was time to explore. Kaz was happy to stay behind on this first jaunt, and after visiting the aforementioned northern tip, I travelled to Dougga, probably the best preserved Roman township in North Africa.

The journey took me west, away from the built up coastal area, into farmland then up onto a plateau. I could just make out the eastern edge of the Atlas mountains marking the border with Algeria, but the most striking feature of the whole scene was this isolated city of ruins surrounded by countryside.

It was clambering time. There were temples, mausoleums, a market place and a wonderful forum. The streets, formerly full of dwellings were now olive groves, and for two hours I enjoyed these almost deserted Roman remains.

The town was well established for over 400 years before the Roman occupation, but the archaeological digs had concentrated less on its Berber and Punic history. Following the fall of Rome there was a Muslim invasion, and the town remained occupied until UNESCO took over and moved the remaining inhabitants a few miles down the road to New Dougga in 1991.

I listened in whilst Faisal, our youthful guide was describing the town's history to two mature American women.

"Dougga may have been the ancient city of Tocae, captured by the Greeks of Syracuse," he explained to the gum chewing ladies.

"Oaawh!" said one in a high pitched drawl. "Are there any Greeks still living here?"

I sniggered, caught Faisal's exasperated glance, and we moved on.

I continued my clambering in the warm sunshine as the cicadas trilled and on the breeze I could scent the Mediterranean pine. I found an olive tree atop the forum, and sat on the steps under its shade to eat my cheese salad baguette lunch.

Back on the bus and we continued west reaching the Commonwealth War Cemetery of Medjez El Bab. There are over 2,900 soldiers buried here, a place which marks the victory of the North African campaign in May 1943.

Further east Montgomery had inflicted the Axis' powers first defeat in the Second World War at El Alamein. The Germans and Italians had retreated to Northern Tunisia where they were joined by reinforcements from Sicily. More Allied forces had landed in Morocco and Algeria, and together with Monty's Eighth Army defeated Rommel's armies in a pincer movement.

As Churchill said, "Before El Alamein we never had a victory. After El Alamein, we never had a defeat!"

The atmosphere was much more sombre now as the tourists respectfully wandered the 18 plots of graves set in three rows of six columns. Each plot held up to 160 boys and men with their neat white headstones. The identities of 385 "known only unto God".

You find yourself with mixed feelings of pride and sadness. Pride that people from all over the world came together to liberate Africa from the fascist curse, but sadness that the campaign had cost the lives of over 400,000 on both sides.

We returned to our hotels on the coast a little chastened by the experience but with a reinforced intention to wear our poppies with extra humility this year.

The next day I visited Carthage with Kaz.

History, as we are told, is written by the winners. Hence we know a great deal more about the Roman Empire than we do of the almost equally successful and civilised Carthaginian Empire. Rome defeated Carthage in a series of three campaigns known as the Punic Wars. These lasted over 100 years, ending 146 years before the birth of Christ.

To ensure Carthage could never rise again, legend has it that following their final victory, the Romans poisoned the land. Beyond the normal raping and pillaging, this was a real act of destruction which also denied themselves the normal spoils of war.

Ancient Carthage now lies on the edge of Tunis. It was founded by Phoenician traders and over centuries grew into one of the most affluent cities in the classical world. In the third Punic war, the Roman consul, Scipio, besieged the city, finally destroying it and selling its 50,000 inhabitants into slavery. It was revived 100 years later as Roman Carthage, their capital in Africa. With the fall of the Roman Empire the city was sacked in 698 AD and became a Muslim caliphate. The Christian crusade of 1270 destroyed the city and massacred its inhabitants.

Now it is a less than impressive ruined city, its building materials having been pilfered to create modern Tunis. The ruins did merit a good two hours of clambering around its streets and houses and workshops, market places, forums, temples and graveyards. Built on an isthmus, although the ruins were sparse, every angle offered a never less than a wonderful view over the Gulf of Tunis.

You cannot leave Carthage without studying the campaigns of Hannibal, son of Barca. He commanded their forces during the second Punic war and is considered one of the greatest military leaders in world history. He most famously took a huge army which included North African War Elephants (a sub-species now extinct) across the Alps to attack Rome through their back door.

He was Carthage's commander in Iberia and drew up plans against Rome. His campaign began with the siege of Seguntum, an important pro-Roman settlement near modern day Valencia. With the city's sacking he had an important base from which to launch his attack, and had provoked the Romans to declare war. He had amassed an army of possibly 50,000 troops, including many mercenaries, 10,000 cavalry and 40 war elephants (historians differ in their opinions) and marched north through modern day Spain in the Spring of 248BC, "persuading" tribes he encountered to support his cause. He needed to secure supply lines.

Crossing the Ebro, his next major obstacle was the Pyrenees, which he negotiated successfully and entered the less than friendly land of Gaul. He then had to cross the Rhone and defeat a powerful opponent waiting on the east bank. It was Autumn before he reached the Alps. He knew he couldn't conquer them before the Winter but risked his force anyway. They ascended via a variety of passes, then descended the steeper Italian slopes suffering great losses.

Marching towards Rome they crossed the Rubicon and won three great battles at Trebia, Lake Trasimene and Cannae. At the latter they routed the Romans and killed or captured over half its legions.

Rome was now ripe for capture, but Hannibal had problems. His supply lines were too stretched, he had no machinery to lay siege, and he was getting little support from the government back home in Carthage who preferred spending their riches on home luxuries rather than support their campaigning general.

Hannibal spent several years in southern Italy with his exhausted armies and one remaining elephant, allowing Rome to replenish her legions. Under Scipio Africanus they attacked and regained Iberia, then crossed the Mediterranean to threaten Carthage itself. Hanniball was forced to return but he was defeated at Zama and had to sue for peace. Years later he committed suicide in Turkey, having been betrayed to the Romans.

And all this happened some150 years before Julius Caesar proclaimed "Veni, Vidi, Vici" on the beaches of Ancient Briton.

But I have ventured into Europe whilst jaunting in Africa. It's time we journeyed south, to the Sahara.

The next day I re-encountered the two American ladies, this time sporting both sunglasses and headscarves. They had become Thelma and Louise.

It was early morning in the hotel reception and I heard Mohammed greet them from behind his desk.

"Good morning ladies, How are you? he enquired innocently.

"Oh, we're good," replied Thelma.

I'd heard this awful Americanism several times. It is just wrong that you should enquire about someone's health, and they reply with a description of their behaviour. "I'm good" is what a child says should you question their conduct in school.

When you are asked "How are you" (or Ca va, como estas, come va or wie gehts?), you should respond with your state of health. "I am well, or very well, or not so well, or as appropriate. (Bien, muy bien, bene. Ok, German is gut, danke).

Once more we have the threat of this horrid Americanism, "I'm good!" entering the English language (you will recall I hate Americanisms ... period). I really hope and expect this not to catch on.

We checked out and joined Faisal in his air conditioned minibus en route to the oasis town of Douz. There were to be several excursions off the trail.

Firstly we rode the Lézard Rouge, an antique former mineral train which traverses the Selja Gorges in the east Atlas. During the laboured two hour journey there were several scenery stops in the searing heat of the airless defiles, though the views never really matched the spectacular posters, as the train had to travel through deep cuttings in the mountains. However, any time spent in a vintage railway carriage is always a pleasure. We enjoyed the Red Lizard but my favourite remains the Petit Train Jaune which follows the Têt valley in the Pyrenees. And of course there is their more famous cousin, the Marrakesh Express.

Returning to Métlaoui station we spotted Thelma and Louise.

"Are you well?" I enquired.

"Yes, we're good!" they replied incorrectly, but I ignored their poor English.

"You're from England," they asserted confidently. "Why are you in Tunisia?" They asked as if we shouldn't be.

"Oh, I wanted to explore Africa north of the Sahara," I replied.

"We're in Africa!" Louise said sounding surprised. "We're on the Mediterranean, I thought it was Europe."

I explained our location mentioning there was also an Asian coastline and that the Romans considered the sea the centre of the world, hence its name.

"You're a teacher," observed Thelma.

"Here we go," I thought, and Kaz winced. She knew what was coming.

"What sort of school do you teach at?"

Kaz breathed a sigh of relief

"A high school, we call it a bog-standard comprehensive."

"What does the B O G stand for?" asked Louise.

"Best Of Grades" I replied, pleased with my acronym.

"And what do you teach?" Thelma had fallen into the trap. Kaz looked away.

I paused. Can I do this to Americans? I thought. Yes. "Little b*****ds" I whispered solemnly (there were children on the train).

There was a long moment and a look of shock, which suddenly turned into smiles.

"Oh. It's a special school!" they declared in unison, pleased with their interpretation.

"Not many children get born in wedlock these days," added Thelma, Louise nodding, sagely.

Thelma and Louise were from Des Moines, Iowa. Well someone has to be.

Leaving the Red Lizard, we found our minibus which took us an hour west to the town of El Djem where we were to discover a most marvellous Roman Coliseum.

The little town's narrow streets of white stone buildings were deserted, after all we were travelling in the searing heat of midday. Not even a mad dog was disturbed.

The amphitheatre, probably the largest outside Rome, was in almost perfect condition, having only been slightly desecrated for its building materials It was wonderful to just wander around the almost deserted edifice. Everything about it, its walls, steps and seating, columns and arena, gleamed white in the sunshine. The small pockets of shade were a godsend, but we had to climb to the gods to look down not just the onto stage, but also to enjoy the panorama of the town below.

Finally to make your way down to that stage and imagine yourself an actor in a play, or a gladiator in a fight, or even the terror of a Christian facing wild animals was the most wondrous escape into ancient imagination. We were even able to explore the underground areas, the dressing rooms/cells, where the stars of the various shows waited nervously for their cue.

Next stop was Matmata, and the bus travelled west into the desert. After an hour Faisal took us up into the hills and stopped at a viewpoint overlooking a rocky gorge.

"Here," he asserted with confidence, "is the hottest place on earth."

Sitting, as we were, in an airy, air-conditioned bus, that seemed hard to fathom, but as we stepped out onto the tarmac, it was a time to gasp in disbelief. It was like putting your face directly against a two-barred electric fire. There was a collective "I've never known heat like it!" and after a few seconds everyone was back on the cool bus chatting about the incredulity of what we had just experienced. I can't say for certain, but the temperature must have been somewhere approaching 50 degrees Celsius.

We wound down into the valley and the village of Matmata, or as it was known in the Star Wars films, the desert planet of Tatooine. Here, the Berber inhabitants live as troglodytes, and with the year round heat it is understandable they should dig caves to try to keep cool.

We were led to the usual tourist tableau of a family living in a cave with crude furniture and open fire cooking. There were breads and oils and dates to sample, as the momma's wizened brown face smiled through a chequered veil, papa turned a chair leg on a primitive lathe, and children played in the dirt. Then the obligatory souvenir shopping opportunity. As we left I noticed the main village had normal white adobe houses, to which no doubt, the families retired once the tourists had left.

Finally we entered Douz, an oasis town billed as the gateway to the Sahara. We were now nearly 300 miles south of Tunis. One imagines an oasis as a small well with perhaps a small copse of palm trees, and the occasional caravan turning up to take on water, but Douz is not like that. It is a modern town built on a grid system with over 500,000 palm trees producing deglet noor dates. It is the biggest producer outside California.

Faisal drove us to the Touareg Hotel. We entered a lovely cool marbled reception and could see a welcome looking pool within pleasant gardens. As we checked in Faisal addressed us.

"Don't get too comfortable. Meet here in half an hour. We must travel into the desert for the sunset."

The Sahara Desert, the largest on Earth. Look at a map of the world, and it looks almost the same size and shape as the contiguous USA. In fact it is larger. 3,000 miles from Africa's Atlantic shores to the Red Sea, and up to 1,200 miles from north to south. Of course it also extends to include the Canary Islands and the Arabian Peninsular. And it may well have been lush as recently as only 12,000 years ago, before the last Ice Age.

Amazingly we walked from the hotel to the desert, which was just behind, and there awaiting us were a group of saddled dromedary camels.

Now, I have ridden on a camel many times, Kaz not so much, but we do actively avoid the creatures. We have nothing against them, always having found camels rather ambivalent to humans, whether mounted or not. They don't smell too badly, drool a bit, and sometimes spit, but we've never been bitten or thrown off. Their problem is they are so uncomfortable. It doesn't matter how cushioned the driver makes the saddle, which perches on the hump, the ride on a camel is always less than pleasant.

I suppose they are called ships of the desert for a reason. The swaying makes you seasick. And it doesn't matter how gently they stroll along, the lurch from the height of their hump makes it impossible to sit comfortably. No rising trots from these saddles.

On this occasion we were introduced to our animals, and dressed accordingly, extravagant turbans wound around each of our heads.

The camels were seated on the ground, therefore easy to climb aboard. Bidden by their driver they first rise onto their back legs, throwing you forward, then ascend onto their forelegs, steadying you as they steady themselves. There are no stirrups for the feet, your legs just dangle. After a while you try to create some sort of crossed leg effect, but you soon realise comfort will be an impossibility.

Anyhow, whilst all this was happening our little caravan was making its way into the Sahara Desert, and what views we had. This was desert as depicted in all the comic books, nothing but fine sand and dunes in every direction, the Great Eastern Erg, the Sand Sea.

We walked for perhaps half an hour, maybe only a mile or so into the desert, then with the shadows of the dunes lengthening, we circled to face the setting sun. Whilst walking south I had looked at my shadow to our left. There was the camel with me atop stretching at least 50 yards. From above apparently, you can see the shadows if not the camels themselves.

With the sun sinking and the desert haze rising, we slowly made our way back to the hotel. A remarkable experience.

Then came the dismount, and you can never get used to it. Urged by the driver the camel falls to its knees and you are convinced you'll be pitched forward onto your face. Then it steadies and falls back onto its rear haunches, throwing its incumbents into a whiplash. Only then can you breath and dismount, back onto dry land.

That evening we dined at a round table that held a lazy Susan. There were nine of us; a German couple, a French couple, Thelma and Louise, Faisal and us. This was our first opportunity to chat socially with Faisal who told us Douz was his home town and tomorrow he would be visiting his parents, his sister and his fiancée, all who worked in the family dried fig business.

Faisal had himself attended Tunis University after High School, and had studied history and languages, he spoke Arabic, English, French and German, as he had proved conversing easily with everyone at the table.

"My specialist subject was Ancient Carthage," he informed us, "and my hero was Hannibal."

"What, Lecter?" interrupted a confused Thelma.

"Who?" asked an equally confused Faisal, and the table broke into laughter. We had to explain to both of them the difference between Hannibal's Lecter and Barca. One was a fictitious psychopathic serial killer with a soft spot for FBI agent Clarice Starling, and the other a brilliant Carthaginian General who came within a cat's whisper of toppling the Roman Empire. We chatted about how that might have changed the history of the world. One of the possibilities could have been that 250 years later Palestine wouldn't have been occupied by a belligerent bunch of Europeans with a penchant for crucifixion. Then the couscous arrived.

In a huge Tunisian tajine slow cooked chicken fillets were piled. The couscous steamed above, with layers of fresh vegetables on top. The dish was quite mountainous and made a pleasant change from the mainly Mediterranean fish diet we had experienced further north, at the coast.

We asked Faisal why he hadn't gone into the family business. He told us that with tourism being such a huge and relatively new industry, he felt he was helping his country by selling it to foreigners like us. He certainly was an enthusiastic guide with a wide range of knowledge for one so young.

After dinner Kaz and I strolled into the desert, not too far, the Sahara would be a hell of a place to get lost in. With the myriad stars above, including the Milky Way, I could find the Great Bear and follow the far side of the saucepan to locate the Pole Star twinkling directly above our hotel.

"It amazes me you ever get lost," mused Kaz.

The next day, our last in Tunisia we took a horse-drawn carriage ride around the oasis town. It was an enjoyable experience but we were concerned for the horse's welfare, working to pull us and its carriage around the admittedly palm sheltered streets, but in withering heat.

We expressed our concerns to Anwar, a middle aged Berber who owned this little business.

"You must not worry," he assured us. My horse is my family, and is fed, watered, and rested well. We follow the principles of the Brooke Foundation."

As we gently trotted around the streets Anwar told us the story of Dorothy Brooke.

With the outbreak of World War One Britain's fields were emptied of horses which were requisitioned for the war effort. Many spent terrible times on the Western Front, as recorded by Michael Morpurgo in War Horse. About 20,000 horses from Britain and the antipodes found themselves in North Africa at the end of the war and couldn't be repatriated. They were sold off to traders in Cairo and forgotten.

In 1930 Dorothy's husband, Major-General Geoffrey Brooke, a renowned horse expert, was posted to Egypt. His wife learned of the plight of perhaps 200 war veteran horses which were emaciated through forced hard work, and resolved to find them to retire them peacefully. She founded a charity to raise funds to buy back these horses and mules, and after four years had rescued over 5,000 of these poor creatures which had been born in the cool green fields of Britain.

She founded the Old War Horse Memorial Hospital in Cairo, which remains one of the most important headquarters for equine welfare in the world. It was located in what is still known as the Street of the English Lady, in Cairo. Dorothy was a Scottish aristocrat.

The Brooke Foundation today helps over 2 million horses and donkeys worldwide, every year, possibly also benefiting up to 12 million people whose livelihoods depend upon them.

We bade farewell to Anwar and his happy little mare, and prepared to leave Tunisia. We took Faisal's bus back to Sousse, and on to the airport at Monastir.

Tunisia is a short haul destination, not much further than Spain's Balearic Islands. Short haul flight passengers are probably the most mistreated people in the world of commerce, and it was following our trip to Tunisia I penned the following article about the joys of returning from holiday.

Homeward Bound

"Imagine you have just had a week or two abroad, enjoying the sunshine, the peaceful relaxing surroundings, which could have been beach, pool, countryside, or a mixture of all these wonderful places. You have met interesting people, dined out under the stars, perhaps danced and partied, but generally now you feel your batteries have recharged, and you have that relaxed, bronzed glow about your person. It is time to go home. You say your goodbyes to people and places, and head for the airport.

The journey home may begin with being turfed out of your hotel room 20 hours before flying so you are forced to pay a small fortune for a courtesy room. And you are eventually seated in reception patiently awaiting a ridiculously early transfer whilst happy holidaymakers mill around. You're in your "home" clothes which probably include socks. This is where the general bonhomie can begin its gradual, inevitable descent.

Or you have been driving, and return your hire car to the dark, concreted bowels of the airport. Some pale foreigner who never sees daylight conducts the rip off inspection. You argue over the dent which *must* have been there when you picked up the dam thing. And the feel-good feeling begins to drain.

Either way you are now in the departure terminal. People seek out their flight desk for the queue to check in, or provided you checked in online, printed off your boarding cards, and have no baggage to drop you can magically head straight for security. This is the first sheep dip moment.

The queue snakes around artificially erected barriers. An official is there at the head of the queue, "Number 9!" he directs and you move forward as bidden. You are instructed to remove your belt, shoes, anything metal in your pockets; keys, money, etc. Mobiles, laptops, tablets must be put in trays. Take off hats, coats. Anything liquid (like water!); yoghurt for your lunch, sun lotion for protection, toothpaste, everything, is confiscated if not in 100ml containers produced in a plastic see-through bag, which you can buy from a special vending machine (Oh! joy, another retail opportunity). Provided your bag passes muster you are then subjected to the pat-down body search, and you are through security. Hooray!

Clutching your worldly goods; shoes, belt, coats, hats, bags, electrical goods, you stagger to a chair hoping your trousers will stay up, and your stockinged feet don't tread in something cold and moist, and sit and slowly attempt to regain your dignity. The reverie is becoming severely dented.

Not long now till the flight; just a couple of hours to kick your heels in the shopping mall that is the departure lounge, where all prices are wondrously inflated way above their High Street counterparts. "I need water," you think because you know the advice of all airlines is to keep hydrated, and now, past security, you are allowed to buy it. £1.50 for half a litre. Robbing bastards.

(The best departure lounge I ever encountered was on the Greek island of Lesvos. Following check-in we were informed, "Sorry we do not have a departure lounge, so if you could sit on the beach, or at the local taverna until you see your flight arrive." I hope it hasn't changed, I fear it may have.)

The next sheep dip moment is coming up. The excitement is palpable as people scan the screens awaiting news of their departure gate. And there it is, B16. And off you power-walk through the two miles of corridors, escalators, travellators and ramps, passed toilets, vending machines, posters advertising this city as being *The Best* for investment, and even more shops and fast food dispensers until at last you join the queue for the boarding gate. Feelings of goodwill are now reaching their lowest ebb, and you would happily empty a cartridge of bullets into the heads of the people who try to push in front, innocently claiming they didn't know the queue for that gate over there started at that distance back there. You are even beginning to snarl.

Finally showing passports and boarding cards for the umpteenth time you are directed onto the plane, and walk five yards to join the end of yet another queue. Not sheep now, you have evolved into cattle and the herding begins. The first obstacle everyone has to overcome is those people who stand idly in the aisles putting their luggage into the overhead compartments, holding up the whole plane. They also need culling.

Eventually everyone having been herded onto the plane and into their seats, you can patiently await departure. You acclimatise yourself first. Now I know that just because it is my experience, that it is not universal. First class and Business class passengers have much more salubrious surroundings, and Emirates for example are much different than Easyjet, but for this account let us imagine Mr O'Leary's Airline.

The seats are plastic, blue plastic. They don't recline so neither do the ones in front. The rest of the livery is a yellow which is so insipid it immediately bleaches any semblance of sun-kissed bronze you may have worked so hard to acquire. There is no basket of brochures attached to the seat in front of you, only a rudimentary tray and a graphic showing you the emergency procedures; seat belt, brace position, drop-down oxygen, and inflatable life vest complete with whistle. Whoopee!

Herding complete, with the last few passengers warned that if they don't take any seat available they will be stowed in the hold, demonstration duly ignored, there are a few welcoming words from the chief cabin crew ("Your crew today includes Donna, Gemma and Andy") and from the captain ("Just waiting for the push back, we'll be flying at 30,000 feet, and the weather at destination is shite"), and we are up and up and away. Ears popping, ankles swelling, neck trying not to loll onto the shoulders of neighbours, you settle into your book.

This is when the crew become the stereotypical trolley dollies, even Andy. Operating in such a restricted space they work the cabin selling warm beer and cold coffee, hugely overpriced snacks, perfumes and for some godforsaken reason, scratch cards. And with the constant, patronising smile which you would slap if you weren't shackled to your seat; a claustrophobic customer, a pinioned passenger.

Landing, and the moment the plane comes to a halt, the passengers are up and emptying their bags from the overhead lockers. There's elbows everywhere and the fact no-one gets brained is more through luck than judgement. No wonder the cabin crew have absented themselves from this scrum. They're at the front of the plane wishing thank you and goodbyes over 300 times. Little wonder their plastic grins.

If you are lucky you avoid the plane to bus to arrivals, and you can walk straight into the building and head for the passport desks. Sheep-like we are once again going back and forth, slowly, painstakingly zigzagging towards the customs officials. One is directing people to number 9, number 5, etc. Is it the same bloke from the security queues? Are people unable to identify a vacated desk? Still, at least it's human and we don't have to suffer that awful "Cashier number four, please" at Post Office, yet.

These days, with just hand luggage, I manage to avoid the most depressing place on Earth. (Not Helmand Province in the Afghanistan theatre of war). The baggage carousel as it circles and circles. Suitcases and backpacks having been thrown down onto it by handlers whose sole purpose appears to be how much damage they can inflict on the belongings of hapless passengers. Look around at the tired, drained, forlorn faces as bag follows bag follows bag. All energy has ebbed away; there is now just a grey, joyless existence. Then the sudden, thrust through the crowd and a surge forward to grab the suitcase before it embarks on another fruitless circuit, and lift it onto the trolley; but the moment of excitement swiftly dissipates and they once again assume the position.

Eventually, all belongings accounted for you push your trolley and drag your depressed, shambolic, and saddened body to the next and hopefully last obstacle; the customs hall.

Guiltily taking the green channel (whether guilty or not, you are made to feel the most awful smuggler), finally you are onto the arrivals concourse and then out into the cold and rain.

All you have to do now is get home (have I mentioned the replacement bus service?).

"Why do we do it?" I hear you say. Why subject ourselves to this demeaning procedure time and time again?

What, why bother going on holiday?

No, why bother coming home!"

Years later I was thinking of and feeling for Faisal, Anwar, and their compatriots when in one sudden act of utmost evil, a cruel and demented individual destroyed it all. When that pathetic excuse for a human being murdered the poor holidaymakers on the beach, he decimated Tunisia's healthy and thriving tourist industry. Thousands of skilled, experienced people lost their jobs and their livelihoods, causing hardship for families the length of the country. This unpredictable atrocity perfectly illustrates the fragility of the tourist industry for any developing nation. Airports and hotels, ship's crews and guides, restaurants and shopkeepers, and many more instantly closed.

From ordinary people to the government, denied the tourist dollar which goes so far in maintaining and preserving the world's great sites of history and heritage, protecting its wildlife and simply providing legitimate and fulfilling livelihoods. All put on hold for at least a decade.

And just when they were getting back on their feet, along comes a pandemic. As I was saying; fragile.

Chapter Three

Egypt

Nile, Tombs and Temples

Egypt is surely the most important country in the world for ancient history. The civilisation of Pharaohs and temples and tombs and marvellous statuary, most of which have endured to modern day lasted nearly 30 centuries. It is so important an 'ology has been named for it, Egyptology, a degree in which all guides must hold.

Cairo, the modern capital, is the largest city in Africa, and the Nile, which flows through it to its delta and the Mediterranean, the longest river in the world. It is a sobering thought that every day 20 million Cairenes empty their waste into it.

My first ever experience of Cairo was in the 90's when our flight landed there en route to Kenya, for refuelling. And whilst the high octane jet fuel was pumping, the rear doors opened so people could go out for a smoke! Different times.

On the return we flew above the Nile and you could clearly see the green arable land on its banks stretching perhaps a mile either side, dependant on how far they their irrigation systems could reach. Beyond this, endless desert. You could truly believe the Nile was the lifeblood that began civilisation.

I love factoids which put context into history. Stonehenge, for instance predates the pyramids by 500 years, and they had existed for 3,000 years when Cleopatra had her dalliances with Julius Caesar, Marc Antony and an asp.

But to return to this, my first random jaunt into Egypt. I flew to Cairo from Heathrow, having overnighted south on National Express, and occupying a seat upstairs on an Air Egypt Jumbo.

It was Easter and I entered the frenetic Cairo airport arrivals hall to be met by a cacophonous crowd of jostling Egyptians, all keen to assure me and dozens of fellow passengers that they could transfer me to the city and a wonderful hotel for the best price. You dare not show an interest in any one offer, as you will be immediately swamped by others craving your custom.

Luckily I had arranged to meet a Mr Salah Mohammed, and there he was holding up a piece of cardboard bearing my name.

"Follow me Mr Hee-off," (he pronounced the G like he was bringing up phlegm) and we set off pushing through the throng, past people who continued to harass, insisting I hear their offer. The kindly Mr Salah pushed me into a yellow Lada taxi and smiled a farewell. I never saw him again.

Cairo

It was near midnight and I recall the journey into the metropolis. Heavy continuous traffic that my driver negotiated skilfully with the heel of his left hand permanently on the horn, changing gears with his right, seeming to operate the steering wheel with his chin, all whilst gesticulating wildly and muttering a string of oaths at all other road users.

Well lit boulevards revealed shops and businesses, wide pavements, trees lit by circular fairy lights, and people in winter clothing busying themselves along. Glowing brightly, huge colourful posters depicted families happily eating together, alongside dark suited and moustachioed male politicians, promising the earth, no doubt.

This was the outskirts. As we approached the centre, the streets narrowed, with darker, taller buildings and an even busier atmosphere. We passed a huge statue of a seated Ramses II outside the joint bus and railway station, and finally my driver halted to deposit me at the hotel Sleepy Dreams.

Let's take a moment to put Egypt into context. It occupies the eastern end of the Sahara, bordered by Libya to the west and Sudan in the south (Sudan used to be the largest country in Africa until it split with what is now South Sudan. That honour now belongs to Algeria). To the east is the coast of the Red Sea which is an arm of the Indian Ocean, and the Horn of Africa.

The Mediterranean sea is the northern boundary. In the Nile Delta is the relatively modern city of Alexandria, founded by Alexander the Great around 300 BC. This land surrounding the ancient capital, Memphis, was known as Lower Egypt.

Egypt is attached to Asia by its borders with Israel and Jordan. This north eastern part of the country is the Sinai peninsular, through which flows the Suez Canal, allowing traffic to flow between the Mediterranean and the Indian Ocean.

This major link was built by the French in the 19th Century, with the British the major shareholder, and we operated it jointly until Gamal Abdel Nasser nationalised it in 1956. This caused the incident (The Suez Crisis) where we tried to seize it back, to the annoyance of the Americans and Russians. Historians believe this cost Britain its status in the world as a great power. God never came under such criticism when he parted the Red Sea for Moses to lead the escaping Israelites into the promised land of milk and honey, the Exodus into the Sinai.

Modern Egypt is a Muslim country, Arabic speaking, with about 15% Coptic Christian. The French have had a great influence here. Napoleon's army first uncovered many temples that had been claimed by the sands of the desert, and found a stele at Rosetta, written in Latin, Greek and Hieroglyphs. This was eventually translated to open the ancient hieroglyphics for analysis. The French were defeated by Nelson at the Battle of the Nile, and ever since the British have been a major influence. Egypt's currency is the Pound, and the Rosetta Stone lives in the British Museum, not far from Elgin's Marbles.

The River Nile floods every year. We now know this is due to the rains in the mountains of Ethiopia where the Blue Nile rises (the White Nile rises in Lake Victoria in Uganda and the confluence is at Khartoum, capital of Sudan). The Ancient Egyptians believed it was the gift of the gods which allowed them to make the land alongside the Nile so fertile. This flooding is now controlled by the Aswan Dam, built with British help, which created Lake Nasser that drowned much of the land of Nubia. This, the land surrounding the ancient capital Thebes, was known as Upper Egypt.

The kingdoms of Upper and Lower Egypt were unified around 2686 BC, with new rulers called Pharaoh, who wore the double crown of unification, the Pshent, depicting the red cobra and the white vulture.

The Sleepy Dreams hotel was a mosquito ridden dump by night and a fly-blown tip by day. A single width, five storey building, it was the sort of hotel which rents its rooms out by the hour. My room had a single wooden chair, a scratched old dressing table, and a hard bed which I lay on fully clothed, not wishing to turn down the grey, stained blanket. A toilet at the end of the corridor had neither a seat nor toilet paper.

Unable to cope in such a sleaze I sneaked out at 2am and checked into the Ciao, next door. The Ciao was nothing special, but if you'd give Sleepy Dreams one star, this deserved five. I ultimately slept well, rose and breakfasted early, and set off in brilliant sunshine on the adventure of a lifetime, to see the Pyramids.

From the door of the hotel I stepped into a street scene of pure chaos. Pedestrians hurried hither and thither, traditional Arab dress mixed in equal measure with western suits or jeans and tee shirts. Merchants of all foods and materials occupied the kerbsides, and the traffic; cars, buses, bikes and trucks roared by in a cacophony of horn blowing. The noise was unbelievable in this heaving sea of humanity.

A man in traditional garb offered me a fez. "Just like that" he shrugged.

"Why did you say that?" I asked.

"Don't know, but all the English say it when they put on a fez!"

Another beckoned me into their carpet shop, and another wanted to sell me perfume.

"I'm going to the pyramids" I cried to be excused.

"Why? They are only old tombs. You must promise to come to my shop," everyone insisted.

I crossed the street to the Rameses station, went down the steps into the metro underground and was instantly transported into a clean, white, modern, even serene, beautifully constructed tube station. Our tube really suffers from its 150 year past, the grime of history, the Victorian architecture. Modern undergrounds have gone to school on our experience. Here I waited with maybe a dozen fellow commuters. I looked up at the screen which seemed to say, "Who cares, we know there'll be another one in a minute or so?" and it was showing instead a an English Premier League game.

The train comfortably whooshed me for 20 minutes to Giza. I wasn't aware there were two Giza stops, and I evidently got off at the wrong one. I emerged back into the bright sunshine, and other than the street being a little wider without a huge statue of Rameses II, I could have been back outside my hotel.

There was the same sea of humanity, cacophony of traffic, and seeming bedlam all around. Was Cairo Latin for chaos? I mused as I looked around for what I thought should be fairly obvious landmarks; the Great Pyramids.

With nothing in sight I set off walking, they must be here somewhere, I thought. Can't be far away. I trusted to my sense of direction, the sun was still eastwards, so I had to head away from it, west. I turned left down a street I guessed led towards the Nile. Seeing gaps in the buildings I hoped I might find a clue. I crossed a canal, and lying in it saw a dead horse, four hooves akimbo. What? But I was getting nowhere.

I made the fatal mistake of stopping to consult a map.

"Hello, can I help you? Where are you from, England? Welcome to Egypt."

"I am looking for the Pyramids," I said forlornly.

"Yes, that is not a problem," he smiled. He was a jovial chap in his forties, wearing sunglasses, jilaba, and brimless cap.

"I am Abdel, here is my business card, you must visit me when next in Cairo. I will walk you there."

"Yes, I promise, but I don't want to be a bother, just point me in the right direction."

"Oh, this is the right direction," and he cleverly steered me into his shop.

Suddenly I was hit by what to me is that awful smell that bombards you as you pass the airport shops heading for the departure lounge. The overpowering mix of blended cheap perfumes sold by what must be very attractive young women, but caked in powders, mascara and fake tan. Sticks in the back of my throat. The smell, not the painted ladies.

"I can't stay here, I am allergic to perfume," I only partially lied.

"Please, you must take coffee with me, and I will show you my scents. The Pyramids are closed today, anyway," (he lied fully) "I am sure you would not refuse my hospitality".

I quickly drained a small cup of coffee dregs and bade him goodbye. He was reluctant for me to leave, acting affronted, but I was struggling for breath. I never did get that business card.

I was back on the street taking in great lung-fulls of African air; exhaust fumes, woodsmoke and manure. Heavenly.

I wandered more, recrossing the canal with the dead dumped horse, but it was fruitless. Eventually I gave up this random searching, flagged down a yellow Lada taxi and wearily got into the passenger seat, "To the pyramids, please" I said with an air of desperation.

My driver set off, expertly weaving in and out of the hectic traffic, blowing his horn and gesticulating wildly and exasperatingly to all around, who were doing exactly the same to everyone else.

After a while he stopped and turned to me. "Where is this pyramids?" he asked.

I couldn't believe it. I was here in Cairo, Egypt with a taxi driver who hadn't heard of the only one of the Seven Wonders of the World still in existence; The Pyramids of Giza, and we were in Giza! Weren't we? I was beginning to think this was some crazy dream. But, although I was feeling slightly discombobulated, I was still fairly confident in the reasonable destination I had asked for. It was just that I couldn't answer his question.

"They are on the West bank of the Nile, surely they are here in Giza" I said, doubting my sanity.

And we re-joined the traffic. Soon we were driving along a dual carriageway with shops and offices on both sides, away from the city. Suddenly between two buildings I saw a sandy coloured, pointed monolith looming mistily into the blue sky and realised.

"There!" I shouted and grabbed his arm as he nearly swerved off the road. "Look, there is a pyramid."

He looked over and upwards and smiled. "Oh. You want the old Giza tombs," he said in a why-didn't-you-say manner, and he turned left, and for 20 minutes followed back streets I could never have navigated. He drove me to the lay-by where all the tourist buses stop, near to the Metro (how could I have missed it?)

"Do you want me to wait?"

"No, I'll be spending all day here, thank you. And thank you for the tour." And I paid and we parted.

Giza, on the outskirts of Cairo is a busy town in itself, located near the river, on its west bank, and if you didn't look to the pyramids you would say quite an unremarkable place, other than the beggars, touts and tourists. But then I climbed the steps and turned the corner to the right, and there, in all its majesty was the magic.

I paid at the booth and entered the complex. The whole 180 degrees in front of me was the desert. I stood where the seats are neatly set out for the nightly son et lumière show, and there facing me were the Great Pyramids.

To the right I could see rows of smaller tombs, and three small pyramids to my left. Ahead and beyond, were the three Great Pyramids, the right hand one dwarfing everything else. This was the majesty of the Pharaoh Cheops' tomb, at 480 feet, the tallest building in the world for nearly 4,000 years. Also known as Khufu, his tomb was constructed with 2.3 million blocks of limestone and granite, each weighing as much as 80 tons. If they laid 100 per day, it would have taken 63 years to construct, indicating they may have begun their work at the birth of the future Pharaoh.

Nowadays we only see the core, but originally it would have been plastered and skimmed and painted with golds and reds and blues.

To the left of Cheops, and slightly smaller is the tomb of his son, Chephren, or Khafre. This still has some of its finish on the pointed summit. And to the left of Chephren, completing the complex, the much smaller Menkaure flanked by three Queen's tombs.

There in front of me was the whole complex, and the most surprising thing of all was that guarding this necropolis, almost at my feet, sat the well known figure of the Sphinx. The head of a king, probably Chephren, with his headdress, and the body of lion, it is a spectacular creation, but it looked tiny, dwarfed by the pyramids in the back ground. The Sphinx is a well known icon for Egypt, of course. It is believed its nose and beard (also in the British Museum) were removed by pot shots from French riflemen.

I began my exploration of the site with the Sphinx. It was sculpted on the floor of the quarry and is the most immense stone sculpture ever created. In advance of the head, stretching forward at least 60 feet are the forelegs and paws. I stood and looked up at his face and the peaceful countenance and couldn't stop myself singing this little ditty, a party piece from Stuart Fletcher (when he's not singing Delilah), to the tune of the Eton Boating Song:

"Oh, the sexual life of a camel
Is stranger than anyone thinks,
At the height of the mating season,
He tries to b****r the Sphinx,
But the Sphinx's posterior orifice
is covered with sand from the Nile,
Which accounts for the hump on the camel,
and the Sphinx's inscrutable smile."

I can report that this inscrutable smile is indeed more than six feet across. I walked around to the rear. The body is 80 yards long, and then there was another surprise you never see in the pictures, a tail stretching around the body's right flank. From the Sphinx (which faces the sunrise. The Egyptians always built their tombs on the west bank, in the direction of the setting sun. To add to the mysticism of the Nile, the sun crosses it every day) I headed left to where I saw a hill. At the top of this hill was a modern cemetery, with many Christian and Muslim shrines, but the view from here was unsurpassed. To the south in the shimmering heat I could make out the much older, step pyramid at Saqqara, a sort of prototype. In front of me was a valley heading to Menkaure. Years later Kaz and I were here and hired horses to trek into the desert. Unbeknownst to our guide, Kaz is an experienced horsewoman and the two raced each other, reaching a terrifying gallop. I was left behind in a cloud of dust. The moment was very special for her.

I descended to the smaller pyramid and enjoyed clambering around the archaeological site. You can't tell, but this whole area has been painstakingly examined over the last 150 years. From the rear of Menkaure I made my way to Chephren. On the north face a wooden causeway had been constructed up to the tomb entrance. At the bottom of the steps a very attractive young policewoman relieved me of my camera with a smile, "Sorry, no cameras allowed"

I climbed the steps, entered the small dark doorway, and descended the stone steps into the heart of the tomb.

Of course, this was never designed to be an entrance. The tombs were intended to be sealed permanently with the burial of their occupant, as that occupant made their journey into the afterlife accompanied by all their earthly riches.

Unfortunately, as future generations were to discover, the pyramids were a huge advertisement for the spoils to be had by looting. Grave robbers over centuries and millennia have stripped these places of their wealth. This was why the hidden Valley of the Kings was created in Thebes for the 18th dynasty and beyond. Here we were looking at 4th and 5th dynasties.

The journey down was claustrophobic, hot and airless. The electric wall lamps created only small pools of light. Eventually I came to the small burial chamber, carved out of the bedrock, so below ground level. I could see where his sarcophagus was partially sunk into the floor, and there was another room, which may have held his offerings. There was no art here, neither in the chambers, nor the passageways, no bright hieroglyphs painted on the walls and ceilings, all lost in time, and the exhalations of thousands of people, from constructors, burial party, robbers, archaeologists and now tourists.

The experience was mind numbing, but with nothing to see, I left, blinking back into the sunshine, once more breathing fresh air. At the bottom of the wooden steps my police officer friend returned my camera, smiled and whispered to me. I hadn't heard so leaned forward,

"Sorry?" I questioned.

"You buy hashish?" she repeated furtively, "Best quality."

"Erm, no thanks," I replied, shocked and surprised.

It was lunch time, and I had bought my picnic from one of the little shops at the entrance, a falafel and lettuce sandwich wrap with fruit juice and a large red apple.

When close to the construction stones you can see they are pitted with the erosion of 5,000 years, and there is an overhang at the bottom around the perimeter. It was under this ledge I sat and ate as incredibly there was a short shower of drizzle. These pyramids exist in the dry desert because it is precisely that, dry. On my visit, it rained. Typical.

Now it was time for the main event, Cheops.

Cheops was magnificent and I gloried in my circumnavigation, but you soon begin to realise, once you have seen one great pyramid, they all begin to look the same. The wonder is purely in their size. This is no Taj Mahal. The best view is from the entrance, or up on cemetery hill, to take in the whole vista. Close up, not so good.

There was a boat house to visit. Excavations had revealed the funerary barge buried with the Pharaoh, then I made my way back to the exit.

On this side of the complex the majority of the tourists can be found. They come to look and take their photographs, and few go much further. Many of the people who can afford this sort of trip are wealthy and retired, and maybe not as mobile as most. So it must seem a wonderful experience, to be driven around the pyramid complex by horse and carriage. And this would be a fulfilling role for the horse, if they were looked after properly, but they are not. (we have already seen what happens to them when they have outlived their usefulness; discarded into the canal like a piece of litter).

There is a tarmac road here that slopes down to the complex entrance, and it has been worn smooth by the heat and wheels of carriages. Here I saw emaciated horses and mules struggling to hold back the carriage they were harnessed to. The driver would whip vigorously and shout encouragement as their beast's poor legs flayed helplessly on the tarmac, desperately trying to maintain traction, throwing out showers of sparks when their hooves struck the road. I could see the whites of their eyes, widened with terror, fearing the heavy carriage would overtake and sweep them away. Meanwhile two fat tourists would sit oblivious to the torture being inflicted. I turned away, sickened and ashamed. At least there was a Dorothy Brooke Foundation water trough provided for the poor wretched creatures (equine, not human).

I returned to the Sphinx to take one more sweeping look at the complex, then found the tube station I should have arrived at, and headed back to the Ciao hotel, tired but satisfied that I had given the Great Pyramids of my best for a whole day, once I'd found them.

That night I walked to Tahrir Square and dined on a local speciality, stuffed pigeon. Imagine a small bird, not a plump looking wood pigeon, its meat removed, mixed with soggy rice and stuffed into its tiny ribcage. I've reported before how some local specialities find themselves on menus worldwide; lasagne, boeuf bourgignon, paella, etc. There's a reason stuffed pigeon hasn't made the grade.

Cairo is as hectic and chaotic at night as it is in the day, but beautifully lit up, especially the corniche running alongside the Nile. I love how they circle lights around the trunks of the palm trees. I found my way to Zamalek Island with the hotels the rich tourists and businesspeople frequent, where it is easier to get a beer, and I deserved one.

At Harry's Bar, it was a quiet night so I sat chatting with Anwar, a young, perhaps 30, married man with two children, from Alexandria.

"You would not like it there, it is cold in Winter. Sometimes there is snow!"

He has a degree in Art History but has to work in a bar to finance his night school where he is training to be a teacher.

"All my friends work in Sharm or Dahab on the Sinai. It is very popular with the Russians. One day there will be a tourist industry all the way up to the Israeli border at Eilat."

Anwar had a ready smile, and was about the first Egyptian I had met who wasn't on the make.

"Historically," he informed me, "most of the tourists on the Nile are Italians. They built the cruise ships that sail from Luxor to Aswan in Upper Egypt."

I told him that was where I wanted to go next, but I had a bus booked the following night to take me into the Sinai, then on into Jordan.

Day three in Cairo was museum day, and I presented myself at the Museum of the Antiquities immediately after breakfast. I was slightly anxious. I couldn't find my hat, a leather Australian Stetson type my mother had bought me for my 30th birthday. In truth she had given me £30 and told me to buy something useful. This hat had been all around the world with me, and losing it wasn't just a sentimental problem, it was an essential property in a sun-kissed country like Egypt. Should I buy a new one?

The problem could wait till later. I now had four hours indoors. The museum was wonderful, if chaotic, just like outside. There was no order to it, there were no indications of which dynasty we were in, or items grouped by location, or exhibits signposted as Pharaonic, Coptic, or Roman or from when or wherever. There were labels; this mummy, that statue, those gods, or these artefacts, but no logic to their positioning.

Having made that complaint, I couldn't fault the quality of the exhibits. Mummies wrapped and exposed, stacked with others of their families. Sarcophagi, various types of Sphinxes, statues, gods as one with the Pharaohs; Amun who fused with the sun god Ra, his brother Min symbol for fertility (all erect penises removed either due to Muslim sensitivities or Victorian prudishness), Osiris and Isis, Horus, Anubis, and many more from the Ancient or Modern, Upper and Lower Kingdoms. There was jewellery and garments, ankhs and hieroglyphs, papyrus and artwork, gold and silver adornments, pots and pans, ewers and amphorae and every conceivable dug-up implement.

But there was one centre-piece in the museum. Every artefact and exhibit led to this one most magnificent of saved adornments. The one perfect symbol, which escaped the tomb robbers for millennia. It was there, displayed in a glass case in all its magnificence, lit on every side, the perfect golden death mask of the boy king, Tutankhamun.

The artefacts recovered from that one small tomb give just a hint of the "wonderful things" lost to posterity.

I eventually emerged into the bright sunshine, keeping to the shadows to save my unprotected head. I visited the Citadel and the Mosque of Mohammed Ali, the Hanging Coptic Church to the Virgin Mary, and finally for this trip made my way down to the river to catch the river bus north into the delta.

I was alone in a crowd of students and young people. This is off the tourist beaten track, a favourite with the locals, the 90 minute trip up the Nile to Al Qanater gardens. What amazed me was the exuberance of these youngsters. They were chatting and laughing, playing and singing and dancing, innocent girls and boys, in western dress simply enjoying themselves. No-one was smoking, there was no alcohol, this was just pure fun, which never disturbed the enjoyment of anyone else, it was very much pro-social behaviour.

Lots of folk chatted with me, eager to try out and improve their English, fascinated that anyone else would be interested in a very much Egyptian working class pastime.

The Al Qanater gardens were colourful and green. Known as the Dams of the Well-Being, they are located where the Nile splits into the Damietta and Rosetta arms. Lawns and lianas, picnics and happy people.

The return journey was even noisier and jollier, as the sun set and the colours of the river and its surroundings changed to pinks and reds and longer shadows.

I packed and checked out of the Ciao, leaving my bags to collect later.

At the Windsor Hotel I met the prevaricating Scot, Andrew, who spent a week in Cairo and saw nothing. We went to Harry's Bar where Anwar seemed genuinely pleased to see me. We drank and chatted awhile, then I had to leave (see my Random Jaunts Through Asia).

"I am very sad to see you go Hee-off" said Anwar, "and I am sad you lost your best hat."

I nodded in resignation, and said my farewells. Andrew promised to go to the Pyramids tomorrow, though he never did. Anwar said he would see me in Sharm, and I headed for the door.

"Oh, Hee-off," said Anwar dolefully, and I turned. Then with a great brandishing Anwar shouted gleefully, "I have your hat!"

Luxor to Aswan

That was Spring, and in the Autumn I flew direct from Manchester to Luxor to be greeted by Egyptologist Sami who first imparted the news that my cabin was not ready and that for one night only, at no extra expense, I would be put up at the Luxor Mercure Hotel.

"I will collect you first thing in the morning," he assured as he signed me in. "You can eat here, we will pay the bill."

Fillet steak and a bottle of red wine it was then.

The Mercure was a posh but featureless hotel, and I was a little miffed I wasn't in my ship's cabin with all its watery cosiness and gently rolling and wooden snugness.

I had chosen my boat carefully. I had seen the ships that ply the Nile. Some are huge white cruise ships with several storeys and windows like portholes. I wanted what I called a "Death On The Nile" boat, where Peter Ustinov might open his slatted door directly onto the deck, not too far above the waterline and walk around the whole ship to take in the views. A small boat with maybe only a dozen cabins (ensuring any murder had finite suspects), wicker chairs, perhaps a plunge pool, and a restaurant with crisp white Egyptian cotton tablecloths and starched waiters. In other words, 1920's style.

Sami collected me as promised, first thing in the morning, and we drove through the crowded streets of Luxor to where the M/S Karim Palace was moored. I climbed aboard. We were somewhere to the north of Luxor town, to avoid the mass of moorings, often three or four abreast, where to get on and off your boat you had to sidle across several other boat decks. I had no time to acclimatise or orientate myself before Sami collected his crew together to begin the first of our many excursions. This was ancient Thebes, the capital of the Upper Kingdom, and the wonders here to discover were many fold.

There was me and Sami, a smiling young man in jeans and tee shirt; office manager Craig and his wife Katie with their ten year old son Harry, who were from Ipswich; and a couple, Steve and Emma from Warrington. Steve was a drummer with rock band, Mere.

We began by driving north, following the river along the corniche to the Luxor Bridge. Crossing to the west bank, the "Theban Necropolis", we passed irrigated fields and small, mud hut hamlets until we reached the Colossi of Memnon. These are two huge statues of the seated Pharaoh Amenhotep III of the 18th dynasty, circa 1350BC (that's the last of the "dynasty circa" boring stuff). They appear to be stand alone monoliths, but are actually the gateway guardians to a huge temple, now long gone. Locally the Colossi are known as Shama and Tama.

Next to these was the mortuary temple of Queen Hatshepsut. This is a shining mausoleum built on four colonnaded levels in the shadow of huge cliffs. It has suffered from thoughtless 20th century reconstruction, and now looks quite modern. It was wonderful walking around the site and enjoying the mostly faded hieroglyphs of both haute (sticking out of the wall) and bas (carved into the wall) relief carvings, you can only imagine the splendour of the original.

Sami brought the history to life with his knowledge of the people. Hathepsut was the aunt of Thutmoses who came to the throne aged two, so she reigned jointly in regency. Thutmoses was succeeded by his son Amenhotep and one or the other is accused of the misogyny that saw all references to Hathepsut being removed or destroyed.

What could never be taken away from her was her obelisk in Karnak, the second largest in Egypt at over 90 feet tall, and that she was the only woman to be buried in the Valley of the Kings.

A similar fate befell Akhenaten about 100 years later. He tried to introduce monotheism to Egypt, the worship of Aten. This was so against the grain that his images were later expunged from posterity. The only likenesses that remain show him with a long nose and full lips. His eyes are so thick with mascara it is thought to "belittle" him as gay, but his wife was the beautiful Nefertiti, and he was succeeded by his youngest son, Tutankhamun. I love the way you can gradually fit together the complicated jigsaw of Ancient Egypt. Sami was brilliant at this. To become a guide, he informed us, you must have a degree in Egyptology.

Sadly, Hatshepsut's Temple is now infamous for the terrorist attack which cost the lives of 58 tourists and four guards in 1997. I am always awed by the story of Adrian, who was there that day.

I was sharing a beer with him in Sochitoto in El Salvador when he told me:

"We had hired donkeys to take us from the Valley of the Kings, up and across the cliffs and down into Hatshepsut's Temple. Twelve were brought to us, but we were thirteen. I volunteered to stay and wait, but the others insisted we go as a group. Exposed to the tortuous sun we had to wait and wait for the thirteenth donkey. It arrived after an hour and we were about to begin the trudge down when we heard the sound of gunfire and grenade explosions. Worried and confused we were turned back. If it hadn't been for the thirteenth donkey we would have been in the complex when all hell broke out."

We drove back towards the Nile, then north and around to the land the other side of the cliffs which had dwarfed Hatshepsut's temple. It looked like a limestone quarry stuck out in the desert, but Sami assured us this was the Valley of the Kings.

The Egyptians of 5,000 years ago were pretty miffed at their Pharaohs' tombs being targeted by robbers, and began to realise that a huge pyramid pointing to the sky was a massive clue as to their whereabouts. So they decided, after about 17 dynasties (sorry) to hide their King's tombs in a valley in the New Kingdom. This valley is dominated by a peak, al-Qurn, which is pyramid shaped, possibly a homage to the Old Kingdom at Giza.

We left our bus and climbed aboard a road train which took us up into the valley. There are thought to be 64 tombs here, mostly raided and emptied before the archaeologists arrived (failed theory, then), and after wandering around in the heat of the complex, we visited three of them.

It is thought the tunnels of the tombs were created from the Pharaoh's birth, decorated with hieroglyphical depictions of his life and reign, and the burial chambers hollowed out on his death. Hence the tomb of Rameses II is huge. He reigned for 66 years, dying at the ripe old age of 90. His tomb would have been full of the treasures amassed over seven decades. This would have been a beacon for the robbers whose frantic excavations probably covered the much more modest tomb of the boy king Tut.

Hence it wasn't until 1922 that Howard Carter, financed by the Earl of Carnarvon, was able to find and open this untouched, pristine tomb, filled with "Marvellous Things", artefacts and treasures which have since toured the world.

The tombs we visited were those of Thutmoses III, and Rameses III and IXth. A 100 years of tourism has managed to bleach most of the murals, many of which now lie behind fixed perspex.

The former tomb was very long indeed. Thutmoses reigned 24 years as co-regent with his mother, and 30 years alone. We shuffled down and down his corridors and two stairways to the vestibule with extensive funerary text. His burial chamber was oval with two supporting columns and a cartouche shaped sarcophagus. The blue ceiling was decorated with stars.

The belief was that every day, the double-earthed goddess, Isis, crossed the ceiling of the night sky, to defeat the serpent of Chaos, consuming the Moon and giving birth to the Sun, in the process. The role of Thutmoses is personified here being suckled by Isis.

The ancient Egyptians knew the constants of their world. Life and death, and the transference to the afterlife, aided by their gods; day and night, the birth of the sun in the east, its journey like a chariot across the sky, and its sinking into the west, so life happened in the east, death celebrated in the west. And most important the Nile flooded every year bringing fresh water and silt rich in nutrients to their fields. The god of this inundation was the aptly named Hapi, a male with a huge full belly and pendulous breasts.

Marvellous things, and indeed marvellous stories.

Leaving the Valley of the Kings we spent a few minutes in an alabaster factory, then visited two tombs in the Valley of the Queens where many Pharaohs' wives were buried. There were not the only top people interred here, other nobles, children, priests, key workers and favoured courtiers also had the honour of being laid to rest in these west bank wadis.

We returned to our boat for a very late lunch. "Probably ruin dinner," I remarked to the Ipswich family.

"I doubt it," said Craig. "You've not seen my wife eat."

Katie was a slight lady in her early thirties, looking not unlike Shelley Duval's character in The Shining. She had beautiful big blue eyes under a small mousy bob, with a constantly smiling countenance. She was perhaps size 10, although I know little of such fashion matters. She did however pile her plate very high at lunch.

Following this incredibly busy morning and meal, I finally had the opportunity to unpack. I was pleased with the cabin; dark and cool, with wood panelled walls and fittings, and a small bathroom. My door did indeed open directly onto the deck and I could walk around the whole boat in a couple of minutes. On the top deck were bamboo armchairs with comfy cushions, and a splash pool. This was where I spent the rest of the late afternoon.

Being north of Luxor centre we faced south, towards Aswan, and across the river I could see the desert escarpment we had visited that morning. Whilst standing at the rail two huge, fierce looking eagles swooped down on the boat. I ducked but was in no danger, they swooped again, and I realised their aerial acrobatics was merely a courting ritual. Sami joined me at the rail, "Egyptian buzzards," he confirmed. "And there are Egyptian doves," he pointed to a pair of cute pink and ivory doves, perhaps a quarter the size of our own wood pigeons. At the shore were some wading birds including the Sacred Ibis, white plumage with a black neck and head, and a long downward curved beak. "There is Thoth, our god of wisdom and magic."

I was enraptured.

Dinner came all too soon. I chose a small portion of roast chicken and potatoes. Katie came back from the buffet with a huge plate of meat and vegetables. Harry was not unlike Danny from The Shining, and although Craig looked nothing like Jack Nicholson, he was plagued at work with the epithet "All work and no play make Jack a dull boy".

Work for Craig was as supervisor of an office of six women working in insurance claims. "I'm the most tolerant person I know," he confided. "I have to be aware of their moods and the catalysts that change them; their romances, their hang ups and their preferences, their families and their living circumstances. I really need some of that god Thoth stuff. My working day is spent pleading and placating people with a hormone count beyond belief. Then I come home to these two."

In fairness, Harry was as laid back as his dad, his head stuck into his tablet screen, but not playing futile games, or watching mind numbing YouTube clips. Harry had a passion for Laurel and Hardy. He knew all their films, even from the silent era. He devoured their whole catalogue of hilarious slapstick. His favourite film was Way Out West, with his best-loved scene, The Trail of The Lonesome Pine. Mine too. What a delightful young man.

Whilst we were chatting about office politics and child prodigies, Katie came back from the buffet with another pile of food which she devoured eagerly.

"She has a fast metabolism" admitted Craig ruefully.

Still feeling energetic, after dinner I walked into town and found the Luxor Museum. This was more modern and more tastefully presented than the cluttered Museum of Antiquities in Cairo, and I enjoyed the brightly lit exhibits and their descriptions. Mummies in their blackened wrappings were given some dignity, whereas in Cairo they were just heaped in a corner. I loved the eight feet tall, red granite sculpture of Amenhotep III, discovered in Luxor Temple in 1989. In 3D you lose the "walking like an Egyptian" aspect of the reliefs and papyrus.

When I retired later that evening I found on my bed a swan fashioned from white towels and scattered with flower petals. That's what I call a quality sculpture.

The next morning after breakfast we gathered for the visit to two of the most beautiful temples in the world. First we saw the Luxor Temple, possibly built for the coronations of the Pharaohs. We walked up an avenue of sphinxes. Ahead were two huge pylons, great walls flanking the entrance, and seated in front of each were great statues of Rameses II. There was one beautiful obelisk to the left. (It's twin can be found on the Place Du Concorde in Paris, a gift, as were the obelisks to be found in Westminster, London, and Central Park, New York, both misnamed as Cleopatra's Needles).

Beyond the pylons were walls and colonnades adorned with hieroglyphs and reliefs of gods like Amun-Ra, his wife Mut, and brother Amun-min, having had his phallus chiselled away. At the rear of the ruins, atop an ancient wall was a shrine, possibly to Amun. During the Roman occupation this was converted for worship to their gods, and in the 4th century made into a church by the Coptic Christians. Later it became a mosque. This temple has been a centre for religious worship for over 3,400 years.

The avenue of sphinxes once linked the Luxor Temple to the Karnak complex. It is still only a short walk. If the former is a wonder, it is overshadowed by the latter, which once even featured in a James Bond film.

The Karnak Temple Complex is huge, a veritable village of avenues and halls, temples and chapels, pylons, precincts, sacred lakes and obelisks. Everything here features reliefs telling the stories of its creators. Thirty Pharaohs are thought to have contributed to its expansion from the dynasties of the Middle Kingdom, through to the end of the Roman occupation, possibly 2,500 years.

(Hieroglyphic reliefs celebrate the achievements of Pharaohs. Many of these tell the stories of great battles against their traditional enemies living outside the Nile Valley, in the lands of Chaos. There were the Nubians of the south, Libyans to the west, and Hyksos, Mitanni, Hatti, Assyrians, Babylonians and Persians from the east. Then there were the Sea People of the Mediterranean, from whence came the Greeks to establish the last dynasty of Ptolomy Pharaohs, and finally the Romans. Many reliefs show Pharaohs in their chariots leading thousands of their enemies, captured and shackled to become slaves. However, only victories are remembered and celebrated in stone. Hence no archaeologist has ever found any records of the plagues visited on Egypt by Moses' God, nor the subsequent exodus of the Israelites and the parting of the Red Sea which drowned the Pharaoh Hamun and his armies.)

We wandered the complex for hours, marvellous things around every corner. At the Sacred Lake, Sami told us how every morning the priests and priestesses would gather and perform their rituals to celebrate the birth of a new day. He also took us aside and we climbed high for a view over the whole complex. He then showed us an antechamber where the rays of the sun perfectly lit up Amun-Ra and Sekhmet, the lion-headed goddess.

Finally we spent time in the Great Hypostile Chamber with 16 rows of 134 giant columns, all carved with bas-relief scenes around their massive girths meant to resemble a papyrus swamp. Great for playing hide and seek, or using your license to kill in the Spy Who Loved Me.

Yesterday had been a day amongst the dead, today we experienced the times of the living, much better. I loved Luxor's east bank.

We returned to our boat which, after an Italian buffet lunch, finally set sail at 3:30. This was what I was looking forward to. We cast off and headed into midstream. It was slow going. Although we were heading south, we were actually sailing upriver against the current. We passed beneath the Luxor Bridge and people on both banks were waving and calling to us. The children actually ran alongside, all in immaculate school uniforms, even at the end of their school day. There were smiles all around. To our right the sun was beginning to sink behind the mountains, now in shadow, whereas the slopes to our left, beyond the twin temples shone brightly and golden.

We were soon out into the countryside, greenery on both sides, desert hills beyond. There were herons and storks and ibis, islands of reeds floated by heading north. Sandbanks were backed by palm trees and we passed the occasional mud hut village, a minaret or a factory. Farmers lifted their heads from their work and waved, families washing at the shore called and waved, fishermen looked up from their nets and waved, if we passed boats going the other way, horns hooted their greeting. I stood at the rail and watched this ancient world go by. I was fascinated by the fisherfolk. They'd be in their little coracles, near the bank, casting their nets, then furiously beating the water around them with the flat of their oars. This, Sami assured me, rather than scaring the fish away, encourages them into the nets. Well, you can't argue with 5,000 years of experience. Some children actually swam out to us to enjoy bouncing in our bow waves.

We arrived at the Esna lock after four hours. A barrage was built here to control the Nile flood over 100 years ago, and frustrating queues can form to traverse the lock, but rarely in the evening which our captain had planned to utilise. I watched, fascinated by the little ritual which had evidently built up over the years.

Entering the lock we were gradually raised up to meet the higher level. As we slowly rose, traders on the dockside were trying to sell items of Egyptian cotton, and shouted up their terms to the tourists overhanging the ship's rail. With a mastery and acquired strength they threw bolts of cloth, table cloths, sheets and pillowcases. As we rose higher their aim and ability became more and more apparent. Theses items were being arrowed upwards into customers' arms, fully 20 yards. What bowlers these traders could become on the village green in England.

Later at dinner as Katie devoured the buffet we discussed dynasties. A dynasty is a royal family which comes to power by battle or treaty (usually following a battle), and reigns until the next war, or the line dies out. Cleopatra was the last here, the 32nd dynasty. It had taken six to build the pyramids and 18 to develop the wonders of Thebes. Cleo was descended from Alexander the Great's general Ptolomy, and after her demise by asp, the Romans took over and Egypt was ruled by puppet Pharaohs. With the decline of the Roman empire, the kingdoms fell into disarray, the desert consumed the glories of the past, and the skills that built Karnak, the pyramids, great temples, sphinxes and obelisks, forgotten. Sami told us we still don't know how to mummify as the ancients did, and even the language was lost until the discovery of the Rosetta Stone.

Strangely it was after the Romans that other dynasties flourished elsewhere. In China there had been 13 until revolution swept them away. Similarly, revolution did for the royal houses of Russia, Greece, France, and most recently Spain (now reformed).

British royalty has managed to cling on, even if now only in a constitutional role. Once Alfred the Great had unified the English kingdoms we have had Wessex, Danes, Wessex again, Normans, Blois (briefly), Plantagenets, Tudors, Stuarts and Hanovers. The latter evolving into Saxe-Coburg-Gothas and then the Windsors. So in all about seven full dynasties. About time we built some pyramids.

The Japanese, Steve the drummer reminded, can trace their royal ancestors back 1500 years. So only the one dynasty then.

Dictatorships, monarchies, democratic republics. History shows it doesn't really matter what type of government you have so long as it seeks to help the poor and those less fortunate, and get along with other countries. In an enlightened 21st century perhaps we can make war history, and realise we are but one planet, where there is no room for xenophobia or jingoism.

Then we got talking about football. Such is the power of beer followed by wine, a few strong cocktails, and Egyptian brandy to take you to bed. My towel sculpture tonight was a horse, or was it a unicorn, and were there two or three or four?

I awoke with a thick head. Too much sun yesterday, I reasoned, and made my way onto deck in the darkest of dark glasses. We had already sailed, Esna was behind us, next stop Edfu.

I grabbed juice and coffee and some Danish pastries from the breakfast bar and returned to the upper deck to watch the world drift by. Schoolchildren, immaculately turned out waved and called from the left bank. Mothers and their smaller children washed their pots, their clothes and themselves among the reeds and rocks of the shoreline (the Nile crocodile was eradicated from these waters years ago). Fishermen cast their nets and slapped the shallows to my right. We passed the occasional cargo barge making its way downstream, and other cruise ships with a toot-toot and waves of hello, bonjour, ola, ciao, or just smiles. Felluccas with their triangular white sails tacked the breeze in the wider sections. There was the sun and the blue sky, the distant baked desert, the closer greenery, and the sound of the river as we struggled against its flow. Wisps of smoke rose from simple villages as we passed, and the smell of Africa, that beautiful, heady, earthy, woody, mossy, spicy air of innocent toil, was all around.

There were minarets and the call to prayer. Young boys tending cattle or goats waved their crooks. Islands passed with buffalo bathing in the shallows, and birds were everywhere, egrets and herons, kingfishers and crows, ox peckers and swallows, all doing their particular thing.

We tied up at Edfu, surprisingly at only 9:30. Ponies and traps awaited us. I wasn't too happy about the state of the horses, but apparently this was the way tourists in Edfu are ferried, to the Graeco-Roman Temple to Horus. Two points here. Firstly, if the horses didn't have this job, they would have no purpose and wouldn't exist, secondly it kept us off the streets so we couldn't be accosted by the locals.

Oh, it was really difficult. I wanted to see this country, stroll around the streets and shops and parks, even just wander along the corniche. But as soon as you walk down the gang plank you are targeted, and a young man is at your side. At first, they are very friendly, smiling, welcoming you to Egypt, innocently enquiring where you are from, and then inviting you to share their humble hospitality. I tell them I wish only to have a peaceful stroll, but they become insistent, eventually even pulling at your wrist to come with them to their shop. Once I have managed to convey my lack of interest in their goods, they turn and grimace and become frowning, scowling children, angry that they can't get their way.

Thus a pleasant walk can become a nightmare and that was why I was happy to be on board this pony and trap, until the driver started the same game.

Be that as it may, we were soon deposited at the Edfu Temple.

Egyptian Deities

"The system of Egyptian gods is complicated, not least because we don't really know how they were created, what they did, nor how or why they were worshipped. We have interpreted their mythologies and metaphors by examining the hieroglyphic records, but our understanding lacks any first hand reports and is restricted by our own contradicting theories developed by a variety of self-taught Egyptologists over the last two centuries.

We can surmise that they evolved from their own creation in the minds of the ancients, and their relationships with man and his Pharaohs for over 3,000 years. We can also assume that whilst their roles on Earth, with the creation of the Sun, Moon, Sky, Land, Nile, Harvest, Birth, etc. were of great importance, they came into their own with the human unknown, our fears since the dawn of time, Death and the passage into the Afterlife, or Underworld.

The most important god was Amun-Ra, a composite of creation and the sun, like the Greek Zeus or Roman Apollo. Osiris and Isis, husband and wife team were in charge of birth, death and resurrection and parents of Horus, the falcon headed god of healing. Their enemy was Seth, the ambivalent god of chaos and strength. Anubis was the jackal-headed god of the underworld, while Ptah, seen as Apis the bull, was also a creation god, husband to Sekhmet, the lioness-headed goddess who was mother to Sobek, the crocodile-headed god. All Pharaohs became gods, as well as some of their advisers, notably Imhotep. Hathor and Thoth represented the arts and knowledge.

There were nearly two thousand major and minor deities, some were assimilated from other cultures like Baal, the Syrian god of the sky, whilst others, such as Isis would be subsequently adopted by the Romans. It must have been interesting when the Upper and Lower Kingdoms united. The negotiations as to whom would be absorbed for what role.

Nut is one of my favourites. She was goddess of the sky, and in the guise of the Milky Way, her naked body over arched the world. She is sometimes seen as consuming the moon whilst simultaneously pooing out the sun."

The Edfu Temple to Horus was built about 400 yards from the river, as were all buildings in ancient Egypt. In those days, before any dams or barrages, the river could flood that far inland.

Sami made us walk to the end of the western flagged approach, then turn to take in the majesty of the twin pylons with their huge symmetrical figures of Horus on the inside warding off attacks from Seth.

Thanks to it having been ignored after the Roman occupation and labelled as pagan, it was covered with sands from the desert and silt from the river to a depth of 40 feet, even houses built on top of it. By the time it was rediscovered and dug out, it had been remarkably well preserved. As we had seen before, some of the haute relief had been chiselled away by Coptics and Victorian prudes, but generally the famous "Walk Like An Egyptian" two dimensional figures were impressive throughout. Sami did his best with his descriptions of the mythology to keep us from glazing over, but we'd now seen five temples in three days, and were suffering temple exhaustion. Loved the temple, loved the reliefs and the statues of Horus, but let's get back to the boat, set sail, and enjoy pottering up the river.

Harry was particularly looking forward to the evening entertainment; belly dancing. What he expected, I didn't know. But what he was hoping for we would soon find out.

Most of the other guests on the boat were Dutch, and many people could have been forgiven for thinking they were a group of loud Germans, for their beer-swilling noisy antics. But they wore orange, and there was a slight difference in their guttural accents. It felt strange as all of the Dutch I'd ever met have been fluent in English and would prefer to use it. Perhaps they were more confident in their rare majority.

With cool drinks in the afternoon, and as we continued south with the Nile scenery gently passing by, I got chatting to Nils and Jan, a young blond couple from Delft who both worked in The Hague, as civil servants.

The Dutch and British share an almost unique position in Europe, having split personalities. As I explained, I was born in England and spoke English, but my nationality was British and I lived in the United Kingdom. They were from Holland, but were Dutch and spoke Dutch. Their country however is called The Netherlands. How come?

"It is like people calling the UK, England," Nils explained. "The regions of Holland are our biggest provinces, therefore over the centuries even we refer to ourselves as Hollanders. It is called synecdoche." With that he proved once again some foreigners have better English than the English.

"But why Dutch?" I asked

"We call it Nederlands," said Jan, "and we like to think it is midway between German and English, not so harsh, more romantic." She fluttered her eyelashes and I felt myself blush.

"No, but why are You called Dutch?" I emphasised. And I explained how, since our differences around the 16th and 17th centuries, with wars over trade routes and spices, the term Dutch had been incorporated into English as a disparaging term.

I listed some of those phrases still in use today, "You can be talking double Dutch (rubbish), have Dutch courage (brought about by drink), go Dutch (pay individually) have a Dutch auction (drive prices down), or just say 'well I'll be a Dutchman' (meaning I've gone doolally)."

"It's your fault again," Jan continued. "The English called all Germanic speaking peoples Dutch, then the Germans became Germans, but Dutch stuck for the Netherlands," she had provided the answer, then added, "We don't find your terms offensive, they date from a different time. Mind you we do refer to the English Disease. This can be anything from football hooliganism to trade union obstinacy or economic stagnation. It is nothing to worry about as it can also apply to rickets, depression, sleeping sickness, syphilis and homosexuality."

Thus we moseyed on south, up the river, drinking cold beer in the relentless sunshine and joshing merrily together, happy in our ability to take the Mick out of each other. And that doesn't disparage the Irish, either.

We tied up at Kom Ombo, but it was too late to visit the temple, so I simply spent a pleasant hour in the cool of the dusk strolling around the well manicured gardens and admiring the imposing pylons of the east bank temple to Sobek, the crocodile god.

After dinner everybody settled down for the evening entertainment, the afore-mentioned belly dancing show, fairly standard tourist fare, but a certain young lad had been very excited about this moment all day. He wasn't even that interested in the show itself. It wasn't until the end, during that embarrassing and awkward moment when the dancers go amongst the crowd looking for volunteers that Harry came into his own.

"Pick my mum!" he shouted, jumping up and down, to the delight of everybody on the boat, and to the horror of Katie. "Pick my Mum!" he insisted again as Katie shrank back, trying not to catch anybody's eye. And Harry stood on his chair, and pointed extravagantly at his poor stricken mother. "Pick my mum, pick my mum!"

And thus reluctantly Katie was pushed forward. She was taken away to be fitted with veils as her son beamed in the corner. "My mum's the best," he proudly asserted.

The performance was suitably embarrassing, and I'll not dwell on it to save Katie's blushes. Suffice is to say neither her tiny belly nor her slender hips managed the gyrations her son was hoping for, but the applause was polite and sympathetic, and Craig praised his wife's courage.

That night my towels had been arranged into a large snapping crocodile.

The Graeco-Roman Temple at Kom Ombo, whilst impressive, fell below the standards of Edfu and Karnak. Funny that these marvellous places, located anywhere else would generate great wonder and awe, but when placed up river of neighbouring monuments, fail to impress. There were however three mummified crocodiles worthy of note in the attached museum, but quite small when compared to Nile crocodile monsters found elsewhere on the continent. Sami was his enthusiastic self as he described all of the temple's wonders, and we sailed after breakfast.

The highlight of today would be our arrival into Aswan.

Aswan is the link between the upper and lower Nile. From here there is an uninterrupted journey north to the Mediterranean, a supremely important trade route for millennia. For all that time granite has been quarried here to journey north, with the flow, to create the Egyptian architectural wonders; pyramid and temple stones, statues and obelisks. Here is the location of the historical First Cataracts, rapids and waterfalls, the natural river barriers. At Aswan, Egypt begins, but south there lies only the Dark Continent. At Aswan it was decided to create the High Dam that generates so much power and controls the flood and in turn formed Lake Nasser that leads to Sudan. Lake Nasser is one of the largest man-made reservoirs in the world, and its control, via the Aswan High Dam, is the catalyst for everything that happens in Egypt. The fact that Ethiopia is constructing their own dam will have wide reaching effects.

Aswan is one of the sunniest cities in the world, on the Tropic of Cancer, and rainfalls can be seven years apart. The Nile here is wide, nearly half a mile, and decorated with white sailed felluccas. There are islands, and Elephantine Island has its own town and botanical gardens. There are mosques, churches, monasteries and temples, museums and souks, a Nubian village and the Mausoleum of the Aga Khan. I wanted to see them all.

We tied up on the east bank and those due to visit the sites gathered on the quayside (having edged across the rear decks of four other boats).

It was a sorry crew. Four days and nights of foreign food had taken its toll. I arrived with Katie, fast metabolism and the constitution of a horse. Harry was not well, and Craig who himself didn't feel 100% was staying behind to convalesce. Steve and Emma had succumbed and remained on board. Of the remainder, mainly Dutch, at least half weren't up to it so there were only 12 souls fit for the excursion. Sami had a word with his fellow guides, fluent in Dutch, and we decided to pool our resources. Jan and Nils and another couple joined us two and Sami, and we set off for a whistle stop tour of Aswan.

"It's eggs," I said to anyone who had the constitution to listen, as we bounced along the rutted streets. "I never eat eggs, and, touch wood, I am never ill abroad." I repeat this mantra every time, but the disinterested green faces that looked away told their own story.

First stop was the old dam where we took motor boats to the island temple of Philae. Approaching by water we first saw the temple pavilion, or Trajan Kiosk, a 12 pillared square mini-temple dedicated to Horus, son of Isis. This was perched on rocks above the river. We then rounded the island to tie up at the landing jetty.

We disembarked and joined the crowds above the diesel fumes. The temple here illustrates a perfect example of how these structures have evolved over three thousand years.

First built in the 25th dynasty by the Nubian Pharaoh Tahaka, it was deified as the burial site of Osiris. Legend had it that no birds flew over, nor animals lived on, nor fish swam around the island. Isis, his wife who resurrected him, was worshipped here, and the original had many additions and extensions for 1,000 years. Isis was also a Greek and Roman Goddess, hence the original Egyptian carvings had been overdrawn. Later still the Coptic Christians defaced what they saw as pagan worship, as did adherents to Islam. Isolated on an island, the temple didn't suffer cannibalisation to build future towns, and the river washed away desert sands. Hence the temple has stood almost pristine for 3,000 years. However with the building of the lower Aswan dam, floods and silt began to undermine the foundations and it started to crumble. Thankfully UNESCO took over and it was taken brick by brick to be rebuilt on a higher island 600 yards away, in the 20th century.

Its repositioning was a marvel in itself, just like Abu Simbel, but it has lost the majesty of the palms, pylons, purple mountains and glistening boulders which used to frame it. Plus, many of its jewels; statues, friezes and obelisks now stand in the Louvre.

I loved the Temple at Philae, I love anything on an island.

Our little boats took us back to the right bank and we visited a papyrus factory, eminently forgettable, really just a shopping opportunity for which I am sure Sami and his fellow guides receive a commission.

Then it was on to the Unfinished Obelisk. This sounds far more uninspiring than it was. It is a broken piece of granite which once snapped became unusable and therefore abandoned. But lying here, still in its quarry, it provides a huge clue as to how these monuments were created.

The obelisk was hewn out of the bedrock on three sides. The planned hieroglyphs, telling the stories of the Pharaoh for whom this was to be created, were to have been carved into those three sides, right up to the needle. But this one, for Hatshepsut, broke in two. And there it has lain, abandoned for 35 centuries. At nearly 140 feet it would have been the largest obelisk ever. Probably why it broke.

If it had been completed, the fourth side would have been hewn out and the obelisk rolled onto a barge using tree trunks. Down the Nile it would have sailed to Karnak where it would have been raised into place using a growing mountain of sand and levers (we think!).

Finally we were taken to see the High Aswan Dam. Nothing like you would imagine, not steep sided concrete like the Hoover Dam. This is a simple embankment dam built jointly with help from the Soviet Union in the 1960's. It is 50 yards across, and to the North the Nile flows, and to the south the huge Lake Nasser stands, which displaced 100,000 people.

Many towns and villages had to be relocated, as well as temples and statues from ancient times. The most famous of these is Abu Simbel, a temple to Rameses II. You can fly there, or go by road, but at the time of our visit, "bandit activity" had closed it off. I'd seen enough temples anyway, my cognitive dissonance told me (c. d.-; when you see a pair of shoes identical but cheaper than the ones you have just bought, your mind tells you these others would have leaked, probably).

It was back to the boat for a light late lunch, then the majority of the walking wounded were able to join us for our evening excursion, a trip to Kitchener Island and Botanical Gardens. We boarded felluccas, four at a time, and took the short trip behind Elephantine Island to the gardens. On the way, and it was a pleasure to be wind driven on the lovely babbling waters, we were pleasantly accosted by a number of children rowing green leafed coracles, and they serenaded us with their delightful soprano voices.

The island was a joy, the gardens brightly coloured with shrubs, trees and flowers from around the tropics, a glorious avenue of tall royal palms ran down the centre, and the place was alive with birdsong. We stopped for a tranquil coffee and returned to our fellucas.

I wandered the brightly lit souk in the twilight before dinner. It was hot, bustling and spicy. The scents of frangipani and sandalwood were almost mind numbing, many coming from the open air hookah and coffee shops, but Oh dear! the butcher's shops were bluebottle central, you couldn't see the meat for the flies.

In the morning there was nothing on the itinerary so I negotiated a trip by felluca to the opposite bank. We sailed towards the cataracts, south passed Kitchener Island to the Aga Khan's Mausoleum, a modern domed building set atop the hill. Here I hired a camel to take me to the tombs of the Fatimid cemetery. I mounted Ganga, my guide Mahmoud mounted his camel, and together we travelled into the desert. Ganga only tried to run off with me twice, but once we were behind the hill Mahmoud led us on a heavy trot to the ruins of the San Simeon monastery. No rising trots on a camel, nor stirrups, you just go with the flow, or to be more precise, bounce.

I dismounted at the Nubian village and walked to the rock tombs, mostly Graeco-Roman architecture, with some dating from the Old Kingdom, 2,500 BC. Hieroglyphs mingled happily with a lovely Coptic Chapel brightly decorated with saintly icons.

I climbed to the top of the hill, to the Qubbat-el-Hawa, the dome of the wind, from where I had a marvellous view of the village, the town opposite, the river and its islands. The hill felt more like a sand dune, and I flowed down to be met by Mahmoud at the bottom. I swam in the Nile, warm and refreshing, and I was assured clean along the west bank, then sailed home. A grand trip.

Aswan to Luxor

We left Aswan at 4:30. "It will be much quicker returning north, with the flow of the river," Sami informed us.

Over dinner Sami had kept us fascinated with his talk of Cartouches, oval hieroglyphic name plates, Ankhs, a cross with a loop, the staff of life, and the Pshent double crown, worn by the Pharaohs to signify the unity of the upper and lower kingdoms. The red honeybee crown surrounded the white bowling pin, and it carried a vulture and cobra. There have only ever been pictorial representations, no crown has ever been found in a tomb or with a mummy.

Most people appeared to have recovered from their tummy troubles. Not that Katie noticed as she demolished her third plate of seconds.

After dinner with a full night of stars we passed Kom Ombo, the golden hill. It was lit up and resplendent. Seeing the fragments of colour in the bas-reliefs made you realise in antiquity these were brilliant gold and reds and blues. Pity the modern technology of electric light hadn't been around when these splendid decorations were brand new. It was warm and breezy on deck, full of the smells of Africa, and a party was beginning below. Traditionally, tonight is fancy dress.

I remember chatting over a couple of scotches with Jan and Nils, looking up at the stars. Katie joined us with a cocktail and a plate of creamy pastries. A boat passed, struggling south, and we exchanged hoots, a call from a minaret echoed over the river, and in the dining room people were walking like an Egyptian. Craig and Harry trekked the trail of the lonesome pine as Steve and Emma played air drums. My towel sculpture as I staggered to bed in the early hours was either a twin humped Bactrian camel or two tortoises. I couldn't be sure.

The next day, as we passed the Esna Lock, the captain invited us down for a tour of the bridge and engine room; all clocks and dials, cranks and pistons, charts and levers, and engine oil. I hadn't been so interested in the workings of a boat since the transition of the Panama Canal, or the Yavari on Lake Titicaca. Good times.

With the trip coming to an end I sat on the upper deck and reflected. The sun was setting behind me and I gazed upon the changing colours of the eastern mountains.

It wasn't just the history and mystery of the people who created the dawn of civilisation, and the legacies of the wonders they had left behind. It was the river, and this thin strip of green flanked by desert. The palms, fields of sugar cane, small poor villages, buildings in disrepair, workers in the fields, children at the shore, fishermen, women at their chores, donkeys and cattle, buffaloes bathing, the birdlife, especially egrets and herons, the sacred ibis. The islands with their grazers, the convoys and their horns, the floating clumps of shrub, the calling from the minarets, "Pick my mum", double dutch, Sami and his knowledge, the mysterious towel sculptors.

Three hours from Luxor.

Dinner was quiet, except for Katie who demolished the buffet again. She would be on a flight tomorrow to Heathrow, I had a 6:45am to Manchester. Most of the Dutch left as we docked, taking the overnight train to Cairo. Steve and Emma had a coach to Hurghada for a week sunbathing on the Red Sea.

I wandered the town, stopping to see the little back street workshops skilfully producing their artefacts in metal and leather. Fires and smoke and hammering and fashioning, age old skills. I bought some souvenirs; a papyrus, cartouches, statues of Horus and Osiris

I returned for an early night (early flight), opened the door to my cabin and let out a little yelp of surprise. There on my armchair was sitting a man, cross legged holding my journal and a pen in one hand, a glass in the other. He was wearing my hat and sunglasses. I had a moment of shock, almost fear, "Who the ...!"

Those darned towel sculptors.

I love Egypt and we've been many times. Five visits to the Red Sea and the Sinai, Cairo four times, and another Nile Cruise. Then the 'Arab Spring' as named by the BBC, threatened to pull the Middle East apart, a bomb brought down a Russian passenger jet flying from Sharm, and the flames of revolution brought violence and insecurity. The country was just beginning to open up again when the worldwide pandemic struck. As I have indicated before, the tourist industry is highly capricious.

I have one more wonderful memory of a Nile Cruise.

Kaz and I having experienced the delights to Aswan and back, returned to Luxor, but instead of this being the last part of the adventure, I had booked a hot air balloon flight over the Valley of the Kings.

Balloon flights are always dawn departures.

We were taken from our boat to the Colossi of Memnon, old friends, Shama and Tama. We watched as our balloon inflated, a huge multi-coloured bulb, and were directed to climb into the basket. There were four compartments and two people clambered into each. The pilot was in the centre controlling the burn to heat air in the balloon. Once airborne you are at the mercy of the prevailing winds. All the pilot can do is take you up, or down.

Up, up and away, as the best songs go. There was no whoosh, just a gradual climb and suddenly the crowned heads of the Colossi were beneath us. There were balloons all around, mostly rising, as we were. Then, to our left we could see the colonnades of Hatshepsut's temple, and the escarpment behind, where lay the Valley of the Kings. But we began going the other way. The pilot explained the breeze mainly blew east to west. We had begun on the west bank, intending to fly over the Kings' tombs and way beyond into the desert. Today, he told us, the wind would be taking us east, back across the river. We rose higher and could plainly see below us the smoke trails from the burning of the cane fields' stubble. We were going the same way.

The temple and the colossi were behind us now and we began floating across and far above the Nile. We could see river boats arriving to their moorings, and white sailed fellucas, and then the majesty of Karnak and the avenue of sphinxes leading to the Luxor temple, but mostly as we crossed the eastern bank, we could see the city, the modern hotels near the shoreline, the criss-cross of roads, the back streets of artisan houses and workshops. Finally, after an hour or so, we were beyond the city and above irrigation canals bringing life blood to the farmer's fields. Then the pilot told us we would be landing in one of those fields.

The pilot led us down slowly, and the basket was skimming across treetops. Strange, but up there everything had seemed so peaceful and serene, just floating. Down here we were frantically avoiding crashing headlong into trees, going at a frightening pace. Then the pilot found a gap, let more air from the balloon and we dropped onto the edge of a field. The basket hit the ground with a bump, and with one last pulse, the balloon pulled the basket over and all the passengers spilled into the field. We stood up, laughing and dusted ourselves down. Some children ran over, pointing at us and our craft and jabbering as if we were invading aliens. The farmer appeared with a donkey and cart and began remonstrating with the pilot. I wasn't sure whether he wanted compensation for his crushed crop, or was offering to taxi us back on his cart. Eventually the following crew arrived, placated the farmer with a hand full of grubby notes, packed away the gear and returned us to our boat. Just in time for breakfast.

Chapter Four

The Gambia with the Beckhams

The smallest country on mainland Africa, The Gambia is a west coast sliver, wholly surrounded by Senegal.

It used to be a reliable pub quiz question. Which is the largest country in Africa? People always think of Africa with elephant and lions and apes, so rarely come up with the answer, Sudan, which is mostly Sahara Desert. But then it split and South Sudan became one of the world's newest countries. The answer now is Algeria. Similarly with cities, with a population of 20 million the largest is Cairo, but many people think of Kinshasa, or Lagos, in sub-Saharan Africa, or even Johannesburg in South Africa.

Anyway, The Gambia is the smallest country, existing either side of the Gambia river, which empties into the Atlantic. It is almost as far west as it is possible to go in Africa. There is a 40 mile coastline on which much of their fishing and tourism industries depend.

We (Kaz joined me on this adventure. I go gallivanting, she lies on the beach) arrived at Banjul airport via Birmingham, a manageable five hour flight with no time difference, and checked in at the Badala Park Hotel.

When we are taking a holiday, I will usually choose somewhere with a coral reef. The Red Sea, Indian Ocean, Caribbean are all fine. I love snorkelling. There aren't coral reefs in the Mediterranean, nor the west coast of the Americas, nor the west coast of Africa. The Med is too cold, and the other two have coastlines have cool currents flowing north from Antarctica, so coral can't form.

I've also previously avoided the west coast of Africa as it is too hot and steamy. Humid jungles riddled with disease carriers, and the countries tend towards volatility and hostility, hardly conducive for a mere cowardly gallivanter. Give me the eastern savannah, a cool breeze and the coral reef, all the time.

However, I felt I needed to explore a west African country as these colonies were originally created for the insidious slave trade, which, evil as it was, proved to be a huge catalyst in the development of the world as we know it today. Huge amounts of people in the Americas, Caribbean and Europe can trace their roots to this area.

The Resort

Kotu is the village, and the Badala Park is on the beach, well not quite. Out the back of the hotel is a little crossroads of dirt tracks. To the right it heads to a river, with a wooden footbridge on the other side of which is a small village of mud huts with straw roofs, possibly housing hotel workers. The women are at the river with their small ones, busy washing pots and clothes. They wear colourful wrap around dresses and turbans, some carry a papoose, front or back. The river is full of egrets and other wading birds.

Ahead is the beach, but there are a number of little stalls selling curios and souvenirs, silk scarves or beach bags. Beyond these you have to cross a field of brown cattle, while pigs scavenge on the verges. The field is uncut bush; grasses wave in the breeze with colourful shrubs and flowering trees. Beyond are paddy fields and mangroves. Marking the boundary between sand and soil, palm trees offer welcome shade for the European sun bathers. Across the pristine beach the breakers of the Atlantic Ocean crash in a burst of white foam. Men throw fishing nets into the sea at the confluence of the river. Large colourful fishing boats dot the shore above the tide line, possibly six or eight oars.

This was the scene that greeted us on that hot, sweltering February morning. We paused to meet the stallholders, browsing idly as they smiled and welcomed us warmly, all women.

One girl, wearing jeans and a pink striped shirt. was seated beneath an umbrella with a small trestle table on which lay three or four well thumbed books, and a pair of binoculars.

"I am Fatou," she introduced herself. Her braided hair fell across her shoulders with colourful beads which also adorned her neck. "If you like the bads, I can take you to see the bads." She opened one book and pointed to a colourful bird. "This is the Blue Spotted Roller, our national bad. He lives here. I can show you". She indicated across the bridge.

We thanked Fatou and promised to take her up on her kind offer.

We had the rest of the day at the beach, returning to the hotel only for lunch and dinner. Kaz sunbathed while I frolicked in the warm ocean, great fun with those big breakers. Around us on the beach were other couples and a few families, of course, but also some singletons, mostly middle aged women, usually in conversation with young local men. The same young men you could find hanging around at the front of the hotel. Non-threatening, just friendly young men. I gave them no more thought.

Ours was a small two storey hotel, and our room, on the top floor overlooked colourful, manicured gardens with trees the height of our balcony. Here we were up in the canopy, and it didn't disappoint. The birdsong was ever present, louder and more insistent at dawn, with a different, calmer tone at dusk. At night the trilling frog songs were punctuated only by the occasional near-silent swoosh of an owl. Our favourite was the superb starling magnificent in its iridescent greens and blues. One would perch regularly on our balcony.

We breakfasted at the hotel, but dined across the road at the Barracuda restaurant, always fish or chicken accompanied by rice and vegetables. Guaranteed fresh, sometimes spicy, always tasty, with names like superkanja, benachin, or domoda on the menu, all washed down with Jul Brew.

We met our fellow guests in the evening, (as the drummers and dancers wearily went through the motions of displaying their village rituals) and at breakfast. They were an earnest lot, disinterested in the holiday experience. They were here to lend their skills to help building a school. Very altruistic. Some said they came every year to saw and fit and paint, mix cement and build classrooms. "If it weren't for us there'd be no education," they insisted.

Around and About

We were advised to travel down the beach, south, to see the feeding of the vultures. Thus one morning we set off, sun to our left, rollers to our right. We kept to the wet sand left by the retreating tide, for a better purchase on your flip-flops. After an hour or so, during which we saw hardly a soul, we came to the Senegambia hotel, and stepped up onto a wide, well-kept lawn. Other folk were gathering and after a while some of the hotel workers, young lads dressed in white came to the lawn, carrying plastic bins.

We knew vultures were about to be fed, but could see none circling like in the old movies. Then we realised they didn't need to circle, they weren't waiting for their prey to become carrion, nor for the alpha predators to have had their fill. All they needed to do was wait in their roosts till 11am, and dinner arrived with a hey presto.

It reminded me of break time or lunchtimes at school. Towards the end, with the children still running around noisily, the gulls would gather on the roofs, in the trees, or perch on the perimeter fence. The bell ringing was like a signal to Pavlov's dogs. With the children heading for class, the birds would come screeching down onto the playground to hoover up the discarded crisps and sandwiches.

Back in The Gambia, ropes were affixed to goat or chicken carcasses, and the boys swung them around in the air. Within moments dozens of huge black vultures with ten foot wingspans swooped down onto the lawns to devour the food. Each was the size of a large turkey. With those bald heads and necks, and their strange loping trot, they fought and gorged on the free meals to the delight of the watching tourists.

There are always controversies about these types of displays (I've seen a similar show for red kites at Bwlch Nant yr Arian, which you might guess, is in Wales). The birds are being encouraged to rely on human intervention; they might, like seagulls, learn to mug humans; they become unnaturally domesticated, and evolve to forget their natural behaviour. But, of course, they're not going to stick their noses (hooked beaks) up at a free lunch.

The biggest question however is why are we feeding these birds all this free meat, in a country where many families and children are starving in abject poverty?

They answer that it encourages tourists, who spend their tourist dollars, and help the economy. But most of that money never cascades down to where it is really needed. I wonder.

After they'd fed, many of the vultures spread their wings to bask in the sunshine as the tourists walked amongst them.

A little further along the beach from the Senegambia Hotel was the Bijilo Forest National Park, a strip of jungle at the back of the dunes, and we spent the rest of the day wandering its pathways, in and around the palms and rich scrub. The forest is famous for its troupes of monkeys, both up in the trees and on the ground hoping to be fed. We also saw birds including our favourite hornbills, and agamas, foot-long colourful lizards.

Butterflies fluttered in the searing heat, and the humidity amplified the aromas of the flora, creating a sultry cocktail for the senses. We were bowled over by this heady experience. And when you added the buzz of the insects blending with the distant roar from the crashing waves, it was all-intoxicating. No wonder we needed to cool off with a swim and thirst quenching beers once we had strolled wearily back to our hotel.

Next day we met Fatou at the rickety Kotu bridge shortly after breakfast.

Instead of using the bridge, Fatou suggested we wade across the river. Under the bridge she pointed out bat roosts and the sticky nests of the swallows, swifts and martins, all fattening up on African insects before making their arduous migration to Europe, and in particular to our barns in England, to breed. At water level we could see the wading birds, herons and egrets. There may have also been curlews and avocets and bitterns, such were the variety. Kingfishers seemed to dive amongst us, both monotone and iridescent. Climbing out of the river we walked through armies of soldier crabs, the males waving their hugely oversized single claw (for them, size does matter) to attract a mate. We walked down to the confluence on the beach, greeting the washer women who smiled happily as their children played. Sandpipers ran skittishly in and out of the wave ripples as the breakers died on the sand.

Eventually Fatou turned right and took us inland where the rice paddies mixed with the mangroves, and the wild bush was a haven for insects and birds. She had her book, and we our binoculars, and every so often she would shush us and point to a distant tree or branch.

"Is a blue spotted roller, coucou, piapiac, drongo, bee eater, long tailed starling," she would whisper enthusiastically. She knew, and enjoyed her 'bads'.

What a morning we spent, sloshing in and out of irrigation channels, climbing around mangrove roots and buttresses, leaping over logs and hedges. We saw harriers and parakeets, plovers and shrikes, grouse and kites. There were all sorts, a twitcher's paradise.

We bought Fatou lunch and she explained to us she had matriculated and was hoping to go to the University in Serekunda next year.

"I want to be a teacher," she confessed. She had already taught us so much.

Then in later conversation she asked "I am troubled. Do you know what is a conundrum?"

We asked what was on her mind.

"Here we are very poor and the government knows that the way out of poverty is education, so we build schools. But the European tourists come to our country to build the schools for free."

We couldn't see a lot wrong with that.

"But the young men who should be busy building our schools have no work, therefore they hang around the hotels being gigolos for the European women!"

Then we could see the conundrum and understood why so many young men were on the beach. The Gambia is a hotspot for sex tourism. As one female colleague put it to me years later; it is just sex with no baggage, no questions asked, no repercussions, no guilt, and then you come home.

(And your cuckolded husbands take away the boys' real jobs.)

Not for the first time on my travels have I had to remind myself of Starfleet's Prime Directive; Never to interfere with the internal and natural development of other societies and civilisations for fear of contaminating their culture with our different values and ideals.

On behalf of Europe, a supposedly advanced society, I could only apologise to Fatou.

The next day Fatou took us into Bakau, a suburb of Banjul, for two important reasons. We first visited The Divine Hope Orphanage School.

Orphanages are now an anachronism in the UK. Youngsters in need are taken into care and foster families sought out to look after them. In Africa, and especially Sub Saharan Africa it is not possible to create that sort of system, the infrastructure and whole of society is still too poor.

Also, and this is the true tragedy, the instance of orphan creation here, is epidemic.

Talk of the greatest killers worldwide, and heart disease or cancer will be cited. Well, in developed countries, we are lucky to be able to live to an age where those dangers are a consideration.

Malaria might be mentioned, especially for people living in the tropics. And yes, Malaria kills over 400,000 people a year, 90% of whom are from Sub Saharan Africa.

But HIV/AIDS kills three times that amount. Over a million people a year die from AIDS in Sub Saharan Africa. over 70% of instances of AIDS around the world are in SSA, and 90% of the children suffering from AIDS around the world are in SSA.

In these countries AIDS has reduced life expectancy in some areas by 20 years, to only 35. A whole generation of parents and economically active young adults have died from AIDS. This is why places like the Divine Hope Orphanage School exist, and why schemes like Comic Relief exist, and why charity efforts need to start from the ground up.

It was a run down building with dilapidated furniture and equipment, but to many it was home and the only prospect of a future. We chatted for a while with some youngsters and their teachers, then left in tears.

"Why are you crying?" asked Fatou, "This is Africa!"

TIA. I'd heard that so many times. Instead of complaining, just know and accept that 'this is Africa'. Previously it had applied to slow service in shops or restaurants, or interminable delays at border crossings. I'd never heard it before in the context of children with no families.

Why is AIDS so prevalent in SSA? This question has been addressed by people much more qualified than me. There has been education and edicts from the well respected, Bishop Tutu, Nelson Mandela. There are free condoms everywhere you look. There should be no more ignorance, but still it is there.

"Lorry drivers," said Fatou. "They deliver goods to towns and villages all over the continent, on long drives where they need to stop over. They look for the young girls, and they have money."

To lighten the mood, (it didn't) Fatou took us to the small History of Gambia Museum. It contained some interesting artefacts and information about the country's flora and fauna, but mostly there were exhibits which related to its colonial past and links to the slave trade.

During three centuries of the slave trade, over 3 million people were sold, chiefly by Africans to Europe and then the New World. These people were usually prisoners from tribal conflict or kidnapped unfortunates. From 1807 when Britain first abolished the slave trade, the navy worked hard to return slave ships to the Gambia river.

Next port of call was the Kachikally Crocodile Pool, surely one of the most amazing places on earth, which prompted me to write the following article.

Tick Tock Croc

"Crocodilia is the term that covers true crocodiles, alligators. caiman and gharials. They are marvellous creatures which lived alongside the dinosaurs and are such perfect predators they have hardly had to evolve in the 100 million years of their existence. We in the modern era find them a sinister creature because, quite frankly they receive a bad press.

I've had a variety of encounters with them on three continents but I've always thought that the blue riband of excursions would be a boat trip in the Northern Territories of Australia to see the "Salties", giant salt water crocodiles, a truly fearsome man eater. *But I can beat that.*

I recall standing on the ramparts of Ranthambhore Fort in Rajastan looking for tigers, but down below at the lakeside I could see what looked like tiny parallel sticks. Focussing through my binoculars I saw they were crocodiles, hundreds of them, lying on the banks, basking in the sunshine. Fish eaters I imagined. *But I got that beat.*

In the Everglades of Florida the alligators boss the canals, about one every hundred yards or so. That is their territory. You see them crossing the roads, and I've approached to within ten feet as they've basked on the banks, and they simply slide off into the water. I don't know about swimming with them but people canoe in flimsy craft alongside them. You can go to shows where wizened rangers will tell you they have a brain the size of a quarter (the alligators, not the rangers), slow metabolisms so they only need to eat once a month, and are very territorial. The ranger will then dive onto the back of one to demonstrate how they were caught, and show that if you slowly put something into their gaping jaws, they can snap shut with an unnerving crack, which is quite startling. I've also seen many of their smaller cousins the caiman on waterways throughout Central America. *But I can beat all that.*

The most aggressive of crocodiles is thought to be the Nile Crocodile which can be found throughout sub Saharan Africa. They have a similar lifespan to us and can grow to about 15 feet. The largest I've ever stroked however was only 10 feet! The ancient Egyptians worshipped Sobek, the crocodile headed god of the Nile, and mummified crocs can be seen at the temple at Kom Ombo. Crocodiles have been eradicated from the upper Nile now, but at Aswan children will bring hatchlings to restaurants for tourists to photograph.

In sub-Saharan Africa every waterhole has a crocodile, and the rivers are full of them. Children and women washing the family clothes are taken regularly from river banks and we've all seen the pictures of crocs attacking wildebeest as they try to cross the Mara River on their mass migration. I've seen the carcasses which all but clog up the river. Crocodiles are still not the most dangerous water based animal though. That distinction belongs to the hippopotamus. If you see a hippo whilst out walking, so the local advice goes, stand perfectly still, bend over and put your head between your legs; and kiss your ass goodbye! *But I've even got that lot beat.*

Probably my most alarming encounter was whilst on safari in Kruger National Park, South Africa. And this was where I felt a certain affinity with Captain Hook whose crocodile nemesis had eaten his hand and liked it so much it stalked him for more. Luckily from the pirate's point of view this crocodile had swallowed an alarm clock so Hook was always alerted to the danger by the approaching tick-tock, tick-tock. Who wound it up? I often wondered as a child.

It was approaching lunchtime and our jeep came out of the jungle and slithered down a dirt track to a rickety looking bridge which crossed a small river virtually at its surface. Slowly we crossed the shaky bridge, and half way across we stopped so the bridge could stabilise. I looked over the side, and there, less than three feet from my head were the open jaws of a huge crocodile reaching up out of the water. I jerked my head back inside the "safety" of the open car. You remember how Roy Schieder delivered the line "We're gonna need a bigger boat!" in Jaws? Well, I simply enquired whether *now!* might be a good time to consider making our way to the other side, Mr Smee! *But I can better even that!*

Kachikally Crocodile Pool has to be one of the most amazing places in the world. It is a sacred site, a sanctuary where crocodiles and visitors alike are allowed to roam free. Located in the centre of a particularly poor district of Bakau, in The Gambia just west of the capital, Banjul, I visited with Kaz and our guide, the lovely Fatou.

The pool itself is about half an acre, set in a depression, and is green with weed. It is surrounded by lush jungle, rocks and strategically placed pathways. Because of the canopy it feels cool, quiet and peaceful. Locals believe a visit can increase fertility therefore washing rituals are performed regularly for barren women.

There are around 100 Nile crocodiles of various ages and sizes living here, and they are fed on fish so don't see humans as potential meals. Mysteriously, there is no aggression, which is attributed to Kachikally's hallowed nature. Whatever the reason, these reptiles are docile and therefore approachable. Not only approachable but you can sit with them and even stroke them. We posed with several, from six foot adolescents to 10 foot giants, all dressed in the bright green algae which covers the pool. I wouldn't advocate sitting on them or putting your hands in their mouths, and they are hardly cuddly or attractive enough to want to take home, but simply being able to wander around in the company of these normally fearsome predators is wondrous in itself.

Kachikally is an unbeatable and astonishing experience which is truly unique. If it were in any other country then all tourist roads would lead there. As it is, it is a hidden gem. Captain Hook would have felt comfortably at home."

South Gambia Safari

We had one last adventure in The Gambia, but Fatou had returned to school so couldn't join us. An open land rover picked us up at 9am, just us, our guide, William and a driver who William didn't introduce. We were heading south.

From Kotu we drove through the village of Kololi, past the Bijilo Forest. We turned inland at Trankill and stopped at the Abuka National Park.

We had driven through several villages, and sitting on the back of an open jeep, stuck out like two sore thumbs. The villages were busy with people going about their daily business. Off the main street all roads were just dirt tracks, a hotchpotch of ramshackle shops and market stalls,but folk seemed happy, jaunty, waving and calling jovially. Women in colourful tops and long skirts carried enormous loads on their heads. Children ran alongside our vehicle shouting and holding out their hands. Once I threw some sweets their way, and the resulting frenzy looked just too dangerous. It was a mistake, it is best not to, it only encourages the begging.

Walking into Abuka park, lush green thick vegetation among mahogany and palm oil trees, William took us to a hide overlooking the Lamin stream. We saw Herons and snake birds, two crocs and a monitor lizard. We continued through the dense bush and came across colobus and vervet monkeys, and then to a rescue centre with baboons, hyena, and a bush buck.

Next William took us to Lamin's Lodge Oyster Farm on the Gambia river where we canoed around the mangrove buttress roots to find kingfishers, soldier crabs and mud-skippers. Back at the lodge we took coffee and were serenaded by a dread-locked musician and his home made guitar. Inland it was hot and humid, and we were glad to get back in the car for the breeze, but not before we had bought a box of lollipops for the children.

After driving through three small, but very poor villages we were back at the coast, Paradise beach, William called it, and there were many brightly coloured fishing boats returning with catches of tarpon, grouper and snapper. The scene was madness with tons of silvery fish, some over four feet in length being thrown onto the sand, fishermen and buyers haggling over prices. Seabirds swooping down for the leftovers added to the disarray.

Just behind the beach was a village with wooden huts for living in, smoking fish, and eating, and at one we had a beautiful meal of fresh fish and rice on the porch overlooking the sea where it was caught (the fish, not the rice).

Behind our restaurant shack was a crèche for mothers with their babies. This was the moment Kaz had been waiting for. She had brought with her two carrier bags full of our granddaughter, Taylor's clothes that she had grown out of. Giving these to the grateful mothers Kaz was overjoyed when seconds later three little girls were playing together wearing Taylor's Mothercare frocks.

A dozen boys were hanging around, kicking their heels, looking glum. I asked William why they were so sad.

"They have broken their ball," he said. "They were playing football and it has burst."

I had seen a shop in the last village so asked the driver to take me there where I bought them a new ball.

They were overjoyed if a little quizzical when I handed it over. They kept looking back at us slightly confused. Understandable really. We had signed the ball "David and Victoria Beckham".

We finished the day with a peaceful stroll around the Tanji Bird Reserve and were returned to the hotel by 5:30. We thanked William and I gave the driver my green and white striped shirt, a favourite, but I was brimming with pride to see him drive away proudly sporting it.

That night, our last, we dined with Fatou. I happened to mention that we were impressed that everyone spoke English fluently.

"I am Mandinka, we are the majority. But there are so many tribes here, we have over 20 languages. It is better to speak one which everyone understands." Wise girl.

Finally, the last few days had been hard for Kaz. She had alternated between joy and despair, thoroughly enjoying meeting such friendly and innocent people, but weeping over the bleakness of their poverty stricken lives.

"A beautiful people at peace with themselves. They have the sunshine, the ocean, the land, their religion, and little else. Their life is hard, but the children play, folk are honest, and their greetings' sincere. Their smiles light up the world. We don't know we're born," she concluded, philosophically.

Chapter Five

Ethiopia. Geldof, Lucy and Haille Selase

Ethiopia was recommended to me by Julie, the accountant from Leeds whose breast I crushed on a volcano in Nicaragua.

It is the former Abyssinia in the Horn Of Africa, one of 17 landlocked countries on the continent, since its civil conflicts with Eritrea led to the loss of its Red Sea access.

Sadly, the name Ethiopia has become an icon for "Biblical famine" since Michael Buerk's report for BBC World News on the 23rd October, 1984:

"Dawn, and as the sun breaks through the piercing chill of night on the plains outside Korem, it lights up a biblical famine, now, in the 20th century."

The pictures beamed back were of a sea of malnourished families living in bleak tents. The children,, their large eyes protruding from gaunt faces, were too weak to wave away the flies. Children with flies in their eyes, another symbol for Africa and poverty.

The scenes roused Bob Geldof and Midge Ure to action, and a couple of average singers in mediocre bands became world leaders in the fight against poverty and famine.

If only we'd known then that the catastrophe was not caused by Mother Nature alone, but government and NGO induced. Oxfam and Medicins Sans Frontieres had advised displacing farmers for work elsewhere. Had they not left, their skills would have been able to deal with the drought. More, essential supplies delivered were mostly lost to bandits, spoiled where they lay abandoned in dockyards, or acquired by forces bent on profit.

Nonetheless, we bathed in the glory of our "doing something", massaged our egos on the altar of donation, and enjoyed "Band Aid", a great concert. It made Phil Collin's reputation, catapulted Freddie Mercury into superstardom, and helped free Nelson Mandela.

The disaster also spawned a genre of telethons, charity concerts, charity hit singles (Do They Know It's Christmas?). Stars each sang one line, and celebrities visited Africa to highlight the plight of those children-with-flies-in-their-eyes, improving their own image, simultaneously.

Many years later for my own adventures in Ethiopia, I reported back with articles called Blogs. Whatever they are.

"Blog One

This is not the Ethiopia of Bob Geldof, suffering drought and famine, torn by civil strife and afflicted by a despotic, totalitarian regime.

30 years on from Band Aid and the Red Terror, Ethiopia models itself as the new spirit of Africa. Modern agriculture could lead it to be the breadbasket of the continent, there is universal schooling, the makings of a national health service and infant mortality is falling whilst life expectancy rises.

Some of the four star hotels would put western equivalents to shame, especially the level of service, comfort and spectacular locations. There are problems, of course, (This is Africa, where poverty isn't measured by obesity) and troublesome neighbours, and China is having an increasing influence, but overall Ethiopia is a nation ready to embrace prosperity. Bring it on.

I began my journey in Harar, an ancient walled city to the east of Addis Ababa, where donkeys, goats and tuk-tuks share the streets, kites snatch titbits from market stalls, and I fed urban hyenas by hand. Spices and a mildly hallucinogenic plant called Khat (chat) are the main commodities, and the people, Habesha, are friendly and curious of the strange white Ferenji invading their busy lives. The strangest man I saw chewing chat also wore a condom tied around his head filled with his own urine. That's what drugs do to you. Turn you into a pisshead."

I had left England at an awkward time. My granddaughter had painful constipation and both mother and grandmother were suffering viral tonsillitis. Still, explorers have to do what they do.

I'd arrived in Addis Ababa via train, tube and Dreamliner and joined the others who had signed up for this expedition. They were all over 50, some approaching 70, and when I broached the skewed age range I was reminded that this wasn't the sort of holiday that Benidorm sun seekers would book.

I reassured myself I was not on holiday, but exploring on an adventure mission. Gallivanting, as those I'd left behind would say.

Our leader was Sue. Tall, slim, long straight dark hair, a bit of a stunner, from somewhere in the Cotswolds, she said, but having lived in Ethiopia for the best part of 20 years.

It was early as we drove into Addis, a hectic metropolis, typical of developing nations; buses, trucks and motorbikes; a few taxis, but not many private cars. People on foot hithering and thithering, busy-busy, commuting to work. Someone was building a huge flyover across the main thoroughfares, probably the Chinese.

We were taken to the Government Hotel to relax for the day. An ageing, tired four star with much leather seating and wood panelling. Its gardens were extensive and interesting. It is a popular venue for weddings, and the mature trees and flowering shrubs were a haven for birds. From the humble sparrow to colourful and outlandish rollers, their birdsong was almost cacophonous.

A white woman with a blue-grey rinse stood sniffily at the reception desk. "You must send someone to remove a lizard from my room," she demanded. "It is constantly beeping."

"Yes, madam," said the immaculate young man behind the desk, patiently, "I will send someone with a new battery for the smoke alarm."

I love those reception moments when the haughty are deflated.

In late afternoon we were returned to the airport for our first internal flight to Dire Dawa, the home of the French built Djibouti to Ethiopia Chemin de Fer. The 50 minute flight was delayed an hour due to unseasonal rains, and we dropped out of the clouds to a sodden landscape of flooded wadis. A rainbow encircled the twin-engined Bombardier as we approached the runway over lines of camels and the strewn debris from previous crash landings.

From Dire to Harar (Hip! Hip!) was a two hour drive through rain and darkness. We ended up at a cheap hotel with simple good food and cold beers.

Over a getting-to-know-you session the group began to gel. I'm always a touch reticent in the first day or so, identifying those I'd wish to join or avoid. I'm also aware that first impressions count, and often people might think you are quite interesting, until you open your mouth.

But the conversation tonight was quite cerebral, there was considerable experience of random jaunting around the table, and we discussed the problems of a violent, tribal continent, cursed by colonialism, bled dry by tyrannical dictators, corrupted by self-serving bureaucrats, and now blighted by naive, do-gooding aid agencies.

Britain, Portugal, Germany, the French and the Belgians had been the main protagonists in the Scramble for Africa. Abyssinia had been targeted by Italy, who colonised Eritrea after defeat at Adwas. Mussolini had felt humiliated, so his Italian forces invaded and occupied in 1935. His Excellency, Haille Selasisie was forced to flee, and was given refuge in Bath, England. Tales of Italian atrocities are everywhere.

The British relieved Ethiopia in 1941, for which we are revered. We reinstated Haille Selassie and gave him Eritrea which created a 30 year civil war. You see, too much interference. Note the Prime Directive.

The ghost of Haille Selassie permeates everywhere. He claimed to be the 225th Emperor, directly descended from Solomon. Like Ghandi in India, and South Africa's Mandela, his influence remains overwhelming.

That evening we were also introduced to two other Ethiopian legends.

Everyone eats the flatbread Injera. It is a cold, sour, tripe looking green towel which acts as a plate. An interesting, acquired taste.

Then there is buying a beer. You become inured to bureaucracy in Africa, as you interminably wait in line for this stamp, or that visa, or yet another security scan, after all, TIA, This Is Africa. But in Ethiopia you queue also for a receipt. I have been in many countries where the cashier is kept distant from the sales staff, to ensure there is no suggestion of fingers in the till, but here, the system goes one further.

You must go to the cashier to place your order, "A beer, please." There is a deal of fussing, the cashier must justify their position of authority, and the transaction is recorded in a dog-eared ledger, before an amount of, say 50 Birr is demanded. On payment there is another round of fussing and recording before a large receipt is issued. You take this receipt and hand it to an ill-trained, underpaid waitress, who examines it with eye-squinting interest before acquiring said product from a fridge and handing it over, then with a flourish, sticking your receipt onto a spike, all before the watchful, nodding eyes of she who raised said document. It all appears to have been designed to make the act of purchasing so complicated and long-winded, that people just won't bother.

We had a day in Harar. It is a walled, hill city in Eastern Ethiopia, an important trade route in the middle ages. It is famous for its mosques, being the birthplace of both coffee and khat, and its hyenas.

I walked the streets inside the pumice walls. These alleys were so narrow, only single file, with wooden balconies looming just overhead. Corrugated cardboard sheets were everywhere, on which stood sacks, full to overflowing of the most colourful herbs and spices, grains and pulses, fruit and vegetables. Women, young and old, squatted amongst the goods, wearing scarves and dresses of flowing pastel colours. They chatted and smiled constantly.

In one small square boys were throwing crumbs for the vultures, kites and buzzards, which would swoop to take the offerings in mid air. The cheeky urchins would shout "Ferenji" with a flourish as the huge birds took the food.

Outside the city walls was equally interesting. All the trees were festooned with the tightly woven, hanging nests of yellow weaver birds which fluttered at the entrances. And there were views across undulating green valleys to the misty mountains beyond.

As a group we visited Rimbaud's House. Arthur Rimbaud was a French poet who settled here to become a merchant. His 18th century house and its fixtures and fittings are now a museum. Sadly we were accompanied by the most soporific of guides. I'm sure this must have been a wonderful experience, but by the end of his talk I recall simply wanting to gnaw off my right leg. It was in the courtyard of Rimbaud's house we encountered the poor, unfortunate condom-pisshead. Although he seemed happy enough.

That evening we visited the hyena man. "In Harar, the people are proud of their symbiotic relationship with hyenas," Sue informed us. "Mind you, they still lock up their goats at night!"

The scrap of waste land outside the city walls was dimly lit by the headlights of three tourist mini buses. A man stood in the middle with a sack of meat and a stick. Gradually from out of the gloom five spotted hyenas appeared. With small nervous chatterings (hardly laughter) they slowly, nervously circled and approached the hyena man. With that stooping, unctuous gait made famous in the Lion King, you would never trust a hyena.

The hyena man threw them goat legs, or similar and they ate greedily while nervous tourists circled and took photographs. Strange, that their circling was not dissimilar to that of the hyenas.

These creatures have jaws so powerful they could bite straight through your leg, and they will often engage in wars with prides of lions for bragging rights on the savannah. They are not the snivelling cowards literature would have us believe. A pack like this could decimate the watching humans.

But the hyena man beckoned me forward and gave me his stick. He encouraged me to throw titbits of meat to two of the younger, smaller beasts which looked a little less threatening, then I was allowed to slink back into the shadows. It was a truly surreal experience.

Back at the hotel we fed ourselves. A hot chicken curry soaked up with injera, and a good bottle of Ethiopian red wine.

The next day we left Harar by minibus, heading back towards Addis Ababa. The first stop was the chat market at Awaday.

There was an immense seething crowd in the market selling what I could only describe as bunches of privet. It was a mad, but innocent, peaceful, smiling, shuffling sea of colour. The stuff sold here goes all over Ethiopia, and into Djibouti and Somaliland, two of the only countries not to have banned what is essentially a dangerous narcotic.

It may be mild, but it does incapacitate, and without it young men can become psychotic and violent. Quite similar to cannabis then.

Somaliland, incidentally, most people won't have heard of. It is a small peaceful nation, therefore never in the news, and not to be mistaken for its southern neighbour, the no-go country that is Somalia, which is regularly newsworthy.

Another feature of this mad market, which I thoroughly enjoyed, were the goats, donkeys and zebu which wandered untethered and apparently unowned, in and out of the milling throng.

Heading east we drove through the fertile Bale Mountains, home to the Oromo people who make up 35% of the Ethiopian population. ("Do they provide a massage service?" I asked, "Oromatherapy!" Collective groan)

Stopping for petrol and a comfort break was an interesting aside. Firstly, because of the conflict in South Sudan, there is a shortage, and shortages mean queues, but our driver was canny and queued behind an ambulance and we joined its slipstream as it was ushered forward. Then we had to guard the bus from a group of poor urchins, barefoot with dirty, ripped clothing, they darted at us like snapping puppies. They threatened to surge onto the bus until Sue shouted at them and they slunk away.

"What did you say?" I asked her.

"I told them the ferenji were pissing on their homes".

We descended into some acacia bush and came across a deep wadi. There was a very colourful market taking place and a herd of camels being driven down through a cloud of dust. These were people of the Bass tribe a displaced and embittered Somali people, but proudly coiffured.

"Blog 2

Anyone who has been on safari will be familiar with the dik-dik. Called a duiker in South Africa, this charming miniature antelope can often be seen walking in the bush close to roadsides. Today we have driven from Harar through the Oromo tribes' lands, a mountainous region of terraces and wadis, to the Awash National Park where the acacia tree dominates and the proudly coiffured Somali tribe live.

We embarked upon a pleasant if unspectacular game drive from the Awash Gorge waterfalls back to the town. After spotting kudu, oryx and gazelle, the driver stopped to track a large male warthog. The rather skittish animal once disturbed, ran into the scrub alongside the bus. On the other side I spotted a dik-dik standing in a clearing, in full view only yards away, and announced it to my fellow passengers. However they were all craning to catch a glimpse of the disappeared warthog and completely ignored my spot.

"Is nobody interested in my dik-dik?" I cried plaintively, and after a momentary embarrassing pause, the bus fell apart!"

Awash National Park was a brief delight. Before entering Sue took us to a rubbish tip. Just like at home, these sad, dumping grounds of human detritus are full of birds. There were vultures, eagles, herons, egrets, flamingos and hornbills, but perhaps the most spectacular were the particularly ugly Marabou Storks rummaging about. With a huge grey wingspan swooping in, landed they are then perhaps four feet upright. They have the the most vicious long sharp bills protruding from warty, puce faces, sporting saggy puce wattles, whilst beady eyes peer from under a bald puce pate.

Further on into the park, after we had walked the waterfalls with crocodile below, we spotted a good variety of game; baboons, oryx, (warthog and dik-dik, of course) gazelle and my favourite, kudu. All this in the shadow of the jagged craters of the dormant volcano, Mount Fantelle.

My second favourite pastime, next to snorkelling a coral reef is to safari, especially in Africa. Away from the more famous savannah regions to the south, Awash was a pleasant surprise. Nothing beats the roof up, standing, peering into the bush, the warm breeze, the bus bouncing along dirt tracks, the patience, the expectation, then drawing to a halt (the driver always spots first), and the excitement of seeing these magnificent creatures in these oh-so special places we have allowed to remain wild. And there are always birds of every hue with the sizzling screech of the cicadas in the background.

Have I mentioned the birds?

I have never known a country blessed with so much birdlife. Every where you look, around houses and villages, up in trees, in the bush, at road sides, and as we have seen, at the rubbish tip, there is a plethora of bird life. And they are not shy about it. Not only are they every size and every colour, but they sing constantly, or even just croaks and squawks; there is a constant cacophony.

It was the same at our next stop, Lake Koka, a man-made reservoir at the northern end of the Great Rift Valley. We lunched on rather juicy Zebu steaks and cold beers, at a shaded restaurant terrace with a particularly scenic panorama.

The rest of that afternoon was less idyllic, the painfully slow, bumpy, dusty crawl back into Addis and the Government Hotel. The evening was good though, a bar with a singer and injera covered in a particularly hot and spicy curry. I'm getting a taste for the injera.

It was time to discover the delights of Addis

"Blog 3

Ethiopia is the cradle of so many things; the Great Rift Valley, Humanity, Christianity. In a museum in Addis I came face to face with Lucy, the fossilised remains of the earliest discovered hominid. She had been waiting 3.2 million and 40 years to meet me, because she was found in Awash in 1974, and was 3.2 million years old then.

Lucy was upright, but outside the museum I came across poor, frail-looking, misshapen women who were anything but. They have taken on a curious and crippling vocation. Every day they walk 10 miles up to a eucalyptus forest high above Addis Ababa and proceed to cut 100's of switches about ten foot in length. These they tie together into an enormously frightening bundle which they strap across their backs. Then, bent double, they slowly make their way back down the mountain to the centre of the city. Here they sell their cargo for firewood and fencing and can make 20 birrh, about a dollar!

They do this once a day for six days a week, and on the seventh they rest their crippled body and go to church to give thanks to God. Maybe it is their way of serving a living penury in the hope of eternal salvation, or maybe they know no better. I just wonder if God could perhaps invent for them a little wheeled trolley, or a beast of burden called a donkey or a mule. Or perhaps not, because then the RSPCA would cry foul.

Either way it is a cruel irony, an inhumane conundrum; the first upright fossil, and the bent-double women."

We saw Lucy in the museum, her bones neatly laid out (she was christened Lucy as the discovering archaeologists were into The Beatles' Sergeant Pepper's Lonely Hearts Club Band, and particularly Lucy In The Sky With Diamonds). Apparently she was an Australopithecus.

Haille Selase's tomb was next. The last of Solomon's dynasty, he came to rather a cruel end when it was all the fashion to overthrow monarchs and install republican governments based on a strict form of socialism.

He had abolished slavery, enrolled Ethiopia into the United Nations, helped create the Organisation for African Unity, improved health care and literacy, and worked to unite the various tribes of his country. To the Rastafari he was the Messiah, but he was murdered by the Derg in 1974, aged 83, and some believe his body dumped in a latrine.

Our minibus climbed a hill, where we saw the bent over women, to the eucalyptus forest and a lovely viewpoint of Addis, nestled below and surrounded by green mountains. We then descended back into the city and passed the American Embassy, and...

"Blog 4

Driving around the city we pass the American Embassy, an imposing white building with columns and such, and we are told not to take photographs; who would want to. However a whistle sounds and our driver has to stop and back up. The door opens and a security grunt climbs aboard. He is chewing open-mouthed. The guide explains that no photographs have been taken, but the grunt has to summon a superior who decides that cameras must be inspected. There are heated words between the driver, the guide and both grunts. I weigh in and tell them in no uncertain terms that their actions are both stupid and idiotic. They then begin to search through the camera of an elderly lady who is clearly upset. Finally Colonel grunt arrives and drawls that the problem is that it is not allowed to take photographs of the embassy. I am irate, "Why on earth would we want to? We are British!" I immediately feel rather foolish at having evoked the "Do you know who we are?" argument. But these are brainless Yankee drongos. Well done, America. You never let us down. God bless you, God bless you all!"

I had been a little upset.

We were up at five for our seven o'clock flight, a 90 minute, 400 mile hop to Bahar Dar, and the Tana Hotel on the shores of Lake Tana, in the north of the country. We spend the time in flight practising how to say thank you to our hosts in their own language, Amharic. It is not as easy a task as it seems. The term "Amasaganalahu" literally means 'I praise you'. It doesn't trip off the tongue, and can't be shortened to Thanks, or Ta!

We barely had time to drop our bags off before a boat was ready to take us around the lake. Once again the birds were a huge feature. In the gardens of the hotel were weavers and warblers galore, and my favourite, the bird of paradise bee eater. We walked to the private jetty, and as soon as we were on the water appeared egrets, cranes, pelicans and geese; fish eagles, heron, plovers, and kingfishers (the Old English Halcyon).

Tana Lake is Ethiopia's largest, and the source for the Blue Nile. It contains over 30 islands, most of which house ancient churches or monasteries. Most of the countries previous emperors and bishops are buried in these isolated holy places, which also house many historic treasures, from ancient writings to art and artefacts. One once housed the Arc of the Covenant, and the Virgin Mary was said to have visited here on her journey back from Egypt.

We landed at Dek island, the location of five villages and churches, and climbed through the jungle past troupes of monkeys to Narga Selassie, a monastery of the Orthodox Ethiopian Church.

We were to find that the orthodox church here is full of symbolism, iconography and apocryphal writings.

The church is constructed in the classic round style with a dome to symbolise the one true God. There are four walls to represent the four gospels, and three inner sanctums which are the trinity. Only priests are allowed in the innermost. "The Arc was hidden here," we are told, "But it is hidden everywhere. How do you find a tree in the forest?" Oh, very clever. Indiana Jones never thought of that one.

We were shown many beautiful paintings and frescos depicting scenes from the bible in vibrant colours, the guardianship for which has been handed down over the centuries. All the saints had haloes, but both they and the mere mortals appeared white, with large Ethiopian eyes and curly black hair. We were told that if the face was facing front, showing both eyes, they were holy people, Satan and his evil cohorts were always shown in profile, with one eye.

To further complicate this symbolism we were shown a drum, the type of which is played all over Ethiopia, a sort of tall bongo. The priest played it and danced a little jig.

"Each skin of the drum (top and bottom) are the cheeks of Jesus, slapped by the people of Jrusalem, the chords tightening the skins are His scars from when He was flayed, and the pebbles inside are from His stoning".

Many of the images, we were told were of the miracles performed by Mary whilst in Egypt, after fleeing Herod, and taken from the apocryphal lost book of Celemente.

I was finding much this symbolism quite befuddling. I didn't remember any of this from Sunday School. Then we came upon an image of St George slaying the dragon. Ah, this was more like it.

Sadly we faced a gauntlet of hawkers on the way down, just to take the edge off our new found sense of holiness.

Back at the hotel I ordered a coffee then wandered off to get a better look at a bird of paradise bee eater. A monkey jumped down, grabbed my sugar bowl and skipped back up the tree to enjoy his booty. Have you ever tried to explain "the monkey stole my sugar" in Amharic to an incredulous waiter?

"Blog 5

Lake Tana, at 2,700 metres is one of the highest large lakes in the world. The lake provides a diet of catfish and tilapia, caught by hoodies in little reed canoes, but there is no swimming here. If the hippos or crocs don't get you the nasty parasite bilharzia which burrows into your skin and lays eggs in your organs, will. On the lake's island peaks lie ancient churches untouched by modern times. The first you know about them is the chanting of biblical chapters through loudspeakers which usually begins at 4:30 am and does not stop. The churches are populated by priests who can marry, and monks who can't. Women monks are also common. The Ethiopian Orthodox church has evolved separately from western influences, and have some different books, what we call the Apocrypha, in their bible. One of these is the Book of Mary of Miracles, which details the life of the Holy Family after they fled the Slaughter of the Innocents, into Egypt, and His mother's works there. The frescos which adorn every surface of the churches are colourful, vibrant, and tell the story of every scripture you have ever heard of, and much more. St. George and the Dragon is a big favourite here.

The Blue Nile drains Lake Tana, controversially known as *the* source of the Nile. Tis-Isat Falls, or the Blue Nile Falls, used to be a spectacular 400 metre cascade array plunging 45 metres. Now, due to the dry season and the dam which diverts the water for hydro electric power, it is simply one flume feeding the gorge below. There are some wonderful walks around the gorges, but a disappointing waterfall. On the return journey we passed subsistence farms and villages where everybody waves happily, and the children shout "Ferenji, Ferenji", excitedly. You want to give the children sweets or pens, but all you will encourage is fighting, and they will continue to follow and harass tourists instead of going to school. Aid has the same effect."

Sundowners were followed by a short trip by tuk-tuk into the small town and a dinner of fried tilapia and rice, with beetroot salad.

We had a sunrise cruise, and at 5am walked through the pitch black gardens to the jetty. The world was waking up from the east as a full moon set in the west. Roosting birds sang and frogs continued to hoot as we saw fishermen paddling to inspect their overnight nets. Near the point where the Nile begins, a bull hippo suddenly rose out of the water. He was protecting his harem and offspring, nine in all we counted.

Later we drove to one of Haille Selasse's palaces where there was a view of the Blue Nile flowing out of Lake Tana. Then on to Tis-Isat Falls, which were turned off. We crossed deep gorges via two bridges, a modern Swiss suspension bridge and an ancient Portuguese stone arch. We took a small ferry across the river then trekked back up to a Habasha village, accompanied all the way by children, who should have been in school.

We left Bahir Dar for Gondar, once the capital, with royal palaces. The three hour journey across the northern plains was punctuated by stops to see the village of Wareta, and the Devil's Nose, aka Finger of God (not much difference there).

On the journey I came across two profound maxims. Firstly we were discussing the nature of time. Not in a Steven Hawking way, you understand, but how, as you get older, time seems to go faster.

"Why do the years go quickly?" Catherine, a tall, slim widow with a troublesome timeshare in Nerja, repeated the question. "It is because each succeeding year is a smaller proportion of your life," she asserted with slight cynicism.

Later, Sue was talking about local village life. "They have a saying here; 'A happy woman has a well to walk to'."

This began a debate on the nature of women's roles in any society. But we couldn't get past the meaning of this aphorism. Are the women happy because they can get away from the household chores with a simple but essential task that doesn't tax the mind, or are they just keen on meeting their friends for general gossip and socialising?

I told the group about how wells in India were closed by the Raj because they became meeting places where revolution could be planned. So we decided on the latter.

Tap water in the home has a lot to answer for. No wells to walk to, no happy women.

We stopped at Wareta to wander the market. Set on an uphill track away from the main road, with arteries running off, it was a hive of colourful activities.

There were tall, slim men in cloaks driving goats before them, children leading cows or donkeys, mule carts fetching and delivering. Tuk-tuks buzzed around, with the only sedentary folk being the Europeans, lazily wandering and observing.

A line of tailors all worked their antique, treadle operated, black singer sewing machines, next to people using irons filled with hot coals. Others were fashioning sugar canes with machetes, or recycling tyres into footwear. The vibe was just busy, busy, busy

Later we stopped at God' thumb (whatever), a rock teetering straight up in the air. This was a favourite tourist attraction, you could tell with the amount of children wanting to beg, or the women selling trinkets. Surely all better employed in their own market place. We didn't stop long, our driver had hit and injured a goat.

We finally arrived into Gondar and took our hotel, the Goha, which stood on a hillside overlooking the town. To the side of the hotel was a large pool where the Timkat celebrations are held. We'd missed them.

Timkat takes place around Epiphany and marks the baptism of Jesus. An Arc replica is paraded around the town whilst clergy in their robes and umbrellas dance and frolic. Men and women chant rhythmically whilst children play, and everyone ends up throwing themselves into the water. Sounds great fun.

We were appointed a guide, Teja, who took us into the town and showed us around King Fasilidas' medieval castle, and Debre Berhan church with its "remarkable ceilings frescoes of painted faces". Sadly Teja was soporific in his descriptions, but did amuse with his use of plurals. (Don't get me wrong, I have every respect for people who are bi, or even tri-lingual. After all, his English was far better than my Amharic). He explained how "thesies thingies" happened to the "kingies and priesties" and "peoplies suffered from plagueies and invaderies". At least he got the faces right, could have been awkward.

That evening I relaxed in the hotel pool as the sun set and swallows swooped to take sips of water. Sunbirds and shimmering splendid starlings also shared the view of the town with me.

The next morning I was up at dawn to enjoy the pool, swimming 16 lengths, but the scene that unfolded as the sun rose was one of the most remarkable I have ever experienced.

"Blog 6

Gondar, a town rich with medieval history, and a place favoured by the invading Italians because of its climate. The British bombed Gondar in 1941 to rid it of Italians, an act for which the Ethiopians are eternally grateful. That is how evil Mussolini's occupation was.

It is a town of castles and churches and I will never forget the morning I came down to the hotel gardens filled with birds and birdsong to take a dawn swim overlooking the awakening town. Mist still lay in the hollows, mixing with wisps of smoke from the emerging kitchen fires. The town had looked magical at sunset but its unique flavour surfaced at daybreak with the sounds emanating from its many churches. Each one musical yet discordant; chanting, calling, singing, shouting, praying, and ululating their descriptions of the scriptures. Surely one of the most unique sounds in the whole of Christendom. Each ancient building using their loudspeakers to glorify the strength of their faith to drum up business. They make the Roman Catholic church look like rank amateurs."

After breakfast, which was the usual porridge gloop, I walked into the town and encountered a demonstration. At the head horse riders were playing to the crowds, rearing their steeds onto their hind legs, western style, "Yeehaa!". Then came the banner wavers, declaring independence for the Agan Qument people, then the marchers, and finally the traffic jam. What better way to see the town, I thought, and joined the march. It took me back nearly half a century to Centenary Square, Birmingham, marching to the chant of "Thatcher, Thatcher, milk snatcher".

Later at a cafe I played table football with some of the local boys and finally picnicked at the Ploughshares Women's Refuge, a self sufficient farming commune. The women and children protected here are recovering from operations, suffering with AIDS, or are otherwise disadvantaged.

We left Gondar, and I was a little worried about some health issues. Ethiopia is a country at altitude, Addis Ababa at 7,700 feet is the third highest capital in the world, and all week I've experienced sleeplessness. This is not unusual at this height; the lungs have to work harder and your natural sleep rhythm is affected. But I'd also had the return of my night najjers and there was a possible problem within my gut. However we were approaching the most anticipated part of my adventure, the Simien Mountains.

Two hours away was Debark, a cold, dusty, poor, one street town which is trying to sell itself as the Gateway to the Highlands and may one day benefit from the tourist dollar, but for now simply remains, basic.

The hotel was basic, but had a bar, and in the bar was a television, and after dinner we were invaded by the young men of the town, all wearing Arsenal shirts. They were here to watch their team play Liverpool and were delighted with their victory. Asking why they supported Arsenal, I was told the whole of Ethiopia follows them. It is often the way in Africa, a country will adopt one Premier League side. Oh, I also had a haircut.

"Blog 7

We drove from Gondar, north to Debark, and I resolved to get a shave and set off to find the local barber. Usually this just involves a mirror nailed to a tree, a chair and a pair of scissors. However, the one I found had his own little shack. I sat down, mimed what I wanted done, and settled in waiting for the tip back, and shaving soap to be applied. Imagine my shock to discover I had chosen the only barber in Africa to own a Philishave. He proudly plugged it in and proceeded to rub my face with it. I even had to do my own facial contortions. Maybe he is just removing the long beard, before using the cut-throat, I thought, but no. With the Philishave and its three floating heads, having done its work he plugged in a Braun to finish the job.

We have a phrase to describe unexpected queues or capricious bureaucracy or irrational activities. It is TIA; This Is Africa. They do things differently here. You can expect to say TIA and shrug at least twice a day."

The next morning we turned right out of Debark and climbed for two hours to reach the Simien Mountains NP. The views all the way were stunning. We had to pick up a guide and two armed scouts. "Don't worry," assured Sue, "there are no dangerous animals here."

It wasn't long before we had our first encounter, Gelada Baboons. These are beautiful, long haired, peaceful grazing creatures. We left the bus to watch them. Babies and youngsters were playing in the meadow, adults grooming.

"Walk around them," whispered Sue, "not at them, and don't make eye contact."

After a few moments we returned to the bus and continued on to the "Heighest (sic) Lodge in Africa, at 10,600 feet. Just past here we encountered another group of baboons, maybe 200, and they were being "behaviourally observed" by two young researchers from Michigan University. While one explained their work, the other herded the baboons away. I tried to tell them that encouraging unnatural behaviour, i.e. herding, would render the results of their study unsafe. They didn't understand which probably meant this was more a learning curve for the students rather than serious research into Gelada behaviour.

Gelada are not real baboons, but have a taxonomy of their own, They are a little like apes, a little like monkeys, but they are the size of chimpanzees. They sleep on the cliffs, coming up to the grasslands during the day to graze, forage and socialise.

Throughout Africa, true baboons are a problem. They are unpredictable, thieving, scratching, biting scoundrels who will terrorise people. This is mainly due to them having been given titbits of food, and being allowed to take food. They now expect food and will approach people to claim what they believe is theirs. When challenged they can become violent and dangerous. Never leave your car door open with a picnic on view. Seagulls, dogs and children can become similarly feral.

Gelada baboons have none of these traits.

We left this troupe and embarked upon a two hour trek around the rim of a ravine. We were looking for Lammergeier, the bearded vulture. As we started the trek I had a nosebleed, further evidence that perhaps all was not right.

I love contour trekking, no ups and downs, just a pleasant stroll around the mountains. The views here, on Africa's alternative roof were marvellous. Distant snow-capped mountains, deep ravines and canyons; we had light scrub with flowering shrubs covered in butterflies and bees, and birds circling in the thermals. We saw kites and vultures, pied crows and thick-beaked ravens, two totally white Egyptian vultures, and, yes, one lammergeier. There were also three klipspringer bouncing around the rocks and bushes.

I was chatting to Sue, she told me we were about to drive through a place called Tigray.

"You would probably remember it as 'War-torn Tigray'", she said, such are the epithets used in the BBC News. "Because of that, it is now quite wealthy."

She explained that being on the northern border between Eritrea and Ethiopia, Tigray became a battle zone. Now a lot of money is being spent on re-building

"A few years back there were some boys hassling tourists, so the UN gave them a grant."

"It's always the same in Africa, you cause enough trouble and you get money thrown at you. It's the same with the diaspora," she added.

This was a new one on me, "What are diaspora?"

"They are returning refugees. These are people who fled when the going got tough, and were given asylum, by law, in safer countries. When they return they are given a grant, so will often set up home, a nice new home with all mod cons, next door to the poor people living in hovels who stayed to support their country. They are not popular"

Once again, I was amazed at how travelling can give you a completely different view of the world.

After picnicking in this in this Garden of Eden we began the journey back to Debark and came across an even larger group of Gelada baboons. The groups grow due to socialising as the day progresses. I asked Sue to stop the bus so I could conduct my own experiment.

We all left the minibus and I slowly walked into the centre of this grazing troop, not walking directly towards any animal, and not making any eye contact. I then sat down and began to graze myself, mimicking their actions. These beautiful creatures accepted me as one of their own by ignoring me, walking around and in front and behind, sitting with me and moving along; grazing, grooming, and basically chilling. They had their babies with them and were quite happy to allow their children to play and gambol in front of me, ignoring my presence, behaving quite naturally. I have never been so moved to have been so totally disregarded. They knew I was no threat, and treated me as a fellow primate. It had been a truly magical experience that went straight into my top ten wildlife encounters.

We left the mountains to return to Debark where I was hassled by a group of youngster, almost mobbed into buying gum. They picked on the wrong one there. As a teacher I hate gum, hate the smell of it, hate the mess it makes, hate the contortions of people's faces as they chew it. It is truly an ugly substance. It was either gum or cigarettes.

I gave up and gave them a bag of boiled sweets. "Here," I said smiling, "treat your teeth to these."

The next morning breakfast was a choice of green or pink gloop. I think one was porridge with avocado, the other with papaya. I mixed them to produce gloop with pink and green streaks. Still didn't improve the taste. I did however discover the source of my apparent health problems.

"Blog 8

I've been at altitude now for over a week and have been suffering a little breathlessness, but suddenly there was a new problem, an altogether more troubling one. I have put up with unpredictable nosebleeds in the past at altitude, but now there is bleeding in my bowel. At least I am hoping it is to do with the thin air. I mentally make a note to see a doctor on my return, because two movements have shown up a lot of blood. Over the next few days I monitor the situation carefully and record the state of my movements, and some do and some don't. Then someone innocently says, "Have you noticed how much beetroot they put in the salads?" Pause, and enlightenment, panic over. I am such an idiot, but a very relieved one. I sometimes wonder whether I should be allowed out."

We travelled out of the mountains on a hairpin road down onto a hot plain. The road from Debark to Axum has been discredited by the BBC in a programme called The World's Most Dangerous Roads. David Baddiel and Hugh Dennis misrepresented both the road (built by the Italians who in a former life, known as Romans, were quite good at roads), and Ethiopians in general. Auntie Beeb has since had to issue a re-edit of the programme.

The road itself spectacularly winds down the Simien Mountains into the Tekaze Valley where youngsters sold us doughnuts, then up again into Tigray (war-torn).

I met some farmers who did complain about the roads. Apparently they are being improved, asphalted. Increased wealth has led to this, which should generate more wealth; surely a win-win situation.

But try telling that to the farmers, who have used these dirt tracks for centuries to drive animals to and from market, or to the families who have quietly traversed these pathways on foot, and whose children use them to go back and forth from school. Speeding lorries, cars and buses now threaten the safety of all. The price of progress.

We arrived in Axum, once the holiest city in Africa, and home to a 10,000 year empire, to the only genuine Arc of the Covenant, to the Queen of Sheba, to King Balthazar (he gave the frankincense), to the Ezana Stone (like the Rosetta), and to obelisk-like stelae. It was a mind blowing location.

We checked in at the Yeha Hotel, which overlooked a field full of these 30 foot stelae, some leaning at crazy angles, some fallen and broken, but mostly upright. The centre one, to King Ezana stands at over 80 feet and was the last of these to be built, around the 4th century.

They are not obelisks as they are not topped by pyramids, but were created in the same fashion, carved from a single piece of granite, and mostly sculpted before erection. They probably served as markers to tombs, in much the same way as we have tombstones, and represent buildings, with windows and an entrance door at the base. The Italians had removed three and re-erected them in Rome with the aid of steel supports which attracted lightning strikes. They later cleaned, restored and returned them.

Tonight we sat and enjoyed sundowners overlooking the stelae field as it gradually lit up. We'd travelled from Gondar, the Camelot of Ethiopia , via the Simeon Mountains, to Axum, the home of the Queen of Sheba. What more wonders could this country provide?

"Blog 9

The sights of Axum did not disappoint. Firstly the Yeha hotel was perched on a hill overlooking the stelae fields, and to the left the Mary of Zion Cathedral. Queen Elizabeth II visited here as a guest of Haile Selassie and gifted its chandelier. Beyond are the mountains from which the stelae were hewn. How they were transported, carved and erected, nobody knows, but there are some wonderful mysteries. They exist to signify royal tombs. That is known, but the tombs have long since been plundered and stripped clean. Of the three tallest, and, presumably newest, it is thought they date from about 300 AD when Christianity was introduced and new burial methods thought up. Only one remains standing, and that at a crazy angle and is shored up. There is another standing, but that was in five pieces when the Italians took it away and erected it in Rome It was returned post-war as compensation. The most spectacular is called the Great Stele and is in about four or five pieces and remains on the ground where it fell, either in the process of erection, or as is thought, felled by Queen Judith the Destroyer back in the tenth century. I spent all day clambering over the stelae fields, in and out of the tombs, saw the Queen of Sheba's palace, her baths, and many other places that archaeologists are itching to begin uncovering. This place is a gold mine.

I also spent time at Ezana's stone, with inscriptions in three languages, discovered by three local farmers. It is now housed in a shed. I saw the Dungar Palace, Royal underground tombs, the tomb of Balthazar (Bazen), The Chapel where lies the Arc of the Covenant (guarded by one little man), and finally climbed to King Kaleb's tomb, atop a hill with wondrous views of my day.

In the evening I ate at the Antica, with a background of music and dancing. You can either have fasting meals (Ethiopians are vegetarian for 200 holy days a year), or non-fasting. The local sauce is Shiro, hot and tasty, or Doro Wat, a fiery chicken curry. Nothing wrong with any of that. It is just the Injera bread they eat everything with. It is grey-green, at best it looks like underlay, at worst, tripe. It tastes sour, and is cold and clammy to the touch. It is served as a blanket with the Wat poured on top. By the end of this trip I'll be glad I'll never see it again. If only they could invent naan or chapati."

The empire at Axum declined with the rise of Islam, deforestation and and incursion of Bedja herders. We left for the airport, but there was drama to come which led directly to:

"Blog 10

Leaving Axum for an early morning flight to Lalibela, my final destination. I enter the airport and go through the usual security scans, then sit to await the flight call. "Let's go and have a look at the canteen, just to have a walk," someone said. I wander upstairs, and there are a group of Dutch tourists hanging around a non-descript coffee shop. Head downstairs and ...What's that? ...No, leave it alone.... No, I can't leave it alone. It's a bullet.

I don't know much about munitions, but enough to know this was a live bullet from a handgun, and it was on the stairs inside an airport. I picked it up and thought I had better hand it in. I made my way downstairs, looked around and saw a security guard, and walked up to him.

"Hello," I said, "I found this on the stairs, and thought you had better have it."

I gave him the bullet and innocently wandered back to my seat. I was just explaining what had happened to the guy sat next to me, Dave, when I suddenly felt eyes looking at me, and people pointing. Well, not everyone, only the official looking people stood around the security points. "I think you may be asked to assist with their enquiries," Dave said, and sure enough, within a few minutes two suits came over and asked me to accompany them.

I followed them to a small room with one table and two chairs. The older man sat down behind the table, I took the other chair and the younger man perched himself on the table and asked if he could see my passport. "Of course!" I said, and the younger man made some notes and chatted to the older man in Amharic. I began to feel a little fidgety.

"Tell me," said the younger, taking the bullet out of his pocket and standing it on the table, "Why have you brought this ammunition into the airport?"

I told him, calmly and firmly, that I had previously been scanned entering the airport, therefore it cannot have been on my person. I pointed out I had found it on the stairs, and had felt it necessary to bring it to their attention as they may have a security problem.

The younger man spoke to the elder who became rather heated and called someone on his mobile phone. I thought, that's it, I am going to spend the next month in an Ethiopian gaol waiting for the British Embassy and maybe the Daily Mail to spring me. I may become quite a celebrity back home.

Just then a curly haired man arrived, and sat on his haunches holding his head in his hands. He was followed by Sue, who asked me why I was being detained. I told her and she immediately began berating all three men in their own language.

The older man nodded and passed me a piece of paper and pen and indicated I should write a statement. I was about to when Sue snatched the piece of paper, screwed it up and threw it on the floor. She shouted at the elder man and pointed at the curly haired man.

The younger man became quite flustered and tried to reassure her I was not in trouble, and they had no intention of detaining me further. He turned to me and said, "If you could just show me where you found the bullet."

"Gladly," I said meekly and left the office. I would continue to feel a little unsettled until we were on the plane. I wanted to give Sue a huge hug of thanks.

Later I rejoined Dave. "I thought you might need some cavalry, so asked Sue to intervene. You'd gone as white as a sheet." I thanked him. "So what happened?" he asked.

"Oh, they handcuffed me and slapped me around a bit, and were just pulling on the marigolds when Sue arrived."

Later as we were leaving Lalibela airport Sue told me the head of security at Axum had been re-located. "Would you do it again?" She asked. I thought long and hard.

"Indeed, I believe I would have to!" I said, confident it was a rhetorical question."

There were wonderful views of the artificial Lake Tekezi as we climbed away from Axum and landed at Lalibela within an hour. I couldn't relax until we had left the airport, then we had an hour's drive up to the aptly named Panorama View Hotel.

We were here to see some of the most remarkable churches in the world, but began by walking downhill to visit the stunning Ben Abena, the Flower on the Hill.

It is an excellent restaurant on so many levels (about seven). Ben Abena is the brainchild of Suzie, a retired Scottish home economics teacher. It looks like a space ship, and shouldn't work as a structure, in an unspoilt landscape of rolling hills, but does. It has launchpad lily balconies, Tardis toilets and circular stairwells.

Suzie fed us with dishes of salads, vegetables and chutnies with chili sauces to dip our home made bread into. She introduced us to her staff, local youngsters she was teaching a trade, and gave us a brief guide to Lalibela.

There are eleven churches here, all built by King Lalibela of Axum, in the eleventh century. He was disappointed that his subjects were unable to make a pilgrimage to Jerusalem because of persecution by Muslims.

He found this area of sandstone and resolved to build a new Jerusalem, even naming the river running through here the Jordan.

All of his churches were hewn out of the rock. Not like in Petra or the Lycian Tombs, out of vertical rock, but dug down into the rock, like underground monoliths. Nowhere in the world has anything similar. At Easter Island, Stonehenge, Aswan, even Axum, obelisks and stelae have been hewn, decorated, transported and erected. Here they have been built out of the ground, The only tools used were hammers and chisels, although Lalibela did cheat a little.

The king himself proclaimed, "Man chiselled during the day, the Angels finished the work at night."

Well fed, we left Ben Abena to visit the work of the Angels, built out of basalt and sandstone, and standing as a testament to unwavering faith.

The 11 churches are grouped together, in what was called little Jerusalem, but the most famous, dedicated to St George stands a few hundred yards away. They are all linked by hidden stairways, ramps and tunnels. An afternoon visiting these unique monoliths is akin to spending time in another world, a different dimension, such is their incomparable power.

Unlike my other favourite rock-hewn place, Petra in Jordan, these buildings at over 8,000 feet high in the mountains, can suffer weathering. Therefore UNESCO, in their infinite wisdom, and with the help of the guilt-ridden Italians, has funded the raising of giant gazebos over them for protection. It is rather unfortunate to see 20th century steel stanchions and dirty white tarpaulins stretched over them like some huge ugly umbrellas.

This apart, it was a great time for clambering in and out of these monoliths.

Most people gape open-mouthed at these astonishing structures and can only reach the conclusion that aliens had to have played a part. That old fraud, Erich Von Daniken would have had a field day with his "God Was An Astronaut" theories.

During my visit, at each church (they are living places of worship) the priests delighted in showing us artefacts, relics, icons, paintings and books a thousand years old. And their drums, they love to slap the cheeks of Jesus.

There is some controversy over when the churches were created. Surely, some archaeologists have argued, they can't have all been built in the lifetime of the King/Saint Lalibella. And why build so many? It is like having ten pubs in a village of 1,000 people. They can't even date which were the earliest or latest, although some believe there could have been 500 years in the construction.

I loved that each had their one claim to fame; the Royal Chapel, House of the Cross or Virgins, Replica Tombs of Adam and Jesus, one was a prison, another the royal bakery, Houses of the Angels, the Evangelist, the Saviour of the World, Golgotha, and the Tomb of Lalibela himself.

To put all this into context: To build one church, a huge area of rock would have been chosen perhaps the size of two tennis courts. They would chisel down and form a ramp leading to and opening up into a square of avenues, sometimes only six feet wide and with a depth of around 30 feet. Having isolated the cube of rock, they then hewed out the insides to create doors, windows, rooms and archways, altars and alcoves. Surely the painstaking work of several decades. Between each of the eleven churches are rock carved chapels, priests' living quarters (still in use), even graves and sanctuaries. The aforementioned most famous, the Church to Saint George is shaped as a Maltese Cross, a masterpiece amongst miracles.

The villagers live in little round houses of stone, probably built with the leftovers from the churches' construction. That evening we dined at Wubita's house with her daughter Betty (not from Elizabeth, but Bethlehem). It was a simple meal of salad and vegetables with honey wine. Then she gave us some local firewater which whet our appetites for a discussion about Angels and Aliens.

We staggered back, uphill to the Panorama View Hotel. The silence and the stars, the huge black firmament, the looming dark mountains, especially atmospheric.

Then dawn in the Ethiopian Highlands and the views, breathtaking. And I could suddenly see why you would not want to be anywhere else in the world. Why you could see yourself building Ben Abena, the Flower atop the Hill.

I met Wubbit the muleteer, and his mule, Muffin. Honest. We were to take a trek up Mount Abuna Yosef to the monastery of Asheten Mariam, dedicated to the scent of Mary.

The journey took us up another 2,000 feet, stunning views everywhere, and many scary moments when Muffin clung to gravity defying ledges. I now know the meaning of sure-footed.

In truth the arrival at the stone cut church was a touch anti-climatic. This was definitely one of those instances where the highpoint (no pun) was the journey, not the arrival. But one priest lives here and he was delighted to be able to show us the treasures of his little church, especially the fully illustrated Bible.

The return was no less hair-raising, but as we approached the lower, gentler slopes, passing tiny villages, we met children racing down to or trudging back from school. They have two shifts. Those going down were really keen to talk with us, no doubt ready to blame their tardiness on those darned photo-obsessed tourists.

We met a farmer Menguishi, who fancied himself in politics. His wife had given birth yesterday to a son, Abraham, and his donkey had also given birth that very day. He invited us into his home and introduced all four involved in the births. I am not sure of which of the newborns he was more proud. They were both very beautiful, and both had big blue eyes.

"Ferenji!" he declared with a huge smile.

The time had come to leave Lalibela and begin the journey out of Ethiopia, home.

"Blog final

Tomorrow will be the first day of Lent. To celebrate Christ's journey and fast in the wilderness, there has to be the traditional feast, what we call fat or Shrove Tuesday. To this end farmers are driving their goats and cattle uphill to be slaughtered for the feast. We are travelling downhill to the airport, and the driver is driving carelessly. He is swinging the bus around tight bends and blind corners. There are people, families and their livestock coming towards us. Children are swinging around wildly flapping poultry. We are hanging on in the bus, being thrown from side to side. "Slow down!" I shouted, several times, but my protests fell on deaf ears, then, bang, and a heifer goes rolling over and over into the bush.

We skidded to a halt, and everyone leaves the bus. A heated exchange between farmer and driver ensues. The poor cow is soon up on her feet, but evidently quite groggy. She has a bloody nose, and damage to her back leg

The custom here is that where livestock has been injured, the driver must pay a notional contribution towards vet fees. We clubbed together and handed over a bunch of notes which seemed to satisfy the farmer, and we continued more sedately to the airport. It could have been a child.

Looking back, our gesture seemed a little futile. No vet would have been summoned, All we'd really achieved was a bit of tenderising."

We flew back to Addis Ababa and the Government Hotel where a lavish wedding was taking place. Big limousines, a band of costumed drummers, a beautiful bride and a large immaculate entourage. For once, even the birds had to take a back seat.

I visited the Red Terror Martyrs Museum in the late afternoon. It was upsetting. There had been a very black period in Ethiopia's history, after the Emperor had been overthrown, and a variety of pseudo-communist militia groups fought for power.

During 1976 and 1977 these factions created vigilante groups called kebeles. These kebeles went on paranoid rampages murdering men, women and children in horrific scenarios, such as herding them into churches to be torched. Gun battles and assassinations were rife. It is thought up to two million people died during the Red Terror.

The museum contained photographs, torture instruments, skulls and bones and other evidence of atrocities. A softly spoken guide told us what happened to dissenters of the Derg, led by convicted war criminal Mengitsu Haile Mariam. It was he who organised the policies that multiplied the effects of the terrible famines of 1983 to 1985 in which 1.2 million died. That's when Bob Geldof came in

The harrowing tale of man's inhumanity to man, which never seems far away in Africa. I wrote in the visitors' book:

"Before I never knew. Now, I'll never forget."

In a daze I left the museum. Just around the corner was the huge city square from where Mengitsu spouted his evil bile. A flyover has now been built over it.

That night Sue took us to a restaurant where there was lovely food, and singing and dancing from a talented and happy troupe of enthusiastic entertainers. A much better final memory of Ethiopia.

My Ethiopia adventure was over. Quite an extraordinary experience. In all my travels I don't think I have ever visited a country that felt so different to the world we think we know.

Harar's hyenas; the Awash dik-dik; Lucy and the bent-over women; the Oromo, Somali, Habasha and us Ferenji; Lake Tana's Blue Nile; Gondar's dawn chorus; Debarks barber, the Gelada baboons, Axar's stelae, the airport bullet, Lalibela's churches, the Red Terror, diaspora, and the birds. Did I mention the birds?

The Ethiopian Orthodox Church, sometimes attributed to the Lost Tribe of Dan, perfectly illustrates the differences between us. Here was the earliest known organised form of Christianity. Here it has been left to evolve in its own way for two millennia. Like the animals of Madagascar and the marsupials of Australia, the same as us but so different. And then we hit a cow!

This has been extreme gallivanting. Amasaganalahu.

Chapter Six

Kenya. East and West

Truly annoying are all those travel companies and Sunday Supplement travel writers who insist that safari in Africa is so expensive.

They sell a week on the Masai Mara for the price of a small family car. One night in a lodge on the Serengeti can cost the equivalent of a week on the Costa Del Sol. Trust me, there are easier, better and cheaper ways to have that holiday of a lifetime.

I'll let you into the secret, but first, my adventures on my quest to see the Big Five.

The East Coast

This was my first trip to Africa, only my second away from Europe, and happened in the days before iPhones, Google, Wikipedia, Facebook and the Euro. People were beginning to become paranoid over something called the Millennium Bug. And that never happened.

The overnight flight had already stopped to re-fuel in Cairo, where some folk got out for a cigarette, then we followed the Nile as it cut through the desert, and over the Horn of Africa, to land in Mombasa, Kenya's second city and a major port on the Indian Ocean.

Before passport control everyone lined up to hand over $50 cash which was unceremoniously swept into an old wooden drawer, for a visa. Running the gauntlet of porters and taxis, I emerged into bright sunny morning to see a Masai warrior, tall and proud with his slicked back red braids, and wraparound red cloak, tending his cattle as they grazed the airport lawns.

The journey through Mombasa, bustling and pot holed, ramshackle shacks next to modern shops, old markets propping up pristine offices, took me to the dilapidated accident black hole which is the Likoni ferry crossing. This joins Old Mombasa island back to the mainland. The ferry consists of four unseaworthy boats that take the population and cargoes south of Mombasa to and from work. A whole city has built around the Likoni ferry.

We rolled off the boat, crowded but subdued, then down the Lunga Lunga Road till we turned off onto Palm Road which runs parallel to the coast. I was dropped off at my hotel, the Shelley Beach, checked in, and taken to my ground floor room by one of the army of smartly dressed boys who have been lucky enough to have matriculated and grabbed a much sought after job, looking after European and American tourists.

The window to my room was covered in a giant spider's web (on the outside), quite an inconvenience to a one-time arachnophobe. In the middle was seated the resident, fully six inches wide.

"Don't worry," assured my porter. "The Momma will only move at night, to feed."

This area has a perfect climate, sometimes very wet, mostly very dry, with a temperature range 28 to 33 degrees Celsius. No wonder it was much sought after by farmer settlers who made a fortune here growing coffee.

I left my room to explore the complex. Manicured lawns with bursting borders of flowers, and lush flowering trees and shrubs everywhere. I passed the restaurant and pool, and came to the wall beyond which was the beach and my first view of the Indian Ocean.

"Hello!", I heard a voice. "Welcome to Kenya."

Beneath the wall stood a young man, barefoot, in frayed jeans, a white tee-shirt, sunglasses and straw hat. There were other locals on the beach, setting up shops, playing football, or just minding the children. All of the Europeans lay behind me, around the pool.

I found some steps, and stepped down past the gun-toting security guard, onto the white sand.

"You cannot do this," my friend sounded concerned. "Here, or you will burn," and he took off his hat and plonked it on my head. We faced the mid morning sun, as it rose towards noon.

"I am Mkunzo, but people call me Del Monte. They also call me Del Boy, but I do not know why," he introduced himself with a wide grin.

Del had adopted me. And I was glad. Because I was his, the other beach boys didn't bother us, the ladies who sold brightly coloured clothes and all sorts of souvenirs, went through him, and from Del I learned a great deal about his country and its people.

"I have to return to the hotel," I said after a while. "Where can I find you later?"

"Oh, I will be here," he said, and he always was.

Back in the grounds I continue to explore. There was a path extending north and south. The tide was out, but close to the hotel, I could see the high tide mark with its long line of greeny black seaweed. Lining the path were palm trees of all shapes and sizes. Occasionally huge light brown fronds lay fallen next to coconut husks. A boy was shinning up one tree with a machete to clear out the dead stuff, while his colleagues stayed on the ground to protect wandering fools like me.

I came across several lizards, some large and very colourful, not skittish at all. Then I saw a spectacular one, just sitting on the path. It was obviously in the business of courting, it was so flamboyant. It had a bright orange head, electric blue feet, yellow legs and a blue spotted body and a tail with an orange tip.

I called over one of the boys, "What is this?" I asked.

"I do not know papa" (they all called me papa), "I will ask my friend."

Before I could protest that it was of no real concern, he had disappeared. I felt obliged to stand guard. Moments later he returned with his friend, and they both pointed at the creature and chatted in Swahili, shaking their heads.

"Sorry papa, we can not help you, I will ask my boss," and they both disappeared. I felt a little embarrassed I had caused so much fuss, but soon they returned with a taller, older man in a posher uniform. All three pointed and spoke heatedly in Swahili before the older man turned to me and addressed me with confidence.

"Sah!" he almost saluted, "Sah!" and he gestured with a flourish, "eet ees a leezard!"

I thanked them most profusely, "Hakuna Matata," they replied happily, and I went on my way.

Some weeks later, and this is how we used to do these things, I visited the local library, procured a relevant natural history encyclopedia, researched and found that our 'leezard' had been in fact a Kenyan Rock Agama, or Rainbow Lizard.

It was time for me to assess the food on offer. For me and most of the people I met on this trip, this was our first experience of a new type of board called all-inclusive. In the early days of this phenomenon people did see this as an opportunity to binge, especially finding themselves embarrassingly drunk. Brits abroad!

The Kenyan cuisine at the buffet owed a lot to Asian influence. Curries of chicken, fish, crab and bushmeat were predominant with chapati and naan breads, as well as the usual international dishes of pizza, pasta and burgers. Local specialities were mainly spicy stews containing sweet potatoes, yams and beans.

The Asian influence came from two direction. The Arabs from the north had been here for many centuries trading up and down the coast, mainly in slaves. And in the 19th century, the British imported many workers from India to work on the railway. They wanted to link the hinterland stretching from Lake Victoria, Rhodesia and Uganda to Nairobi and the port of Mombasa.

These Asians worked very hard and became very successful in their adopted countries. So successful in fact that the dictator of Uganda, Idi Amin, chucked them out in the 1970's. These expelled unfortunates had British passports so settled mainly in the UK, Canada and Australia.

In the UK they revived and made successful an ailing textile industry, and became famous for taking on the 'corner shops' in which families worked from 6am till 10pm. They have become so successful that second and third generation youngsters went to university and became accountants and lawyers. They probably won't want to take on the family business when their parents retire. Interesting times ahead.

Over dinner I met Martin, a tall, black financial adviser from Bristol, Yvonne and Debbie, Jewesses ("but not orthodox, you understand") working in catering, from London, and a couple from Leeds, Ann-Marie and Pete. Martin and I hit it off straight away, both with an interest in the local wildlife, so we decided to source a safari.

The next morning, not long after dawn the tide was out and Del offered to take me to the reef.

"By boat?" I suggested.

"No, we will walk. You will need a hat, sunglasses, sunscreen, water and some reef shoes."

"But you are barefoot," I said

"I know where I can put my feet. You do not. There is sharp coral, urchins, and stone fish. They can kill you.

I fetched my shoes.

When the tide is low, it exposes the barrier of coral about a mile out from shore. This extends down the whole of the east coast of Africa. Inside this barrier the coral is many thousands of years old and is mainly turned to rock, so there are many rock pools and coral gardens to explore. On our walk we also swam in the warm water between outcrops, mingling with the many smaller fish living here, butterflies, damsels, sergeant-majors, wrasses. We picked up starfish; red, blue and white, the size of a football, foot-long sea cucumbers, and Del showed me how the crimson urchins move and feed and mate and give birth. He told me about native cures should you step on their spines. We saw sea spiders, sea worms, sea slugs, and the occasional pair of cuttlefish changing their colours whilst swimming by. He found a stonefish, looked like a stone!. He poked it with a biro and purple venom squirted out.

"If you tread on its spine, the venom will go into your foot. If it reaches your heart, you will be dead," he told me, chillingly.

We reached the sand bar at the end, over which crashed Indian Ocean breakers. Out to sea I could see large tankers and container ships, this is a busy sea lane.

"Out there is the big fish, tuna and shark, in here, the lagoon is protected."

We walked and swam back, chatting as we went. Del was 24, he had lost his father when he was sixteen and had become the main breadwinner. His family lived hand to mouth so if he went home from the beach with no shillings, they stayed hungry. Del was undoubtedly bright, both numerate and literate, with good communication skills, but as he had not matriculated, with his father's demise, he would never be able to have a job with a salary, unlike the boys in the hotel.

I had a chat with several of the guests later, some of whom had felt quite intimidated about going outside the grounds of the hotel to mix with the locals. With the next low tide, for his reef walk Del had ten customers.

Martin and I booked a safari through the hotel, one night away in the Shimba Hills. A minibus came to pick us up late morning and we drove south to Diani Beach for lunch.

Colobus monkeys, with blue testicles (only the males) were playing and swinging from the trees outside the restaurant, and there was a small table upon which we could put our drinks. One of the boy monkeys climbed onto the table, knocked over a bottle of Fanta and began lapping at the spilling contents. A waiter came out and threatened him with his teatowel, and the monkey cowered and sped off. When the waiter went back indoors, the monkey returned and tried the same trick. Confidently I stepped forward to shoo him away as the waiter had done. I was not the known waiter. The monkey flew at me with a hiss and threatening teeth. I jumped backwards in fright, emitting a fearful little gasp, like "Ooer!" and the witnesses fell about laughing.

"It was like something out of Alien," I tried to splutter, but everyone was too convulsed to care.

We arrived at the gates to Shimba Hills National Park and so began my very first safari game drive. The driver raised the roof so we could all stand up for a better view, there were six on board, two at the front, two in the middle, myself and Martin in the rear.

What followed was two hours of pure magic.

A slow drive on unmade roads through the bush of thorny trees, flowering shrubs and high dry grasslands waving in the hot breeze. There were occasional views through the green hills to the blue ocean beyond, but all eyes were on the adrenalin filled business of spotting game.

Firstly, bird life was everywhere, from buzzards and eagles circling to bee eaters perching, weaver birds nesting and storks and cranes striding the savannah. We saw a secretary bird, like a crane, but with a pot full of pens on its head, which wonderfully kills its prey, snakes by stamping on them. There were water buffalo, warthogs and bush pigs. At one point we came across a family of pigs, startled by our presence, who were crashing through the bush. We laughed when a baby somersaulted into the open to join them. We saw sable antelope, gazelles and impala, zebra and wildebeest, and the stars of the show, giraffes. When you have seen giraffe in their native habitat you will never want to visit a zoo again. (Sorry to all those wonderfully caring places which look after, breed and work to reintroduce our valuable animals). We saw two giraffe necking, not the violent, swinging, fighting behaviour known of males, these were merely cuddling.

Our first game drive ended with our arrival at the Shimba Hills Lodge, built in the style of Treetops where half a century ago a princess arrived, to leave as Queen Elizabeth II.

The open plan bar, lounge and viewing platform of polished wood overlooked a watering hole. The plan is to sit and drink, and whisper and enjoy the best of nature. Whispering is very important. Nothing scares game away more than noise, so the atmosphere of almost monastic silence was exceptionally peaceful and relaxing.

We had another game drive at dusk, then a five course dinner where we fed morsels to the resident bush babies, and an early bed. We were up before dawn for a final game drive, returned to the lodge for breakfast and were back at the Shelley Beach before lunch. A magical 24 hours. Shimba Hills is a fantastic taster for safari, but it is small, so most of the Big Five are absent.

Over night I had had a strange dream. Like most dreams, the exact nature quickly escaped me, but it involved Carol Vorderman who had 36 pierced nipples.

I recounted this to Martin, who nodded sagely, and an American couple as we breakfasted.

"Who's Carol Vorderman?" the lady asked.

"She's a celebrity mathematician," I explained .

"Why would you dream about a mathematician?" she drawled incredulously.

"I met her once," said Martin. "I got aroused. Not bad. Seven letter word!"

The American lady's jaw remained dropped. Her husband chuckled.

The next day I met up with Del and he took me into the village of Timbwane, behind the hotel. The village had lost its freshwater well (contaminated with seawater) with the building of the hotel. But this was offset by the jobs and tourists the hotel provided. Children took their handcarts and plastic drums every day the five miles to the nearest stand pipe.

There was a coral quarry here digging limestone, and the village was built on this dark grey, sharp stone. This was evidence that the reef had been created over millions of years, gradually moving further out into the ocean.

Later I went home with Del in a tuk-tuk so he could introduce me to his family in Likone.

He had told me previously he was of the majority Kikuyu tribe, Muslim, like most coastal dwellers, and came from the village of Shimba. He was hoping one day to save up 30,000 Shillings (about £300) so he could buy two cattle and a plough and return to his village

I was shocked by his living conditions, but retained my, hopefully not patronising smile. He lived in a warehouse divided into living quarters, for perhaps twenty families. His nine foot by six foot room was cordoned off by rough wattle walls and a single curtain for a doorway. There was no ceiling or windows or water, but a tap within 100 yards made this a much sought after accommodation. His wife looked embarrassingly shy as she held their one month old daughter, and together they were seated on the tiny bed. There was a single gas ring, a broken mirror and little else. I didn't ask about toileting.

Later as we wandered the rubbish strewn streets of Likoni, I told Del about our safari and he asked whether we had seen hippopotamus. I said we had not because the water holes had mostly dried up.

"You know the hippo is the most dangerous animal in Africa. If you see one and you are between him and water, there is only one thing you can do," Del sounded very serious with his sage advice.

"You must stand still and bend over as far as you can until your head is between your legs."

I was captivated by his bush knowledge. "And then, Del, then what happens?"

"Then," he widened his eyes and lowered his voice to a slow whisper, "Then, you pray to your God and kiss your ass goodbye." and he roared with laughter.

That evening I spent with the locals in Timbwane's small bar, watching Premier League football. Such a small world. Afterwards, back at the hotel there were Masai dancers, resplendent in their red tunics and clay red hair. They are tall and slim with proud high cheekbones and facial scars borne of coming-of-age rituals. They no longer have to kill a lion, but they do bleed their cattle from the neck for lunch. They held their spears and chanted and jumped up and down, very high, and moved around in a circle. The objective appeared to be to out jump everyone else in the troupe.

I finished my week with more reef walks, snorkelling and a dhow trip from the southern tip of the peninsular, out onto the open ocean to spot dolphins. No dolphins, but fantastic snorkelling over electric blue and green and pink coral outcrops. We stopped briefly to walk across Chale Island, a jungle with the biggest land crabs I have ever seen, and we received an apology from the captain.

"I am sorry we saw no dolphins. You can have a free trip tomorrow and I guarantee dolphins."

Not for me, I'm afraid. I was flying home tomorrow.

I gave Del £100 and a shopping list to buy me some souvenirs, a lion, a hippo, an elephant, a dolphin, a safari hat.

"I want the best quality, mind, but if there is any left over, you have it." I was very happy with what he bought me.

*

I'd had a taste of safari and I wanted more. Within twelve months I had returned to the Shelley Beach (a mistake as it was full of ghosts, no Martin, Yvonne, Debbie nor Del although I asked about him extensively), but I only used the hotel to bookend my adventures. I was going to Tsavo East and West, and Amboselli. Here was the perfect base.

Two days in and Francis picked me up in his nine seater safari bus. There were six companions already on the bus, trying to catch up on sleep. We crossed the Likoni Ferry very early. I was amazed at the style of commute. At four in the morning the urgency of the foot passengers, jostling to be first onto the ferry, rushing to the front to be the first off, then running off the ferry as soon as the ramp was lowered. People were eager, no doubt, to be the first into the office, or more likely, to open the shop. The Rat Race, Kenya style.

We passed through the city and out the other side, and were soon on the main route to Nairobi, following the railway. It was a long morning on a difficult road, but we covered the 90 miles to Voi in about five hours. Air conditioning helps.

Here we entered the National Park. These are not like our safari parks at Woburn or West Midlands. Combined, Tsavo East and Tsavo West are at 9,000 square miles, the size of Israel.

Francis, our driver and guide raised the roof whilst we stretched our legs. Our party include Sharif and his wife Melissa, from London, Jackie, a doctor from Oxford, Paddy, an Irish property developer, and a French couple, Carole and Ouafi from Nantes. Sharif was an interesting character. He was the manager of the Oxford Street McDonald's which he claimed to be the busiest in the UK. We had the usual fun but wary introductions, my ice-breaker about teaching young rascals hit the usual amusing spot, even with the French whose grasp of the idioms of the English language was most impressive.

We climbed back into the minibus and assumed our positions for the game drive. We entered the park and began our adventure. The grass was high following a successful wet season, which didn't bode well for game spotting. Lions in particular use the long grass to camouflage their stalking. But Francis drove slowly and we spotted zebra and impala, then the most majestic family of giraffe browsing the acacia trees, including a calf no more than a month old, but already over six feet tall.

We came to a waterhole and were overjoyed to meet a herd of elephant. They were red. The land here is red, the dust red, so these wonderful creatures are permanently red, even whilst wallowing and playing in the water. The family comprised mothers and aunts, with adolescent sons and daughters, and babies. Francis explained that the bulls were solitary and wouldn't bother a group like this until the mating season.

We came across a herd of water buffalo, the second most dangerous in Africa, next to the hippo. I told the group the drill should you be confronted by a hippo, according to Del. As they laughed Francis, whom I was sure knew the joke, said the mosquito was the biggest killer. Jackie asked about crocodiles and leopards and lions. At this Francis stopped the bus turned and very seriously said "later I will tell you about the town of Man-eater."

There was a serious pause before he restarted the bus and we continued.

Before we reached our goal that day, the Voi Safari Lodge, we encountered antelopes; eland, hartebeast, kudu, oryx, waterbuck, wildebeest, dik-dik, impala and gazelles; Grant's and Thompson's. Of the big cat predators, we saw none. The scavengers, jackals and hyena, were around, but cats remained hidden.

We saw warthogs, huge termite mounds, tortoise and porcupine. Occasionally we spotted monkeys in the trees and the less timid baboons on the ground.

Birds included herons, storks and geese, secretary birds, crowned cranes, bustards and buzzards, hornbills, egrets, ibis, eagles, spoonbills and flamingoes. There were herds of ostrich, and families of guinea fowl and myriad colourful unknowns.

Everywhere was butterflies and the constant buzz of insects. We heard elephants trumpet and observed dung beetles do their thing. Where we we crossed the Tsavo river, crocodiles basked in the sunshine while hippos cooled in the water. Kingfishers fished and oxpeckers pecked, and at a wider stretch an osprey waited patiently on high.

We stopped briefly at an overhang to see the Taita hills shimmering on the horizon, and met rock hyrax, tiny guinea pig look-a-likes, related to the elephant. Lizards skittered in the heat haze and mongooses sought out snakes.

The Voi lodge was a touch modern, but the rooms were decorated Masai style. We had three hours to relax before our evening game drive, so made use of the pool. Set in the middle of the African savannah the views around were sumptuous.

We gathered again just before dusk and Francis took us back into the bush. We were less than a mile from the lodge when we heard something thrashing about in the bush alongside us. Then we heard angry trumpeting. Francis was noticeably nervous, and when a huge bull elephant crashed through the bush onto the road behind us, ears flapping angrily, we sped off.

Later when relaxing I mentioned to Francis that if he had given us another moment we could have had a great photo of the charging elephant. "If I had waited another moment," he said, "we could all have been dead."

Dinner was taken in a hushed atmosphere and Francis informed us that the next day we would be crossing the Tsavo river and the railway track to enter Tsavo West, at a place called Man-eater. He told us its history.

Here in the late nineteenth century the building of the railway came to a halt because of the continued attacks of two maneless lions. It was reported at the time that over a period of nine months they took and devoured over 100 Indian workers, attacking and dragging the defenceless unfortunates from their tents. They would have been terrified, and one can only imagine their agonised screams The army was deployed to track and destroy the man eaters, but the cats always remained one step ahead. The project leader was Lieutenant-Colonel John Patterson. He described how the attacks grew more brazen and frequent. One officer, a Mr Whitehead set an ambush for the lions, but they were too quick for him, killing his assistant, Abdullah and clawing Whitehead before he managed to escape. Patterson eventually tracked and killed the lions, but each had Patterson in their sights before they died. The second lion took nine bullets over eleven days, and only succumbed when Patterson shot into his heart as the monster launched into one last desperate attack.

Before bed Francis led us from the hotel via a network of tunnels to a hide which overlooked a floodlit waterhole. We saw families of mongooses at play, and late in the night some adolescent elephants came to drink and play. Just one more magical moment in a day full to overflowing. We'd even had the best bedtime horror story.

Early to bed and early to rise. I was loving it. Up before dawn for collective yawning over coffee and biscuits, and we were on the road as the glow of sunrise grew brighter in the east.

With three game drives behind us Francis knew not to dwell on impala or zebra or tommies. We could begin to concentrate on tracking lion, leopard or cheetah. There would even be a collective groan if we saw a peacefully grazing herd of impala. It meant there were no predators in the vicinity. Girafe, elephant, buffalo, or the more exotic antelope like kudu or okapi still merited a photostop.

As the bush grew brighter and the shadows shorter Francis drew the bus to a halt."Yonder", he said pointing left, "there are two lions."

We peered and saw nothing, used our binoculars to scan more distance and still saw nothing. Francis tried to help, "Behind the line of acacias, to the right of that dark green scrub, see the boulders? Follow to the end of the boulders, there are two heads."

And we could see them. Or we could see two distant fuzzy round things which if you used your imagination could be construed as a couple of adolescent lion heads. I couldn't in all honesty confirm we had seen lions.

Safari can be frustrating like this. You can go for long periods of time seeing nothing, but looking tirelessly. Then you see a dik-dik. Oh, it's only a dik-dik, carry on looking. Then your spotter (the driver) who has all the experience, may see something and get very excited. But we don't want to see anything a mile away, we want cheetahs on our roof, to feed giraffe through the window, rhinos to chase us, elephant to crowd us, and to be there, yards away when a group of lionesses bring down a wildebeest. But it's not like that. For now the dik-dik will have to do.

We returned for breakfast and Francis explained we would be spending most of the day driving out of Tsavo East, and continuing west to Amboselli.

Leaving Voi Lodge, my abiding memory will be the viewpoint over the wide savannah, under a wonderful African sky. As I recorded in my journal "We watched showers sweep across Tsavo as we sat beneath the biggest piece of the world I have ever seen."

The drive to the Manyani gate took over two hours, and we saw game and farming coexisting with each other. There were Masai goat and cattle herders, their dung hut villages, and fields of maize and millet. We also passed Kikuyu bungalow settlements, and began playing a game of spot the weirdest shop name. At the park exit we picked up another passenger, one of Francis's friends I thought, a young soldier evidently going home on leave. They sat and chatted in the front as we passed the town of Man-eater with its railway bridge that crossed the river.

Approaching Amboselli we were close to the Tanzanian border, and a feature is Mount Kilimanjaro which rises up and bulges almost into Kenya, and overlooks the Amboselli game reserve.

Animals, of course, don't observe artificial borders, or fence lines, and even on this main route we saw many giraffe and buffalo wandering along or across the road.

We eventually arrived at the Iremito Gate and said goodbye to our guest as Francis organised our entry permits. We could see the park's crowning glory to our left. Unfortunately on this occasion, Kilimanjaro had its cloud hat on so we could only see the lower slopes, and none of the snow caps.

"Nice of Francis to give that guy a lift ," I mentioned as we stretched our legs in the midday sun, warming our bodies after the air conditioning.

"He was no passenger," Sharif smiled. "Did you see his rifle? He was our protection through bandit land, our shotgun". I stood corrected, feeling a touch embarrassed at my naivety.

Amboselli was flat and wet. We saw fields we assumed were grass, only for hippos to emerge out of the bog. This was a very wet land. We also saw giraffe and zebra and wildebeest and very strange elephants. They were natural grey, not the earth red of Tsavo.

We were making our way to the heart of the park, and our lodge, the Ol Tukai which overlooks the central lake.

Once again this was a sensitively built wooden complex, open plan with small twin cottages. Being so close to water the beds were protected with mosquito nets. This probably also accounted for the many lizards and iridescent blue splendid starlings which seemed almost tame, sitting on chairs and balconies to welcome you.

We relaxed in the heat of the afternoon in the pool, then gathered for the dusk game drive. It yielded one magical moment, the sight of thousands of flamingos on the lake, pink, and growing pinker as the sun set.

That evening over a wonderful hushed dinner, the peace was occasionally disturbed with loud buzz-splats. The mystery had to be investigated..

We found the culprits lying on the floor outside some of the cabins. They were Rhinoceros beetles, and they were displaying what I can only describe as the 'dying fly' dance. They were on their backs, drunkenly waving their six legs in the air.

These insects, some the size of a man's fist, are heavily armoured with a black, polished exoskeleton, and a large horn (hence the name). With some of the cabins being whitewashed and a lightbulb shining, they became irresistible. Myriad moths of all sizes and colours were dancing around the bulbs.

The beetles weren't as clever as the moths, they just dive bombed into the shining. Hence the noise we heard, and their incapacitation.

We tipped some of them over so they could find their feet. But they would flex their wings, cautiously fly off, then moments later, "buzz-splat". So we gave up. Francis said they had been known to knock motorcyclists with hi-viz vests off their bikes.

At dawn the sight of flamingo awakening was even more spectacular. Not far from the lodge we found a lion kill, a wildebeest, but the pride had taken its share, and now hyena were clustered around the carcass as vultures and jackals waited rather impatiently for their turn. We saw half a gazelle high in a tree, carried there and partly consumed by a leopard. An elephant cow came up to us as we took photographs, and nervously paced, waiting for us to move. As we drove 50 yards down the track she crossed to what was evidently her favourite tree and began vigorous backside rubbing.

Thus our latest game drive continued until we circled back to Ol Tukei for breakfast after which we left for Tsavo West. Leaving Amboseli that early morning gave us wonderful views of Kilimanjaro. We were driving east into the sun and the mountain was to our right, bathed in that sunshine. The iconic views of the green savannah, spreading acacia trees head height to the giraffe, with elephant and zebra around, then beyond to the green then brown slopes of Kili and its snowy crater peak, high above us. Unforgettable.

We rejoined the Mombasa Nairobi road, passing the railway with its crash debris of decades pushed to the side, and ultimately came to the village of Mtito Andei, and entrance to our third National Park.

It was a four hour drive to Tsavo West, but at the gate we could still see the slopes and snows of Kilimanjaro beautifully framed against the blue sky. The park was hillier, greener, and wetter, as Sharif would find to his cost, than our previous safaris.

Thirty miles in and we came to the natural oasis of Mzima Springs where, and it was a bit of a novelty, we could get out and walk.

Charlie was our guide here, a white man with flowing golden locks. He was permanently tanned. As a white Kenyan, he explained, he is known as a Kenyan Cowboy.

He led us through the lush forest to see four natural springs fed by the Chyulu Hills to the north. The first looked no more than a pond, but we could see the arched backs of at least 50 hippo wallowing in its shallows. From here we descended some stone steps to two of the larger pools.

"Be careful" Charlie warned, "the steps can be a touch slippery."

Indeed, the damp atmosphere and mossy stones were a lethal combination, and Sharif fell heavily. He was a big lad. Although relatively unhurt, he was shaken by the fall, had turned his ankle, and had nasty grazes on his arm, hip and right side, which Charlie soon daubed with pink lotion; the same stuff you see on Tour De France riders who've come a cropper.

First aid complete we found the underwater hide. It looked like a wartime pillbox, but down some steps and there was an all around window into the lake. It was green and murky and all we could see were some large fish, when suddenly a baby hippo swam by, heading for the surface.

Leaving the hide we continued our stroll around Mzima, spotting more hippos, crocodiles and cheeky monkeys only too keen to relieve you of any snacks.

Next stop was the Shetani lava flow, a prominent black scar which erupted and was deposited 200 years ago. The flow is about three miles long and half a mile wide and is an area of black folded magma. Local people believe it was the source of the devil. Wonderful views from here to the hills around and Kilimanjaro now in the distance.

We spotted all the usual game, now mostly sheltering from the hot sun, as we drove to Kilaguni Lodge to check in and take lunch. The viewing platform from the restaurant took in waterholes and forest, savannah and hills, Kili in the distance, and impala, zebra, giraffe and elephant in the foreground. You could sit here forever.

The evening game drive was as exciting as anything we had previously experienced, although Sharif didn't join us. He reckoned he'd had enough of being bumped and bounced about. His bones needed a rest.

After dinner we relaxed looking out into the night. At least a dozen elephant came to entertain as rhino beetles bombarded behind. A pair of hornbills, who should have been in bed, joined us on the railing.

Later I was woken by crashing and splashing outside my room. I stepped onto my balcony to see an elephant just below enjoying himself thrashing about in the mud hole emitting little trumpets of excitement.

Sleep overtook me. Cats tomorrow? Hope so. Just not the musical!

There was a final pre-dawn gathering and game drive. All the usual suspects, just no cats, and the group were resigned to not seeing lion, leopard or cheetah. Poor Francis had spent hours on his walkie-talkie, in contact with other guides, but the amount of shaking of heads we saw indicated no-one was having any luck finding these elusive felines. "Grass is too high," he continued to complain.

We weren't downhearted, we had had the most wonderful four days and three nights in the African bush, in excellent company, not to mention all the animals.

On the tortuous route back Mombasa we continued to look for unusual shack names. Firstly there were the butchers, or as how they termed themselves, "Butchery", a word which these days carries a slightly more sinister connotation. Then, many shops aligned themselves with their Christian religion. I was most impressed with the pub which named itself, courageously if a little foolhardily, " The Alahuak Bar".

Here are some of the names that gave us a giggle:

Hope Butchery, Bethlehem Butchery, and the Precious Hotel and Butchery.

Covered in the Blood of Jesus Bothique (sic), Mama Mary Bothique Shop, The Fatirash Shop and Beauty.

There were many hotels, restaurants and bars (including the Alahuak one above); Little Joy Hotel, Glorious Morning Hotel, Jambo Guest Hotel, One Love Hotel, Paradise Guest House, Full Moon Stopover Pub and Hotel, New Sabrina Joy Hotel, The My Faith Guest House and the Max Joy Hotel.

Come Back And Eat Restaurant, Garden of Hope Restaurant, Vision Lady's Plaza and the Promise Seekers Emporium.

Bishmillah Bar, Cool Base Pub, Flyover View Bar, Calvary Bar, Jericho Bar, Pain Baby Bar, and a lorry delivering beer declaring it was also Covered in The Blood Of Jesus, and the Camel's Joint.

Then there were a variety of businesses; Mum Hope Shop, Blessing Salon and Massage, Star Of The Sea Greengrocery, Bethlehem Electricals, The Faith Victory Intergration (sic) Centre, Morning Star Agro Vet, and my favourite, The Grim Reaper Gardening Services.

We returned to the Shelley Beach, bade a fond farewell to Francis, and indeed each other, and I had two more days relaxing and snorkelling in the Indian Ocean before ending my second random jaunt in Kenya.

One final postscript though. Our take off from Mombasa airport was delayed because a passenger had been taken ill. The plane had to stop taxiing, and a team of medicals came on board to take the poor malaria-stricken man to hospital. His wife obviously stayed with him. The rest of us had to wait whilst their baggage was located and removed (a security measure, you understand).

I looked through the porthole as the man, his wife and their belongings were loaded into the ambulance. Blow me if it wasn't poor Sharif, the manager of Oxford Street McDonald's who had fallen at Mzima Springs. No luck, that bloke.

Kenya West

Some years later I flew to Nairobi via Amsterdam, and took a taxi to Karen Camp, the headquarters of African Trails, my host for a three safari extravaganza. The highlight would be the Masai Mara, so beloved by TV's Big Cat Diarists, and two of Kenya's Rift Valley Lakes, Nakuru and Naivasha.

You may have read Sunshine On The Water, my random jaunts through Asia and will know that I famously visited ten different safari parks before ever encountering any of the big cats. Finally, number ten was Ranthambhore, India, where I saw a tiger.

By this time in my safari career I had seen all of the African big cats, lion, leopard and cheetah although strangely not a fully grown male lion. And unlike my daughter who witnessed one on her very first safari, never a chase and a kill. I've always been a Jonah for these specialist trips. One tip for a dolphin watching cruise, make sure the name Leo is missing from the passenger manifest.

My taxi took me along the Langata Road, which has the Nairobi National Park game reserve to its south and the Kibera Slum to my right.

The Slum is a shanty town, and the biggest in Africa, housing the most awful levels of poverty. Perhaps a million people live here (officially half that). If you have a job you may earn a dollar a day, but mostly it is unemployed degradation where AIDs, violence and rape are endemic, clean water and sewage treatment almost non-existent, and the hope for a better life in Nairobi's rich suburbs like Langata and Karen, an impossible dream.

We passed the Karen Blixen museum, M'Bogani House, her of Out Of Africa fame, and landed at the African Trails complex. There was little here but a bar, a table at which to eat, a patch of grass to pitch your tent, and a bus park. I was booked on a truck safari.

Having dropped my backpack, a beer was thrust into my hand and the little group I had joined introduced each other.

Robert was our tour leader, driver and cook, he was Kikuyu, in his early thirties and father to a small daughter. Patrick was a granddad, a Masai, who would be our main driver and guide.

My companions had already been here a day and had visited the National Park and the famous Giraffe Manor, where you feed them from the upstairs windows.

Vicky and Jack were a young couple from Croydon who were "travelling till the money runs out, probably a year". David was a tall Irish hunk, newly married to Marie, an elegant slim Swiss, and they lived in Lucerne. They were both taking a year off from their NGO agency work, a sort of extended honeymoon. Todd was ironically newly single, a quiet 34-year-old from Colorado travelling around for five or six weeks, "to get the divorce out of my system."

"I'm here for a week, flying back next Friday," I explained, to their collective shock.

"Why, what do you do," asked David.

"And what do you teach?" Marie added when I had answered.

And thus the ice was broken, although Todd wasn't totally sure about my stock answer. But over more beers he loosened up.

Patrick and I could have been parents to the lot of them, hence we had the most empathy. He ensured he showed me how to erect my tent, before the beers took hold.

"Never leave it till dark for your tent," he sagely advised. Sobriety is supremely important, apparently, when setting up home.

The next morning, up bright and early to break camp, stow your tent and belongings, and to breakfast. We were soon on the road.

The truck was marvellous, easily several decades old. Robert and Patrick occupied the cab, us six had the whole of the coach compartment to ourselves. Built with tables and double seating to accommodate 16, we had plenty of space to stretch out. And we were high up, with huge open windows, perfect for surveying the world about us. And, we were soon to realise, perfect for being seen.

Climbing those precipitous steps up into the bus was like scaling the north face of the Eiger. You often needed a friendly, if forgiving hand, to offer help via the buttocks.

The journey was slow going. We didn't mind, because half the fun was waving to the people as we went. This was the main route west of Nairobi, direct to Uganda and Kampala, so there were plenty of cargo trucks. Some of the albeit slight inclines had lines of lorries dawdling up, not in the slow lane, but in the only lane.

We were able to pass villages, and schools, and markets, full of people, all smiling and waving and shouting "Mzungu, Mzungu", a popular term for white people, literally meaning those who swan around aimlessly. Sounded good to me.

Sometimes if we were near enough I would shout back "No, you Mzungu," and it was as if I had told the best joke ever. I have never known such mirth. So much laughter amongst the poverty.

Our first overnight was outside the town of Eldoret. We had gone into the town, and at a modern shopping complex bought provisions. Marie would only drink percolated coffee and we spent some time searching for the appropriate equipment whilst Robert and Patrick sought out the important stuff. In the end we gave up and just bought a tea strainer.

Outside the town Robert drove us to a viewpoint. We hadn't realised how high up we were until we looked down into this wide, lush valley. We were in fact upon the plateau on which lies most of south west Kenya, including Nairobi. At nearly 6,000 feet it is the tenth highest capital in the world. That was why, even though we were virtually on the equator and at the autumn equinox, the nights were so cold.

"Here," announced Patrick with a great deal of pride, spreading his arms wide, "is the Great Rift Valley, birthplace of mankind!"

There were steep escarpment down, and across many miles we could make out the steep sides of the mountains beyond, but this was like looking down into a new world. Verdant, flat, hot and protected, this was where aeons ago, apes took the first confident step to walk upright, and never looked back.

We made camp at the Naiberi River, and trekked its banks to discover trees and shrubs displaying the most colourful flowers, and equally majestic birdlife.

That evening in the lodge bar we were joined by Aron. I wasn't sure of his role, other than to be the butt of his colleagues' jokes. They teased him mercilessly, but he never lost his smile, which in truth was more like a silly grin. He was smaller than the other two, with protruding ears and a slight squint which made him look cross-eyed. I was just glad he wasn't driving.

I felt a little sorry for him, but as is said worldwide, there is one in every village. Robert laughed as he told us how they had plagued him when he was apprenticed, "Fetch me that left-handed screwdriver, ask the shopkeeper for striped paint, go and find a long wait." He was particularly proud of the time he injected a doughnut with hot chili sauce. "Oh how we laughed as Aron was doubled over with pain." Aron continued to giggle at the tales of his misfortunes and waved us off after breakfast.

Leaving Eldoret we headed for the Ugandan border and Jinja on the northern shore of Lake Victoria. Once again we were like royalty, driving through villages waving at the children who ran to greet us. Each school had its distinctive sunshine colour; pink, white, orange, red, bright blue, matched by the kiddies' immaculate uniforms washed in Tide, Omo and Oxydol. Customers and staff idly chatted around the colourful displays of the shops, kiosks and market stalls. Carpentry, butchery and motor mechanics mixed innocently with goats and cattle. There were fields of corn, maize, millet, then rice paddies, and wild bush. This was Africa, and I loved it.

We finally arrived at the border, and after a two hour festival of bureaucracy, crossed over. (For our adventures in Uganda, see chapter 8)

Four days later we re-entered Kenya at the same crossing, with the same futile paper chase, said goodbye to Patrick who was leaving to spend time with his family in the north, and welcomed our new guide, Aron.

We stopped at the same shopping centre in Eldoret to re-provision and late in the day arrived at Lake Nakuru, to set up camp at Punda Milias.

Aron was now in the elevated position of assistant to Robert. He appeared to be very laid back. Nothing phased him, not even when his two mates had been ribbing him previously. Everything just passed him by and he smiled sagely. Either that, or he really didn't understand and the easy smile was more an inane grin. We quickly came to realise it was probably the latter. And now Aron was to be our game driver.

It wasn't his fault that he began our first Lake Nakuru game drive with some bad news. We had stopped at a marvellous viewpoint taking in the lake and its surrounding rolling savannah.

"Here is Lake Nakuru." He spread his arms Patrick style. "It is a very shallow lake, only a foot deep, and is a soda lake, very alkaline with minerals due to its evaporation. Although today it is deep blue, up until last year it was pink with a million flamingos, but they have moved to Lake Baringo."

This was a disappointment. I had seen great flocks of flamingo at Amboselli, and most people come to Nakuru for just this reason. But you cannot second guess nature. The flamingos had gone, probably for a better bloom of algae, only handfuls remained.

We weren't downhearted, there was so much more to see. Close to the lake were 'flanges' of baboons, and from behind one hillock lumbered a very rare sight, a black rhinoceros.

They are not called black because of their colour, although they are darker than their white cousins. They are also smaller, solitary, and a touch more belligerent. And they are browsers, feeding on leaves from bushes, hence their prehensile top lip Their cousins graze on the grass and have a wide mouth. These were named "weiss" which is German for wide, but this was corrupted into English as white, so the smaller variety simply became black creating the black/white confusion. White Rhino, and Black Rhino. To save possible offence their names are now preceded by Southern and Eastern.

Later we also saw buffalo and giraffe, oryx and kudu, gazelle and antelope. We followed a hunting group of lionesses, and late in the day also saw hyena and jackal. But Aron's driving was a nightmare. He was always late following our directions. He was too slow to slow down, not quick enough to speed up, and his reflexes on right or left were woefully lacking.

He found potholes which could have been avoided, and slewed down flooded tracks nearly flinging his passengers through the windows. He was less than sympathetic to the needs either of his vehicle, its occupants or the game. Sometimes he came so close to the animals, we could see they were harassed. Thank goodness he never had to parallel park.

The highlight of our game drive was taking lunch on Baboon Cliffs, overlooking the lake. We shared our picnic with a colony of Rock Hyrax. About twice the size of meerkats, and looking like big guinea pigs, these scampering little creatures are actually the closest relation to the elephant. Hard to believe.

That evening we turned our banter compass onto Todd. Jack, David and I, and our Kenyan hosts discussed football. Marie and Vicky being European women were quite happy whilst their menfolk engaged in this ritual. Robert asked Todd why he was so quiet and what game did he play. Todd perked up and said hockey. We explained to Robert that hockey was a game played on a grass pitch with sticks and a hard white ball, most favoured by schoolgirls. Todd took the bait. He blustered that real hockey was played on ice with a puck and skates and rousing music. Robert caught our wink and asked about another American national sport, baseball. "Isn't that like rounders, also played by schoolgirls?" he asked cheekily. And whilst Todd was desperately trying to save the honour of his national sports, Marie, a Swiss, interjected that American Football was like rugby but with too much armour and too many time outs. "And that ridiculous Superbowl with its advertising hype and half-time rock stars, is the height of flashy nonsense. Typical brash, arrogant Americanism." I liked her style.

Todd realised he was outnumbered and overpowered, and with no allies to come to his aid, accepted defeat. So we had another round of beers and laughed around the campfire as Aron roasted more marshmallows. He was just pleased he had escaped the ribbing.

Later we sang Simon and Garfunkel songs, and Todd was happier we admired his countrymen. He especially enjoyed our rendition of America, laughing on the bus (a brilliant concept), and the reference to Joe DiMaggio in Mrs Robinson. I told Todd that I had written The Boxer on the trip from Tsavo East to Tsavo West, or had it been in Cuba heading for Fat Mary's Bar? By this time his mind had been so messed with he had no idea what to believe. And he had drunk a lot of beer.

The next day was really exciting, we were going to the Masai Mara, probably one of the most famous game reserves in Africa.

We broke camp at dawn for one last game drive around Nakuru Lake. The flamingoes still hadn't returned.

It took us all day to drive south west over the Olooloo Escarpment, via Naivasha and Narok to arrive at the Masai lands, their ancestral home following their emigration from the Nile Valley. By late afternoon we were driving on a long, straight road, fringed by Masai villages. Between the villages we passed many herds of goat or cattle, the herdsmen or boys standing proud with their iron spears, red or chequered 'shuka' robes, and hair plaited and slicked down.

We arrived at the Masai Mara Camp, just outside the reserve, in time for dinner, (goat, I was unimpressed), then settled down around the campfire, for beers and marshmallows.

We discussed our favourite places in the world. Being the eldest and most travelled, my companions were eager to discover my preferences. I 'ummed and 'arred, and talked about Paris, and the Taj Mahal, and Nile cruises, and Iguazu Falls, but eventually chose the place both Kaz and I have always felt the most welcomed, the island of serendipity, Sri Lanka, to our minds the most friendly place on Earth.

Vicki was shocked that I liked the people of Sri Lanka.. She had never been there but knew a community of Tamil refugees living in London who had escaped the civil war there. She related tales of atrocities allegedly committed by the army of the Sinhalese majority.

The Tamil Tigers of the north had wanted a separate state and had fought with guerrilla tactics for a quarter of a century before being defeated in 2009. In truth there were probably war crimes from both sides, but a defeated minority will always claim the most pitiful events. In fairness Vicki hadn't known the history from both sides, and in fairness, neither had I. It just goes to show how complex every part of Planet Earth can be, and how far we still have to go. How paradise can co-exist with hell.

At any given time there are about 20 major conflicts on Planet Earth where perfectly normal people are trying to kill other people to force their issue. Peace, when it happens is so very fragile, and so very precious. As someone once said, let's give it a chance.

Sadly, in Vicki's eyes I was supporting an evil regime, and there remained an atmosphere until we departed.

But for now we were on the Mara, so named for the river that runs through it which is the major barrier faced by the wildebeest in their annual migration as they follow the rains north to the sweeter grass.

The Mara itself is only a small part, about 5% of the similarly famous Serengeti of Tanzania. Animals know nothing of borders of course, and as they travel north through Tanzania into Kenya, from Serengeti to Masai Mara, they don't even bother to get their visas stamped.

The gates to the park open at 6:30, but for reasons known only to Aron, he couldn't get us there before 8, by which time the nocturnals have retired to their beds, and the diurnals, having breakfasted well would be sheltering from the increasing heat of the sun.

The previous night, however had been a marvellous experience First the night sky full to overflowing of stars spilling from the Milky Way, then under canvas, drifting off to sleep with the throaty roars of lions and high pitched growls of Hyena so tantalisingly close.

A truck safari has its downside. We are high up, giving a better vantage point than jeeps, for instance, but we are denied some of the smaller trails that can get closer to waterholes, or go deeper into the bush. What we saw as we progressed into the park was evidence of kills, not necessarily from the night before, but there were many carcasses, mainly wildebeest. There was a giraffe, mostly intact, but part of its insides devoured and its head and neck at a fearful angle. Then we saw a pride of lions, there were females and adolescents, and for a fleeting moment before he disappeared, a magnificent male. Already the safari magic was casting its spell.

Not far into the park we came across an airstrip with the occasional Cessna type landing or taking off. These were ferrying rich Americans from the cruise ships off Mombasa. Fly in, see some game, fly out. It doesn't really give you the safari experience. Seems a bit of a cheat.

We headed for the Mara river to cross by the Purungat Bridge in the south. On the way we had elephant and dik-dik encounters, zebra and giraffe, wildebeest and antelope, warthog and bush pig. There were secretary birds and vultures and storks, and lots of smaller colourful birds. When we reached the bridge we could see crocodile and hippo and in the eddies of the river were piled bones of wildebeest, easily recognisable by the horned skull. These were the poor creatures who failed in the frenzied crossing of the river during the migration, to be taken by leopard and crocodile. We crossed into the Mara Triangle and took lunch in the shade of an acacia tree. We had been entertained by a young lioness and five wildebeest who played a cat and mouse game around our truck and in and out of a few copses. She wouldn't let them rest or graze, and they always trotted just out of reach. I imagine they were confident there were no mothers or aunts around waiting to ambush.

The lioness had gone now, hence we could alight from the truck. I couldn't help thinking what kind of a mad scramble it would be trying to get back up into the truck, one at a time, if she returned.

In the afternoon Aran took us on a soporific drive through some empty plains, then seemed to panic a little as he headed for higher ground, ignoring many good encounters trying to find leopard or cheetah. We didn't, but still a fantastic experience.

The evening, my last, was a bit quiet. Vicki was still in a mood, and Marie was tired, so the lads just drank beer around the campfire. The shrill insect noise of the hot day had been replaced by the soft whooping and burbling of frogs. The occasional throaty lion roar mixed with the crackling of the fire and the boys laughter as we bantered into the night.

This would be my last under canvass for a while and I was contemplating this when I took my wash bag to the toilet block to clean my teeth. Often in these campsites, the solitary electric bulb is the only artificial light around, therefore attracts all the night insects. No rhino beetles, but all kinds of weird creatures from little bugs to gnats and mozzies, crane flies to moths, and the moths can be really huge, some as big as your hand. I resolved that Kaz couldn't do this, she has a phobia of moths, she's a mottephobic. Strange, she loves butterflies.

The next morning disaster struck. Todd's tent had been robbed. Someone had got into the compound, raised his zip just a few inches and got away with his wallet and iPhone. In his words, "Robbed my pants, man!"

Understandably the morning was taken up with trying to report and resolve the crime, and discussions about what may have happened. It left a bitter taste as we left the Mara, and we didn't roll up to our camp at Lake Naivasha until four in the afternoon.

I had the luxury of wandering around the campsite as the others prepared their sleeping quarters. There were plenty of birds here, peacocks, rollers, bul-buls, pelicans, plus a family of white-furred colobus monkeys playing in the trees. We were told to stay in our tents at night as hippos were known to roam. Marvellous, but wouldn't affect me.

We said our goodbyes over a couple of beers as I awaited my taxi to Nairobi. Then it turned up. It was Aron! Fair play to him, it was three hours back to Nairobi and I flew in five. The lad done well and had me there on time. Jambo!

"Goodbye Africa!" I wrote. After all, you never know when you will return.

*

Footnote

I did return to Kenya some years later, with Kaz to experience her first African safari. We stayed at the Papillon Lagoon Reef Hotel on Diani Beach to enjoy the delights of the Indian Ocean. Beautiful white sand, reef walks, snorkelling, dhow trips to the distant sand bar. Outside our room stood the oldest and largest baobab tree in Africa, 500 years and over 100 feet around, and in the gardens were monkeys, tortoise and butterflies galore. Galagos, or Bushbabies, joined us for dinner.

I negotiated our safari with Robby of Robby Tours, in his office outside the hotel. For a fraction of the cost of booking in the UK, we tailor made our safari. Four days and eight game drives, three superb lodges, all included, and all in our own bus with our own personal driver and guide, Kenyatta.

Kaz wept when she saw her first giraffe family in its own habitat, and loved every moment. The lodges, the service by such friendly people, the food, the viewing points with elephant and leopard and innumerable birds; the game drives with everything from lions to flamingoes, a cheetah chase, and views of the snow-covered Kilimanjaro; more giraffe, red elephants, stampeding zebra and kudu, rhinoceros and hippo.

At one point she wrote; "Feeling poetic. The red earth sets off myriad shades of green against a white flecked blue sky, all framed by the shaded black mountains and Kili's icy hat. The butterflies, birds, heady scents of perfumed flowers and herbs send an exotic thrill into every sense. Then you see animals, at home."

Papillon Reef bookended our safari, and we left with the most wonderful memories.

We flew from Mombasa to Istanbul for our connection. In Istanbul airport many people wore masks. Three weeks later the UK and indeed the world were in lockdown. Gallivanting had been brought to a premature but necessary halt. Whence it will return?

Chapter Seven

Conquering Kilimanjaro?

Extreme adventuring is not what I do. Intense gallivanting, maybe, even concentrated random jaunting. But anything dangerous that you have to work hard at, I tend to avoid. Trekking to the poles, climbing Everest, going into outer space or diving the Mariana Trench. These take too much time in planning and training, or are simply too expensive. Everest, for example costs about £40,000. And you might die or worse, not summit.

Kilimanjaro on the other hand, as I was once assured, is merely a long trek. About 30,000 people attempt it every year. Of those only 60% summit, over 1,000 need to be rescued, and perhaps 30 lose their lives. Not for the faint-hearted then, so I thought I'd give it a go.

Mount Kilimanjaro is the highest mountain in Africa. It is a stand-alone monolith, rather than part of a range. At over 19,000 feet, it is about three quarters the height of Everest, and stands wholly in Tanzania, on the equator. In just a few days climbing, the climate can go from equatorial to polar. Pretty extreme.

I signed up for an expedition run by Explore Worldwide in the Spring of 2008, better known as February half-term.

I flew in on Ethiopian Airlines via Addis Ababa. Two old crates, but comfortable and good service. On the second leg, a near empty plane meant I could make the middle four seats into a bed. Luxury. Stopped to refuel in Nairobi, then on to Tanzania.

A taxi deposited me at the Mountain Inn in the small town of Moshi, and on checking in I received the instruction to meet at 5pm for the "extremely important" first briefing.

The afternoon was very relaxing, a hot 35 degrees with a warm breeze ruffling the palm trees around the pool. I sun bathed, had a few dips and a beer, then dressed and made my way to the meeting room.

Daniel, our expedition leader, took the briefing. He was a fit young man in his late twenties with a shock of golden hair and a ready smile. This briefing, however, was anything but fun. He spoke to the assembled group with great gravitas, explaining that he had never lost a client, and he wasn't about to lose one on this climb. We would have to follow his instructions to the letter to ensure our safety.

He spoke of our diet and the need to eat when altitude takes our appetite. We must drink water, at least three litres a day or risk oedemas, and carry this from the start. He spoke sternly about toileting using long drops in the camps. He warned gravely over the need to have the correct kit and clothing, and that we would be able to hire extra in the morning. He spoke extensively of the need to rest and sleep and how to concentrate the mind to achieve this. He explained the role of our porters, all Masai, who would simply instruct us "Pole, Pole", slowly, slowly. He finished with a solemn warning.

"You must, on all occasions, follow my instructions. I cannot be responsible for the consequences, if you do not!"

"What sort of consequences?" I asked, trying not to sound too flippant.

"You may die!" he added, and the room was silent.

Danny said we would meet at eight for dinner, and left the group to get acquainted, with one final warning:

"From now, no alcohol and no smoking."

I was to be sharing my tent ("You must have a buddy. You have to look after each other") with Roland. He was a retired head teacher, tall and thin, and like me had been a little shaken by the ferocity of the briefing.

Catherine, at 64 was the same age as Roland. She was a Scottish farmer. Patrick, 54, introduced himself as an Irish businessman, then there was Lesley a 38 year old Scottish nurse, and youngsters Paul, Gary and Rob, all 35. Paul was manager of a Toys 'R' Us outlet, Gary an American attorney, and Rob a management consultant.

Dinner was an unconvincing fish curry, and I had a nightcap of one last beer and cigar. (With the hindsight of all these years I look back on this as an idiotic moment of bravado). I slept fitfully, worrying about the stern nature of the briefing, fretting over not having enough underpants (no kidding, I was in a state) and troubled over whether I had sufficient cash for the extra kit needed. I had already forked out $50 I hadn't budgeted for a yellow fever shot. And my ankles were still swollen from the flights.

I rose and breakfasted well before being introduced to the colourfully attired Gladys, our quartermaster. She supplied me with an extra thermal top, a heavy down jacket, and a brilliant toothy smile as she relieved me of more dollars.

We gathered, suitably kitted out, and Gladys and the hotel staff waved us off in our coach. It was a 45 minute drive up to Machame Gate at nearly 5,000 feet

There was the usual "This Is Africa" license issuing bureaucracy, and we met up with our crew of 25 guides and porters inside the gate. We began our climb at 12:30. This first day was to take us from the gate up to Machame First Camp, a climb of 4,000 feet.

The going was a tough but regular trek, upwards all the way. It was hot and sticky as we strode through the verdant, damp rainforest. I don't recall birdsong, nor any animals or much colour, but mostly you are watching one step carefully being put in front of another to prevent tripping, to ensure grip, and to concentrate on taking regular breaths. There were breaks which were necessary to rest, but I hated them as the sweat cooled on your body and became uncomfortable.

I should explain, all we were carrying was a daypack and our water. The porters took everything else, and went ahead to make camp and prepare our sleeping and eating quarters, and our meals.

We made it into camp at 5:30. We had left the rainforest behind, transcended the temperate forest, and were now amongst low scrub.

We took a meal of soup and potatoes and pasta in the mess tent under candlelight, and we were in our tents, snuggled into tight sleeping bags by 8:30. With the struggles of the day behind us, this was our first real opportunity to chat, and Roland and I got on well. Our subject, pedagogy. Whose bright idea was it to put two teachers together?

It matters not if you don't sleep, just the act of resting is enough. Sleep did eventually overtake us, but was fitful and interrupted by many pee breaks. All that water. The air was now thinner, so your normal breathing rate (the one which has been developed over many years) becomes too slow, not taking in enough oxygen, and occasionally, suddenly, there is a panicked sharp intake of breath. I was still worrying about my kit, not realising the futility of underpants when you are up here. Tomorrow we trek up to the Shira Plateau, through an alpine desert.

Early to bed, early to rise, and camp is waking up around 6am. Bowls of hot water are placed outside the tent, and we stretch, dress, wash, and clean teeth, usually whilst walking around taking in the views and greeting fellow trekkers.

"Sleep well?" is the standard question.

"Fine, and you?" the stock answer. Whether you did or not, nobody really needs to know. Sufficient to be aware we all survived the night.

We toilet with as much dignity as one can muster in one shared loo, then find the mess tent for breakfast.

The mess tent is pretty grim. The boys do the cooking outside with calor gas (wood is too precious here), and we enter the dark green tent to sit at a table of six fold up stools either side. The choice is simple, porridge or pancakes, or both. It was here, at this precise moment I discovered a taste and combination which has stayed with me ever since. Pancakes with chili sauce, simple, yet enticingly spicy. Wakes your day.

Pack the day bag, check there's sufficient water, squeeze the sleeping bag back into its ridiculously small nylon carrier, don socks and boots, and off we go.

Day two was another exhilarating trek up to Shira Camp. We were out of the forest, so the views all around were superb. This was boulder strewn moorland. The boulders in question were once bombs ejected from the crater when Kili was an active volcano. They've weathered smooth over millions of years. Our constant companions were hooded crows hopping around searching for food, while eagles and vultures circled to find carrion.

It was cold and windy all the while climbing higher onto the plateau, through the alpine desert. When we reached camp at 1:30 we were at nearly 13,000 feet, which is about three times the height of Ben Nevis. Only another 6,000 to go.

We'd snacked during the trek, and therefore dined early in a mess tent being increasingly buffeted by high winds. Pasta, soup and potatoes, to make a change, and some biscuits with our hot chocolate to take us to bed.

I lay there for a while, resting, if not sleeping, but Roland was becoming increasingly agitated. It didn't help that the wind made us feel like rag dolls, tossed about continuously. He'd lost his appetite, had a headache and was feeling nauseous. Danny asked me to keep an eye on Roland and to find him if the situation worsened.

It was a difficult, unnerving night. Neither of us slept well, nor did we feel we could talk about our feelings. I just tried to snuggle into my sleeping bag and think positive thoughts. Alone, in the pitch black, partner moaning in pain, wind howling, incongruously worrying about the state of my underwear, positive thinking was hard to come by. It proved a long night.

After almost 12 hours in our sleeping bags we were up and out by 7:30. Camp wasn't so jolly whilst cleaning teeth in the freezing cold, but pancakes with chili sauce readied me for the day.

We battled inevitably upwards, through the lava strewn moonscape. Little vegetation, just mosses and lichen clinging to the boulders. There were still wonderful views all around, even if the peak itself was continuously covered in cloud, as if too shy to reveal itself to would-be conquerors.

Day three on the mountain was a time to reflect. I was coping with the altitude thus far, even if others weren't so lucky. I was certainly feeling grateful to my constant companions, my Lichfield walking sticks. Thick socks and sturdy boots were also a boon. I was wearing four layers which helped with the cold winds, although sweat wasn't being wicked away. I had begun to assuage my worries for the lesser important parts of my kit, namely underwear. Finally I was beginning to be thankful for my rugby playing experience. I hadn't undertaken any particular training regime for the trek, happy that 30 years playing back row had given me the stamina and strong legs I would need.

We were still crossing the Shira plateau, heading for Barranco Camp, and hoping to climb up the Lava Tower.

We took lunch under an overhang to minimise the effect of the cold wind and then realised Roland had gone missing. I thought he must have sought a little privacy for a toilet break, but it became increasingly clear he hadn't found his way up to the lunch site.

When we eventually found him, he was safe but cold and a little confused. After he had peed he saw the porters leaving for Barranco and followed them. They hadn't realised he was following and kept their own pace, much faster than his. By the time he realised we weren't with him, the porters were out of sight ahead so he stopped and waited. Although he had taken a wrong fork, Danny and the lead guide found him and led him into Barranco Camp where he was given a warm drink and put to bed. Danny was concerned altitude sickness had taken hold.

Following the Roland scare, and after lunch we climbed to one of Kili's lesser peaks, The Lava Tower at over 15,000 feet, was exhilarating. Then we climbed down to Barranco Camp. On the way there was some welcome sunshine which we enjoyed in sheltered rock armchairs. It was on this path that we came across Kili's Giant groundsels, pineapple shaped cactus like plants up to 20 feet high.

Today had been hard work. We'd ascended 2,600 feet to the Lava Tower, then descended nearly 2,300 to Barranco, covering eight miles of difficult terrain. And we'd lost and found Roland. After a well earned rest we took dinner, soup and chips, then settled down for the night. I was just beginning to think sleep was coming easier when the heavens opened and began to give our little tent a terrible battering. This disturbed Roland and he became very ill, having to leave the tent nine times. He made the decision to go down.

In the morning of Day 4 I helped him gather his things and we all said goodbye as he was despatched with two porters to take him back to Moshi.

His departure left me depressed. I felt I had let him down. I was supposed to be his buddy, but I had let him get sick, I hadn't encouraged him enough to eat and keep his strength up, and I'd carelessly allowed him to stray off. Not only that, but I had lost my buddy too. Now who was going to help me get up this mountain?

I went to retrieve my kit and found to my horror that the tent had leaked all into my left boot. It was soaking wet. I wouldn't be able to go on without boots. What was I to do? I couldn't even walk down the mountain with Roland. I was stuck. The whole thing had been jeopardised by this stupid leaking tent. I was, to say the least, crestfallen. I asked a porter if he could dry it by the calor gas. The lad returned after half an hour and gleefully handed me a warm damp insole.

Breakfast was pancakes and chili sauce, then the remainder of us climbed down into the Barranco Valley.

"Give your poles to the porters," Danny announced, "they'll only be a hindrance here, you'll need all four contacts on this climb."

We had arrived at the near vertical face of the Barranco Wall. This ridge, measuring over 800 feet was formed when the volcano was still active, and is one of the most feared yet anticipated sections of the climb.

It took nearly two hours to scale the wall, no real technical issues, we didn't have to be roped together or anything like that, but it was still an exhilarating climb. I kept thinking my climbing buddy, Roland, would have loved this activity. It got the blood flowing, and cleared the airways, and we could exercise our muscles in a different way then the endless plod of the icefields.

There were two more valleys to lower ourselves into and climb out of, before we stopped for lunch. Now it was almost over, it was back to that plod. "Pole, pole!" the guides kept reminding us.

Danny explained that this next section, up to camp four, our final camp was an interminable ascent, a slope open to the elements.

"Just go slowly, at your own pace. Don't wait for anyone and don't try to catch anyone up. We'll get strung out, but try to conserve your energy."

The climb was indeed a trying experience. Not long into the start, there was a sustained snow blizzard with rumbling then startling thunderclaps. I couldn't speak for anyone else, (because you couldn't speak) but my spirits began to drop. There was no rest, just this slow endless plod into the face of the storm. To keep ice out of my eyes I could only look at my feet as small step followed small step, only occasionally squinting to look upwards to ensure you were still on the right path.

As on many occasions when I have faced bleak climbs or stressful moments, I tried to lift my spirits through singing. Nothing uplifting like gospel, just remembering the music of my youth. I began with Carole King, her Tapestry album then James Taylor singing Carole's You've got a Friend. I graduated to The Beatles and Queen, then the Eagles' Desperado and Hotel California, you can never leave. I tried to sing Harvey Andrew's Margarita, then into the modern era with Cold Play. Katie Melua helped me up the mountain with her Beijing Bicycles, and Thank You, Stars, which I always sang to Taylor, my little grand daughter. But I was struggling with the lyrics. As I trudged higher and higher, there was far too much dooby dooing. I couldn't think straight

I reached Barafu camp, 15,350 feet at four, and collapsed into the shelter of our mess tent. Someone thrust a mug of steaming hot chocolate into my hand, and I sipped, gratefully. There are several routes up the mountain, but they all culminate here which is the starting point for the final ascent. Hence over 100 tents could be seen scattered about the desolate site. Danny pointed out mine, it was quite some way below.

It took an hour for everyone to reach Barafu. We had tea to warm us, and then, when we had all gathered a huge bowl of steaming stew was placed on the table. Everyone was saying how hard they had found the climb.

All I could manage from the meal was a few potatoes. My appetite was going. It should have been a warning sign, my buddy should have encouraged me, but he was gone. I was left with my own conscience, my own thoughts, and they weren't in a good place.

It took me half an hour to scramble down to my tent, and now I had to rest and psyche myself up to face the task ahead. Following the delight at scaling the Barranco Wall, the trek up to Barafu had all but done for me. I had six hours to prepare.

One step at a time, "pole, pole". Concentrate on the heels in your head torch. Think happy thoughts.

Happy thoughts. Dad's birthday. I hadn't realised the summit attempt coincided until someone mentioned Valentine's Day. He would have been 85. Mum to get better, continue recovering from her stroke. The kids, all starting off with their careers and homebuilding. Wishing them success. Kaz to be less busy, find time for herself, stop worrying. Taylor, our first grandchild, such a joy as she begins nursery. I thought of family, friends and colleagues and on until 11pm. Time to get up and pack and dress ready.

Then in the 100 foot climb back up to the mess tent, everything was destroyed, ruined. Huffing and puffing I scrambled up, feeling totally devoid of energy.

Be that as it may, we took tea and biscuits and set off for the summit at 11:30.

We have to climb at night, Danny had explained, to arrive at dawn. Any later and the sun comes up melting the glacier, making it less stable.

Michael, the chief guide took the lead. He was followed by Paul, Rob, then Gary. I was to follow Lesley's heels, Patrick and Catherine to follow mine, and Danny brought up the rear.

The thin air creates crazy thoughts. I convinced myself I was overdressed, carrying too much weight. But if I stopped to adjust my clothing I would chill and lose the group. I would have to carry anything I jettisoned anyway, and would gain nothing. I worried about my water. Would it freeze, could I stop to drink and not lose the group, could it freeze me. Almost delirium.

We climbed for an hour. Inexorably upwards, one slow, small step after another, keeping those heels in your head torch, trying not to stumble over the uneven rocks, on and on. Where it became too steep, we zig-zagged, crunching the volcanic gravel beneath our boots, following the well-worn path.

I began to grow contemptuous of the heels ahead of me. I hated them. Especially that walking pole that Lesley hung lazily around her waist. She was not using it and it was just clanking uselessly behind her. It reminded me of the awful scene in the film Shenandoah, set in the American Civil War, when a Union soldier climbs the stairs intent on rape and murder, his sword's scabbard clanking menacingly on the stairs.

Danny called a halt to rest and drink. Catherine asked if she could return to camp. She was spent. The days' climbs had been too much for her, and she had been unwell. Danny instructed a porter to go with her. We wished her well. Then with a last second decision, Patrick said he would have to quit as well. The pair left and my brain was screaming to go too, but I refused to give up, and we five got up to continue.

It didn't take much longer. My lungs were bursting, my legs like jelly, and I was falling off the pace. Those cursed heels and clanking pole were getting away from me. I had no energy (damn appetite), I was close to collapse, and in desperation called for a rest.

Danny came over, concerned over my condition, my despair

"It not going to get easier, is it?" I gasped dolefully.

"Honestly, Geoff. If you're struggling now, you're not going to make it" He spoke calmly but forcibly, and I knew what I had to do. I stepped aside and hung my head over my poles. I wouldn't let the tears come yet.

I was given a guide, and once the trail had cleared we made our way down the mountain, which, as far as I was concerned, remained unconquered.

It took over an hour to return to Barafu and as I had guessed, the trail had been fearfully steep.

Back in camp I felt a sort of strange elation. The pressure was off, the attempt over, now to sleep. I slept the best I had in a week, and in the morning, around 7am, with snow settled everywhere I took a photograph of the Kibo summit, Uhuru Point. I'd made it to about 16, maybe 17 thousand feet.

I was to learn later that it was about this time that Paul and Rob made it to the summit. Gary and Lesley had reached as far as the rim, at Stella Point before turning back. All described how distressed they felt, in amongst the euphoria, with both Paul and Rob confessing the guides had virtually carried them to Uhuru Point.

Patrick, Catherine and I met up at 8am to begin our walk down to Mweki Camp. From arctic waste, through moonscape, and alpine rocks, to low then higher green shrubbery and eventually rainforest, it took us five hours. The others joined us eventually which was how we learned of their exploits.

At dinner the mess tent was leaking like a sieve so I dashed to my own tent, alone, to read by the light of my headtorch. As the rain hammered down I spent a little time in reflection. I was feeling slightly depressed. It had been an adventure, not necessarily a successful one, but an adventure nonetheless. I'd done Kili, if not summitted Kibo (Apparently you are not supposed to call it Kili unless you have summitted).

And Patrick was a catholic priest. He had confessed at dinner he was taking a sabbatical. No wonder he had always seemed so calm and content. It was his calling. And no wonder he had kept it from us, we'd have all called him Ted. (Except Gary. He'd have been confused. Americans, eh?)

We were up at six for a breakfast of pancakes and chili sauce, then the final trek though lush but silent rainforest to Mweki Gate.

Our team of 25 guides and porters gathered together and they sang to us a morning farewell before we took the bus back to the Mountain Inn to reunite with a reinvigorated Roland. He had used his extra free time, once recovered, to take in a safari, lucky sod. We lunched together in Moshi, relaxed around the pool and dined at the hotel where Danny presented the four of our party of eight with their "I Have Climbed Mount Kilimanjaro" certificates.

I flew the next morning via Addis Ababa. It took nearly 24 hours to reach home, and it was when I was relating to Kaz, the tale of my exploits on Kilimanjaro, that the tears finally came.

*

In 1970, the golfer Doug Sanders had a three foot putt on the eighteenth to win The Open. Had he made the simple task, riches and fame would have been his. He missed, the crowd groaned and he held his head in shame. Jack Nicklaus went on to win the play off.

Doug would be asked many times during his subsequent career and retirement whether he ever dwelt on the moment.

"Nah!" he would assure everyone listening, "Only about every five minutes."

I'm the same about Kilimanjaro. Every day I regret that I failed in my attempt. At least I am able to console myself with what Danny told me at dinner that last night.

"If I had let you go on," he assured solemnly, "because of your reaction to the altitude," he continued, "you may have died!"

Chapter Eight

Mzungus In The Mist

We are on the A104 driving from Eldoret to Jinja, from Kenya into Uganda.

We are on the African Trails bus being driven by Robert, our Kikuyu leader and Patrick, our Masai guide. They both drive, they both cook, we just have to sit the bus and erect our own tents. "We" are me, Todd, our lone American, getting over his divorce, Irishman David with his new wife, Swiss Marie, and Vicky and Jack, our Londoners "travelling till the money runs out."

There is plenty of laughter on the bus as we are made to feel like royalty. Every time we pass through a village the children wave and shout and run after us. Men and women pause from their daily tasks of work or just socialising to look up and smile and sometimes wave. These are a happy people on the streets of East Africa.

The river Lwakhakha forms the border at Malaba, where we crossed after the interminable wait to have passports and visas checked for departure from Kenya. Then we found ourselves in almost the same tin roofed hut having our passports re-authorised, and filling out the forms for visa application and subsequent approval for entrance into Uganda. Two hours of my life I'll never see again. We were the lucky ones, tourists, mostly harmless and bringing in dollars to spend. The drivers of goods vehicles wait immeasurably. How grateful we should be for a Europe without borders.

Nothing much changed on the other side. Endless villages of waving children, schools with distinctive sunshine colours, shops, kiosks and market stalls, carpentry and butchery, then fields of corn or paddies, bush with goats and cattle. Huge African skies, sun baked and dry.

We were in Uganda for a variety of adventures, but we had one goal; to walk with mountain Gorillas.

Uganda is a poorer country than its neighbour, Kenya, so there is more evidence of a mud hut lifestyle, and people gather around the village water pump. Remember, a happy woman has a well to walk to.

The shout is still "Mzungus", the light-hearted nickname for white people, busy, running around in circles, achieving nothing, like a buzzing wasp. It is how Africans view the European, basically a blustering waste of space. They see theirs as a more relaxed, laid back lifestyle, one where things get done, eventually, and there is less likelihood of high blood pressure.

We wave back regally, smiling gracefully, as we swan by in our ancient truck/bus.

It is the children who wave and shout and run after us hoping we will distribute bon-bons. The women might look up as they continue their daily chores of cleaning, shopping, cooking, collecting water. They may smile coyly.

The men are the busiest and most productive, seated on benches in the shade of trees, smoking and discoursing seriously with their companions, righting the wrongs of the world, keeping the planet turning. They know we are there. They don't look up.

We took lunch with a rare and brave family. These were Asian diaspora, returned refugees. After being unceremoniously thrown out of Uganda by the tyrant, Idi Amin, you could excuse people being happy to settle in Britain or Canada. Jaz and his family had courageously come back, opened a restaurant, and were now enjoying life amongst a freer, more welcoming people.

Late in the day we rolled into Jinja, on the banks of Lake Victoria, and set up camp at the Bourbon Campsite and Resort, which overlooks the White Nile as it leaves the mighty lake.

We were just in time for a boat ride, a "Sunset Safari Cruise" which took us onto Lake Victoria ostensibly to spot birds, but the highlight was seeing the actual source of the White Nile. Here a spring bubbles up to the surface to begin its 2,300 mile journey to where it joins the Blue Nile (source Lake Tana in Ethiopia) at Khartoum. It is now the Nile, Mother of Life, and has a further journey of 1,830 miles to its delta on the Mediterranean.

We spotted eagles and herons and ibis, but it was on this small excursion that I learned a lot about what married life was going to be like for David, a laid-back, softly-spoken hunk of an Irishman.

Marie, his wife, asked, "Geoff can I borrow your binoculars to look at the ibis in that tree?"

"Of course," I replied and handed over the glasses, never to see them again. Marie hogged them, to such an extent that I was made to feel embarrassed to ask for them back.

Good luck there, Dave.

Enjoying the sunset on the water meant it was dark arriving back in camp. Patrick had set up our tents, and Robert had cooked our chicken dinner. All that was left for us was to enjoy beers at the Waterside Bar overlooking the Nile, and ensure we'd dosed our bodies with sufficient repellent to discourage the hordes of flying and biting insects that swarmed around.

Such is camp life that I was up four times during the night, just to stroll around, look at the stars and watch the river. Sitting around on a bus all day doesn't tire you out.

We broke camp at 5:30 anyway, hurriedly breakfasted and were back on the road before dawn. It would be a long day.

We soon reached the capital, Kampala. There was a great deal of busy street life as the shanty slums spilt onto the main road. There was some evidence of opulence behind high guarded gates, but the hectic toing and froing you expect at rush hour appeared to be replaced with intense hanging around, mostly at the little food vendors and motor bike repair shops.

You could be forgiven in assuming this part of Africa was full of Marlon Brando aficionados, the amount of youngsters you see in motor bike gangs. But no, these are the Boda-Boda, taxi drivers. And the gangs, the taxi rank. You need to go somewhere, hop on as pillion, and enjoy the ride. I've seen three on the back of a bike, complete with worldly goods.

We were soon in and out of Kampala, and as the day began to heat up, skirting the northern shores of Lake Victoria, to come to the little town of Kayabwe.

As you pass through this little town you move from the Northern Hemisphere into the Southern Hemisphere. Yes, here was the Equator. You don't feel anything, there is no Equator crossing ceremony, but a nice man puts a flower into a sink to show you water going down a plughole, clockwise, then walks twenty feet away to show you water going down a plughole, anti-clockwise. A neat trick, but pure hokum. If anything, at this exact latitude, the water should just go straight down (but it depends on the spin he puts on the flower).

Presently we turned right and began climbing into the mountains. Moving away from the lake, there was a significant change of character in the countryside. There were still villages every five to eight miles, schools of excitable children, and farmland, but we came across dozens of ovens firing clay bricks, and herds of those marvellous Ankole cattle, with the huge horns.

Then we came to the town of Mbarare, and I could scarcely believe my eyes. Here were all the trappings of a modern, wealthy community. Well maintained tarmac roads and marble footpaths. Gleaming white office blocks and shopping malls, busy people in suits clutching briefcases, new four by fours parked in the street, or cruising the main road.

I asked Robert how, amongst all the rural poverty, this affluent city existed, which stuck out like a sore thumb.

"Many Government ministers hail from Mbarare," he told me, "There is a well-respected university here, and other well-funded public projects. I think the Americans call it Pork Barrel Politics."

It was gloomy and misty when we arrived at our campsite in Kigali, the gateway to the Mountains of the Moon. We were on the edge of the Virunga Volcano National Park, where Uganda meets Rwanda and the DR of Congo. We were three days and 700 miles from our Nairobi starting point. Bob and Paddy, as they were now called, had got us here in their luxury truck (now there's an oxymoron), "Overlanding" as it is called here, and the budget way to see Africa.

"Do you think someone pumps in the mist?" asked Jack.

"There has to be mist, it's in Dian Fossey's book, Gorillas in the Mist," replied David.

I was putting my sleeping mat in my tent and emerged to hear this exchange.

"But we're just Mzungus to these gorillas," I added.

"That's us, Mzungus in the mist," Vicky said, with an air of mystery.

Then George arrived to brief us on our requirements for the following day. We gathered around, eagerly.

"Take plenty of water, walking boots, hat, trousers and long sleeves. The forest will tear at your skin!"

George would be our driver up into the mountains where the gorillas lived.

He returned at 5am as promised and we dragged ourselves sleepily into his minibus, six of us in an eight seater, quite cramped compared to what we had become accustomed. And we began our climb. It would take two and a half hours.

There was a half moon and stars twinkling brightly and in the pre-dawn cool, George a middle aged Bantu, played his rap music tape very loud. It was nerve-jarring and I was shocked to find the lyrics offensive, and the rhythm and tempo suicidally mundane. But the Ugandans love it, so what do I know.

Dawn broke greyly and gradually, and the isolated and tiny communities we bumped and bounced past were waking slowly. Smoke from the cooking fires rose thinly and mixed with the valley mists as the young boys and girls returned with their yellow jerry cans, filled from their first visit of the day to the village well. Smaller children were already playing happily in the dirt.

All around was cultivation, not as heavily terraced as in some countries, but the surrounding hillsides were ploughed and planted right up to their peaks. Before man this would have all been jungle. We eventually arrived at one of the islands of jungle that remain.

There are thought to be only about 700 mountain gorillas left in the wild in two isolated and now protected communities. We were in the splendidly named Bwindi Impenetrable Forest Gorilla Reserve.

Our trek began with another briefing, this time from the forest rangers. We had been joined by 18 more tourists and three separate groups of eight would be allowed to venture into the forest to hopefully encounter one of five families known to live here.

Ranger Sarah was allocated to us and she told us we were searching for the Bwuza family. "Beware forest elephant, and mountain ants they will disorganise you. Don't cough or sneeze or eat in front of the gorillas. Keep voices down and do not approach within seven metres of the apes. If we find the apes we are only allowed one hour with them. Be prepared for a long search." She had emphasised the "If", and knowing my record, I was not confident.

Sarah was a youthful looking 30 year old Ugandan who was clearly in charge and would take no truck from any over-enthusiastic tourist who could endanger themselves or upset her beloved gorillas.

"The Silverback can lead," she smiled at me, and I took up my appointed position. Increasingly in late middle age I am chosen for this role. I like to think it is because I am a pioneering, trailblazing adventurer whose courage and wise fortitude make me a natural leader. But it's because the group can only go as fast as the slowest person. A cross I have to bear.

Almost immediately we plunged into the jungle. I was led by a ranger armed with an AK47, to scare any elephants, and a machete to gamely try to penetrate the impenetrable. And they were not exaggerating.

The forest floor was wet and treacherous, slippery on the leaf litter and you could sink up to your ankles in the wood pulp and soil beneath. Every step was hampered by roots and brambles, vines, saplings and fallen branches, all of which served to trap you and entangle your boots. I was constantly having to pull and drag my legs free, which then slid and slithered with the momentum into more entanglements.

Higher up and thorns and stingers clawed and tore and ragged and pulled at my clothing, arms and legs. I was constantly pushing away branches and thick huge leaves from my face simply to try to see where I was going. Every piece of vegetation seemed protected by wickedly sharp thorns, which embedded into my fingers and hands if I should attempt to hold on to steady myself.

The terrain itself was also tricky. Falling down a non-existent foothold was as common as tripping over moss covered rocks. Then there were the lung-bursting, calf-burning climbs and the back-breaking, ankle-twisting descents. The going was laboured to say the least.

After nearly an hour of this, Sarah called a halt in a clearing to take on water. Thank God it wasn't too hot; and thank God it wasn't raining. She explained that our trackers had yet to catch up with the Bwuza family. "If we struggle on any further we might be going in the wrong direction," she warned. "So we will wait."

Mountain Gorillas spend their days moving through the jungle feeding (they can eat up to 25 kilos of leaves and shoots a day) and socialising. They plait together leaves and branches to make new sleeping nests every night. The trackers start where they last saw the gorillas yesterday, then find last night's sleeping arrangements, then they call in to Sarah. We welcomed the rest and watched black and white Colobus monkeys playing in the distant canopy.

I had envisaged meeting with the gorillas David Attenborough style, in a clearing where they would wander around happily ignoring my presence, or even playfully engaging with me. Of course, the editing of natural history programmes for television gives us this false honey-coated image. Reality is very different, much more painstaking.

At length Sarah beckoned us forward, the trackers had located the gorillas. I was to lead again, and off we plunged for a further lesson in labyrinthine jungle trekking. We met up with the trackers who showed us last night's nests, just flattened rafts of vegetation. Beneath each one was a huge pile of poo. How very like us they are. It was easy to follow their progress from here as there was a distinct trail of trampled jungle. These were big families in every sense of the word.

The excitement was tangible as we knew we were very close. We followed the piles of poo until there was a new crushed pathway which fell steeply down to our left. We could hear branches crack and the rustle of shaking leaves, then it was evident they were aware of our presence. We heard a long, low throaty rumble, which was joined by higher pitched cries, and what seemed to be the excited sound of jumping up and down.

The ranger pulled back a branch and there in front of me were two gorillas, adults, one probably a female as her facial features were slightly softer and she was smaller in stature than the blackback young male with his larger head, and more prominent brow and jaw. They don't seem to have come far from their overnight nests, but they would have been up and about for at least three hours. They both moved off and we followed. I was aware that those behind me were keen to catch up and crane for a better view.

I saw a baby dangling acrobatically in a tree, showing off. Sarah whispered that we had met her mum and dad, and that she was two years old. Then the Silverback, the family alpha male, emerged no more than ten yards ahead of us. He was showing himself to us, perhaps a warning, or even a greeting. He walked slowly on all fours, then sat and nonchalantly broke off a branch He stripped it with his teeth and proceeded to chew. At no time did he make any indication he was aware of our existence, but every time we inched forward, he moved off himself.

In this initial breathtaking encounter I was struck firstly by their evident power and strength moving with ease through this dense jungle, then with their shyness, not caring to share their time with us, their cousins. Finally, it was their peaceful countenance, an air of confident contentment. In the next all too few, precious minutes I spent in their company I marvelled at their sleek beauty and their handsome features. They were obviously intelligent yet nervous; noble yet vulnerable. My most enduring concluding thought was of their gentleness. It may be a cliché, but these were truly gentle giants.

I was awakened from my reverie by falling into a tree recently vacated by the baby. Gorillas are sure footed and excellent climbers. We on the other hand, slip and slide and grope uselessly, fumble with our cameras and binoculars, and strain and stretch to get better views. The rangers are able to get up close and pull back branches to reveal these poor, shy creatures who just want to eat and socialise with their family in peace.

Increasingly I felt we were intruding. I sensed we were not merely observing, but driving them through the forest. We had, after all, come some way in a short while since our first encounter, yet the family had not initially moved far from their overnight encampment. It was not what I had envisaged.

Sarah eventually called our encounter to a halt. We were fairly certain we had met up with the Silverback, two blackbacks (probably his sons) two females and the baby. Six from a known family group of ten, and they had led us into a narrow, steep-sided ravine. The climb back out was a tortuous, strength-sapping ordeal.

I left the valley feeling a little guilty at having imposed my presence on these shy, gentle creatures. But this was tempered with the satisfaction of knowing that my tourist dollar (600 of them) would help to ensure not only their continued existence, but also the industry for local people built around them.

A weary troupe ultimately fell into George's taxi. "I pick them up early and they fall asleep," he complained. "I collect them five hours later and the Mzungus sleep again!" he continued to the slumbering passengers. Soliciting no reply, he just shrugged and switched on JayZ.

Arriving back in Kigali, Paddy and Bob had broken camp, and we simple transferred from one small bus to one big one, and we were on our way back to Jinja and the Adrift Lodge, a Riverbase Activity Centre. The only activity tonight was to drink beers overlooking the White Nile and reminisce about our Mountain Gorilla experience.

That night there was a huge thunderstorm with spectacular lightning over the river. I snuggled tightly into my sleeping bag and prayed not to be washed away by the deluge.

The next day, feeling fresh after the storm, an open truck arrived to take us to the Wakitaka Primary School, to join in with painting some classrooms. Apparently it is what some folk enjoy doing. It gives them a buzz to help out a poor community. We had not been painting long when I was hi-jacked by Millie, the headteacher. She had heard I was a retired teacher and now governor of a primary school, and wanted to perhaps forge a link.

She asked If I could observe some teaching and address some of the classes. I happily and enthusiastically agreed, and she accompanied me to meet some ten year olds as my friends laboured with buckets of yellow paint and rollers on 12 foot poles.

We had a lovely day with the children. David was amazed at my ability to avoid physical work. He wasn't the first. In the afternoon we played sports with the children and were shown around the school and learned how the children's education was subsidised by cattle farming on site.

Our final day in Uganda was a white-water rafting day organised by the Adrift Lodge.

We were taken on a long drive to where the Nile was an extremely wild river. Sadu, our guide briefed us before we kitted up, entered our boat and practised a few manoeuvres in the calm headwaters. We were then let loose on the rapids, up to level 5.

Number one rapid was called the Waterfall, and although we approached it with confidence, the turbulence grabbed us before we had full control, and we ended up going over backwards. But at least we hadn't flipped. We gave the customary, but in hindsight premature, high oars.

Approaching rapid two Sadu asked if we wanted the easy or hard route. We chose the latter and he turned the rudder for midstream.

"This is The Bad Place," he said, "Approach slow, when I say the word, paddle full speed ahead. It is level five."

I was behind Jack, at centre stroke. Usually you can see a wall of angry water ahead. At the Bad Place all I could see was the water falling off the edge of the world.

We could hear the roar of the angry water, when Sadu called for action and we began working hard, padding for all we were worth to maintain control of the boat. But as we were about to drop off the end of the world we seemed to hit a rock which slewed the craft around and suddenly the bow rose into the air then crashed down vertically. This propelled me forward and my head smashed into Jack's helmet and the boat flipped.

I was in the water dazed and struggling. I realised I was beneath the boat and heaved against it and eventually caught a breath before the water sucked me back under. By the time I broke the surface, we were in calmer waters and I could signal I was safe with a thumbs up. No matter, someone grabbed my life jacket from behind and hauled me up to the boat which had ended up upside down in an eddy.

Sadu and the rest joined me, no-one had lost their oars. Together we righted the boat, hauled ourselves in, convulsed with laughter, checked we were all in one piece and headed for the next set. Great fun.

Seven adrenaline filled rapids later, and there was flipping going on all around, but not us. We were now kings of the Nile.

It was time for lunch.

On a lush island surrounded by rushing water, with high jungle on both banks, we took a rather magnificent lunch. There was guacamole and salads with a selection of cheeses and chapatis filled with beef and pineapple, all washed down with ice cold beers. We stood around and chatted about our white water experience with other crews, and watched videos of some of the more spectacular spills. Some people had been catapulted out of their boats and sent cartwheeling through the air into the water.

Back at base we enjoyed the sunset with more beers, watched some footie on the TV, and admired the posh weddings taking place on the opposite hillside.

Later we took boda-bodas into town, danced to the noisy music in the friendly and crowded Queen's Palace Club, and enjoyed some midnight street food before getting boda-bodas back to our tents.

The next day we returned to Kenya West.

Chapter Nine

Zambia. Walking The Falls

I decided I wanted to see the world's greatest natural wonders. I had trekked deserts, climbed mountains, flown canyons, snorkelled tropical reefs and gaped into volcanoes. I had tackled forests and jungles, safaried savannah, steppe and prairie, traversed great rivers, and cruised island chains. I decided that the most spectacular single visit objectives must be waterfalls.

Everybody loves water. It could be going to the beach and watching and listening to the waves, visiting rivers and marvelling at their inexorable flow, sometimes slow and meandering, or at other times fierce and terrifying, or driving to a lake, a peaceful, placid, freshwater pond. Who doesn't enjoy walking alongside a babbling brook, and paddling and swimming in the outdoors? It is what holidaying is all about. And boats. Don't get me started on boats. Rowing, paddling, tacking, sailing, chugging along. Kenneth Grahame assured us that there is absolutely nothing better than messing about in boats. But as Terry Wogan used to warn, "A boat is just a hole in the water you throw money into!"

Waterfalls are the tracts of water, usually rivers, that join a higher piece of land to a lower one. Having chosen the world of waterfalls, almost immediately I discovered they are by no means as simple as that. Which are the greatest waterfalls? How are they measured; height, width, flow rate? There are even different types including plunge, step, segmented, horsetail, cascade, and more.

Most people would put Niagara Falls at the top of the list, but other than greatest number of visitors, they 'fall' well short of any other criteria. A far more impressive array of horseshoe falls are those on the Brazil, Argentina, Paraguay border, on the Iguazu River. Niagara is miniscule in comparison. The highest, Angel Falls, is a mere stream falling off a Venezuelan tepuy (flat top mountain). For most of the year it evaporates before reaching its forest floor. The general consensus is that simply because they are near the top of the list of most criteria, Victoria Falls are the greatest of them all.

Moshi-Oa-Tunya, the Smoke That Thunders was first seen by European missionary and explorer, Dr David Livingstone in 1855. He named them after his queen, and they join the Upper Zambezi River to the Lower Zambezi. The falls are nearly a mile wide and plunge 355 feet into a chasm. 33,000 cubic feet of water a second flow off the precipice, and all this water flows out of the chasm into the narrow Batoka Gorge, a veritable boiling pot of white water fury. The town that grew up in the 20th century to exploit the falls' tourism value was named after the explorer doctor.

Livingstone

I left Birmingham on a Friday evening and flew via Dubai into Johannesburg. There was then a short, early morning flight north into Zambia with excellent views over the Zambezi river, and after a quick yellow fever inoculation I was met by a cheerful young man, Evans. He drove me five miles across sun-scorched rocky scrub to the Jolly Boys Hostel in the centre of Livingstone. Evans introduced me to the most elegant, tall, beautiful, smiling receptionist. Grace was resplendent in a shining blue green traditional dress and turban. She showed me to my dorm and around the complex, and advised that nowhere in the town was off-limits during the day, but only to travel by taxi at night.

"Oh, and your safari on Monday is cancelled. Not enough customers. I will try to find another one for you," she apologised.

I had slept well on the flights, and had neither gained nor lost time as we were on GMT, so after a swim in the pleasant gardens and a brief lunch I set out to explore the town.

Livingstone is a one street town but quite wealthy for a provincial African outpost. There are modern buildings housing banks, businesses and the council offices. Over the high street were a few shops which mainly sold essential provisions. The road itself had plenty of potholes and the kerbs were sometimes gigantic where water had caused the surface to sink. Behind the main carriageway was a no-go area for cars, but cycles and motorbikes were able to negotiate the broken roads. In some places the roads appeared to have suffered earthquake damage the holes were so wide and deep.

Barefoot children played in the red dust among the overgrown remnants of some attempted lawns, and large shrubby weeds erupted from the broken tarmac and concrete. A misshapen old football was being chased by all.

I wandered randomly and eventually found my way back to the main drag. The shops were small and the insides kept dark to stay cool. Africa has discovered self service but the shops' aisles were so narrow and gloomy it was difficult to navigate your small trolley. There are still many products sold loose and unpre-packaged. And not just fruit and vegetables, but also herbs and spices, dairy produce, meat and dried goods. And there are brands we haven't seen in decades, like Tide, Oxydol and Omo, bought to ensure African children are turned out immaculately for school. And there were proper size Mars Bars, not the tiddly ones sold in the UK today.

That night I dined on pasta in a spicy cheese sauce, and the excitement of seeing the falls the next day.

I woke early and caught the first available shuttle to Victoria Falls National Park, about a ten minute journey. The car park was already full of vendors selling souvenirs, but I rushed past them to buy my ticket. A short walk on a well marked path through a thicket and I came upon the gorge created over millions of years by the falling Zambezi river. However it wasn't as I expected. Opposite, instead of the postcard image of a wall of water flowing over, there were perhaps a dozen or so smaller cascades. These fell into the rock strewn floor of the gorge and met up with water from the Zimbabwe side to flow out of the narrow exit in an absolute torrent. Ahead and on the other western side I could see the privately owned Livingstone Island, and beyond that, in Zimbabwe, the tell tale cloud of steam which does indeed thunder into the Batoka Gorge.

I walked along the knife-edge trail, marvelling at the diverse colourful flora. This owes its existence to the constant cloud of vapour the falls produce. I soon reached a small wooden bridge. Crossing it I arrived at the end of the track. Still only able to see the steam cloud, and the small rivulets falling into the gorge opposite, this apparently, was as close as you go in Zambia.

Alone in the early morning sunshine I opened my hands, stared in disbelief, and cried out, "Is that it?"

Resigned to this being the end of the trail I sat for a while and sketched this Eastern Cataract, and eventually headed back. At the beginning of the gorge instead of turning right for the car park, I struck out left and reached the shore of the Upper Zambezi. I could see there was a route across the river towards Livingstone Island, and indeed some children were already playing in the pools, alongside mothers slapping their washing against the rocks. They must feel safe, I thought, next to a river in Africa famous for its crocodile and hippo.

I began to walk along the edge of Victoria Falls.

No-one had told me that October was the end of the dry season and that the mighty Zambezi is reduced to a comparative trickle. Compared to the Victoria Falls picture book views, they looked like they were turned off. This drawback however presented me with the opportunity to walk across the falls instead of just viewing them.

I set off and was enjoying hiking alone, and I felt much better about the situation. I leapt from rock to rock, waded across still pools of warm water, and peered over the most amazing drop to the rocks below. There were rivulets gushing over the edge but these were safe to cross far enough upstream.

I came to one such waterfall. To my left was the edge and oblivion, upstream to my right I could see where I could safely wade across, but I calculated that I could climb across this small torrent. Too far and too risky to jump, I simply managed a controlled fall forwards so that my hands were planted on the rock on the far side, now all I had to do was bring my legs across. Too late I realised that I had overstretched. Releasing either leg would result in a fall, there were no nearer footholds to be had, and I couldn't push myself back. I could possibly lower myself into the rushing water and hope for a foothold, but the force of the flow would more than likely just throw me over the side and to certain death on the rocks below. I was stuck.

Neither able to go forward, nor even back or down, I began to despair. Strangely, my mother's warnings came to me "Don't do anything foolish" she would always chastise. I now felt rather foolish. I raised my head to look around, but there was no-one idiotic enough to be walking across Victoria Falls. Then, about 200 yards upstream I saw a group of people. Two young tribesmen were leading four European women the safe way across the Zambezi. I shouted for help, but my voice was drowned by the roar of the water. I risked releasing my right hand and waving as frenetically as my parlous position would allow. But this was tiring for my standing left arm, and anyway they were walking away from me. I resumed my position and once again weighed up the options. There was nothing for it, I waved again and again calling forlornly for help each time.

I don't know why, but for some reason one of the lads turned and saw me. Without hesitation he nudged his friend and they both set off across the rocks and rivulets. Leaping like sure footed mountain goats, they negotiated the jagged rocks with ease and were with me in no time. The rescue was simple, they held and supported my arms as I stepped across.

"Thank you! Thank you!" blathered the red faced elderly white man to his young black rescuers, boys no more than 13 years old.

"No problem, Sah!" they both said and rushed back to their other charges before I could say any more.

I sat down on my rock to catch my breath and contemplate the fate that could have befallen me, and took in my surroundings. A torrent below my feet disappeared over the edge and crashed down onto the rocks to join the swirling, foaming white water of the lower Zambezi. I gazed across the chasm to the cloud forest owing its very existence to the spray of the waterfall, where I had sat and sketched earlier, and to my right the huge cloud over Livingstone Island which is literally "the smoke that thunders".

"That's where I'm heading now. No more risks," I thought, and chuckled to myself. I stood up, dusted myself down and set off again. Along the edge.

I reached Livingstone Island, intending to skirt around it to see the falls on the other side, but was almost immediately challenged.

"Excuse me, Sah. Where do you think you are going?" a waiter in a starched white waistcoat and black trousers asked in a slightly threatening manner.

"I was trying to see the falls from the other side" I explained innocently.

"You cannot come upon here. This is a private island," he announced, haughtily

"I see, then I will walk around this way," I indicated to my right.

Twenty minutes later I had still not found my way around when I realised I was back in the same place, and the same boy accosted me. I tried to say that I had inadvertently become lost, but he was having none of it.

"I must arrest you and take you to my boss" he announced indignantly.

I found the prospect fascinating so went along with him.

His boss, a young man with more worldly airs recognised me for what I was. In well-worn hiking boots, safari shorts, a decidedly threadbare shirt and a battered sun hat, a doddery old fool looking for free entrance across his island. Although I smiled and asked to see the falls from this side, he smiled similarly and just shooed me away. I made my way back safely, lazing in some of the pools along the way.

I had walked across Victoria Falls, a feat I hadn't known it was possible to do, and something I would never have guessed, when I woke up that morning. I just wish someone had mentioned it was the dry season when I was planning this months ago.

Reaching the car park I noticed a path into the jungle and it took me about 20 minutes to clamber, scramble, slither and slide down to the edge of the lower Zambezi, and marvel at its rushing waters at a place called the Boiling Pot, where it turned towards the Indian Ocean. Little did I realise, I would be entering at that same point in three days. I spent some time looking up at the impressive Victoria Falls Bridge spanning the gorge and watching the bungee jumpers plunging down and bouncing like human yo-yos.

I climbed back to the top and made my way to the bridge. Sad to report that on that bridge I was harassed and hassled at every step of the way by trinket sellers. It was really quite tiresome. The only way I could see the full part of the falls was to go across the bridge and pay the $70 fee for a visa to enter Zimbabwe. And there was no way I was going to give the murderous Robert Mugabe any money. So I settled for the return to Jolly Boys where Grace greeted me with the news that she had found a safari. It was on for the next day. Result. Did I mention I had walked across Victoria Falls?

My safari the next morning was in the Moshi-Oa-Tunya National Park, and I was taken to the park from Jolly Boys by our old faithful, Evans. This was a walking safari, one without the safety and anonymity of being in a vehicle. I was accompanied by two guides carrying rifles.

The most dangerous creatures I could meet were the buffalo, which are totally unpredictable and may charge for no good reason. They are the second most dangerous animal in Africa, second only to hippo, and mosquitoes. Sorry, third most dangerous. Anyway, you must concentrate on being downwind. When you don't have a vehicle to escape into, you try very hard to keep to that little rule.

The highlights were giraffes with very faded markings; they used to be called cameleopards because of their spots. This lack of marking was apparently due to the inbreeding that is difficult to avoid in a closed National Park. We also met a white rhino. Sadly she had an injured left leg, and it was being debated whether her horn should be removed before she became a target for poachers. What a sad predicament. And there were plenty of apparently bad-tempered buffalo.

That evening I went on a cruise. It was advertised as a sunset cruise on the Upper Zambezi, and was a very pleasant interlude. The boat ride was sedate, you could occasionally see elephant or giraffe on either bank, the sunset was pleasant if unspectacular, and I fell into the company of Ryan and Sarah. They were an engaged and indeed engaging couple who had both recently completed post graduate courses at Birmingham University, and were now having a few months out prior to launching themselves into the world of work. They were doing the popular, as I had discovered, Nairobi to Cape Town route, totally ad hoc, using the Lonely Planet as a guide to bus timetables and cheap lodgings.

"So what have you been studying?" I asked over sundowner beers.

"Nuclear Science," was the reply.

"And have you found jobs in that area?" I continued to probe.

"Yes, we've both got positions as nuclear physicists in different plants" they confirmed.

"Ah, that's hardly rocket science!" I said with a grin. But, of course, it is.

Later on we were talking to Stacey and James who were two very earnest young Americans working with the Peace Corps. It sounds military, but it is their equivalent of our VSO, Voluntary Service Organisation. Both of these youngsters had been working in the local villages and were very eloquent about the failings of the aid system.

"Money is being thrown at Africa by the developed nations, and in countries like Zambia which are enlightened and have removed the stains of corruption, the money is being filtered down to the villages where it is needed. But it is very slow, only appears in a trickle, and is baulked at every level by stifling bureaucracy."

The biggest problems, they explained, were tribal favouritism and gender discrimination. Most tribes operated some form of caste system, and all women suffer just being women. Village elders were still universally male, drank beer, and would rather have soccer on Sky TV than vaccinations for sick children.

This was a very sobering message, and the five of us agreed that as either developed or developing nations, we'd still got a long way to go.

Oh! those Russians (and Americans)

With the sunset cruise and walking safari behind me I signed up for a slightly more active adventure. It almost sounds like a cliche, just to write it down. White water rafting down the Zambezi.

I woke at seven and was picked up and taken, by Evans, to the Waterside Lodge for breakfast and a safety briefing. The Lodge is a large complex of luxury wooden chalets overlooking the upper Zambezi. Here, where we cruised last evening, the river is wide, calm, slow flowing and seemingly benign, although it does have populations of crocodile and hippo.

There were about 20 of us, and after signing the obligatory disclaimers we were taken by Simba, a tall handsome Zambian, to the rafting departure point. The calm upper Zambezi cascades over the mile wide Victoria Falls, and is squeezed into the narrow Batoka Gorge where it becomes the raging torrent we were about to do battle with. The departure point I had visited previously, and is called the Boiling Pot.

We clambered down through the jungle to the edge of the river. To the right was its entrance into the gorge, and even in this dry season, the compression of these billions of gallons of water made for an impressive wall of angry water. Opposite were the sheer walls of the gorge, eroded by millions of years of this inexorable flow, and to the left, the Victoria Bridge off which even at this unearthly hour, bungee jumpers continued to tumble. In front awaited our flimsy, rigid inflatables.

Simba organised us into the boats. "Anyone with any experience?" he asked. I sheepishly indicated I'd done this sort of thing once or twice before, and he gave me a group of Russians to lead. "They haven't a clue, and are probably tanked up with vodka, but Choonga will look after you."

I was introduced to Choonga who would steer the boat by sculling from the rear and shout instructions to me at stroke (positioned front right, or is that starboard), and the Russians will copy me. Well, that was the plan. I met up with the five portly, chubby-faced, merry Siberians who shrugged and grinned inanely, and cheerily chanted "Wodka".

The instructions were fairly simple: "Forward", to begin our approach then, "faster right, or faster left, or backstroke", and finally, "Down!" This latter was for when we had correctly negotiated the entrance into hell, and must now hold on for grim death whilst being tossed about like aqueous pancakes, and praying to be spat out safely the other side.

We entered the water and practised a few times into the Boiling Pot. We paddled up to and entered the swirling malevolence that threatened to totally engulf our flimsy craft, then reacted sharply to Choonga's "DOWN!" We were then thrown about in a mad Roller Coaster of white water death for a few seconds of pure adrenalin-inspired ecstasy, and emerged soaked and exhausted into the calming eddy which is the other side. And there were to be 23 of those. Some rapids are so famous, or should I say infamous, they have been given names, Stairway to Heaven, Washing Machine, Oblivion, Morning Glory, and the Gnashing Jaws of Death, to name but a few.

The important thing to remember was that you must be in control of the craft as it enters the rapids. This way you can avoid the rocks, go in at pace, choose your entrance, and hopefully avoid being flipped about and over like some flimsy piece of driftwood. Do it right and you emerge exhausted but filled with joy from the thrilling ride of a lifetime. To go through a set of rapids, then wait in the eddy for the other boats, then see them flipped over and the paddlers thrown into the water like broken match sticks, is truly frightening. Then you have to rescue them and put them back into their boats to do it all over again.

One thing I discovered was that the Russians were brilliant at this latter operation. They were so strong they could reach into the water and lift someone out and into our boat one handed and with comparative ease.

There were in between bits, where we just paddled calmly and enjoyed the surroundings and the serenity of the river, and could almost relax and slumber. Occasionally the Russians would sing, and I would teach them to stroke to the rhythm of "Yo-o heave ho". Then you may spot a slight disturbance up ahead and the quiet and slowly foreboding, chilling but irresistible instruction of "Forward," from Choonga, and you knew you had to arm and brace yourself for the thrilling battle to come.

At the Stairway to Heaven, Choonga pointed out a colleague on the cliff opposite who was filming our battle with the rapids. "This is a good one to impress for the video," he informed us.

I readied myself ("summoned the blood, stiffened the sinews") and when the instruction came, paddled like a whirling Dervish, wielding my weapon furiously like a mighty sword against the dragon of the river. Time and again I plunged my blade into the swirling foam, and forced the water back and was out and back in an instant to grimly and defiantly hold our course through the white water. It seemed like an eternity, and I was nearly on the brink of collapse when Choonga shouted to relax, and we were through safely and drifting towards the eddy. The Russians behind me threw up a great roar of victory and lifted their paddles into the air to touch and enact some sort of high-five salute. My arms just felt like dead weights and I was left exhausted and bedraggled and bushed, and slumped in the bow like a wet fish, but grinning inanely.

We stopped for an excellent picnic lunch on a beach following rapid number ten, during one of the quieter passages. After lunch we were introduced to a middle aged American couple who were briefly joining us to experience one of our less scary white-water encounters.

"Would you like to have a go at paddling?" I asked the American lady.

She looked at me astonished and drawled, "I'm sorry, I only speak English!"

I was outraged.

"You foolishly arrogant colonial. I *am* English, and I am speaking the language in its purest form, the way it has evolved over two thousand years of history, not a couple of centuries of corrupted Americanism. Admittedly it is with perhaps a slight Black Country accent, but obviously your inherent fear of foreigners meant you had closed your cloth ears and assumed gobbledegook, whereas if you had the slightest tolerance for other people you may have attempted some semblance of understanding, then you may have recognised, understood and appreciated your adopted language, enunciated in precisely the manner in which it is supposed to be spoken"...is what I wished I'd said. Instead I just ignored the woman.

They left us and Choonga asked if I'd like to experience free swimming. The river was flowing fairly fast, but unencumbered through the narrow, high-sided gorge, so I slipped into the water and thoroughly enjoyed being swept along at seemingly breakneck speed. Eventually I had to get back into the boat as we approached another rapid, but I had floated too far so was picked up by kayak and hauled onto another boat and was forced to experience the crashing, tumbling, roaring, plummeting surge from a seat in the middle, unable to exert any control. When the boats joined up again in the eddy, I was transferred back to the Russians who were so overjoyed to see me, they greeted me like a long lost hero.

That was rapid number 18, and five hair-raising, swash-buckling, rumbustious adventures later we beached for the last time. Leaving the boys to dismantle the boats we climbed some rickety stairs and there, in the middle of the jungle was a funicular railway. Utterly bizarre. This took us finally out of the steep gorge and onto the plain. Here was a coach filled with cold beers which kept us all going for the two hour journey back to base. A dirt road firstly took us through the bush and passed four or five villages, and at each one we were chased by barefoot children, gleefully waving at us, hoping for "bon-bon" handouts.

Back at the Waterside Lodge it was already dark and we were treated to a tasty chicken curry dinner whilst we drank and chatted excitedly, recalling the adventures of the day. Simba announced that the video was ready to buy for a huge amount of Kwacha, and put it on the big screen to enhance his sales pitch. I spot our boat as it entered the Stairway to Heaven, a set of three, level five rapids. There was I, front right, head down, paddling furiously and frenetically through the boiling, seething fury of the surging torrent. And there were my companions, the five Russians behind me, totally ignoring the predicament as the boat was thrown about and hurtled through the water, and happily waving nonchalantly yet enthusiastically, at the camera.

The next day was still hot and sunny and dry, and I pottered about the town, visiting the railway sheds, talking to people, lunching in the Fezbar, shopping for souvenirs, then sunbathing back at Jolly Boys.

It was whilst I lay enjoying the sunshine that Grace woke me with the news she had found me a safari in Botswana for tomorrow. Precious Ramotswe and her wonderful world. I'm coming to see you.

Chapter Ten

Botswana

Elephants In The Sunset

I had dreamt of visiting Botswana ever since reading the wonderful Alexander McCall Smith's stories woven around his creation, Mma Precious Ramotswe, the beautiful, level-headed, intuitive, traditionally-built, First Lady Detective.

Precious, full of empathy for her clients and home-grown wisdom, was married to the shy proprietor of Tlokweng Speedy Motors, Mr J. L. B. Matekoni, and they lived with their two adopted children, Motholeli and Puso. He had two troublesome and workshy apprentices, like teenagers everywhere, and Precious worked with her secretary (and sometime partner), the highly strung Grace Makutsi, awarded 98% in her secretarial exams.

Was Botswana, the former British Protectorate of Bechuanaland, really peopled by the innocently naive, peace loving Batswana as described? I had to find out.

My own Grace, receptionist at the Jolly Boys Hostel, had arranged a two day safari for me. I wouldn't be going as far south as Gaborone, the capital, and Precious' home, but I would be in Botswana.

Evans, my constant taxi, picked me up pre-dawn for the one hour journey to the Kazungula Ferry, to cross the Zambezi into Northern Botswana. Like border crossings everywhere there were lorries lined up waiting for their papers to be sorted and loads to be checked, and I had to fill out endless visa applications and customs' assurances that I was not importing something sinister into the country. On the ferry, as Evans left me I was joined by two American girls who could have been Rachel and Monica from friends, and by two Flemish Belgians, Sabine and Carole, who as one would increasingly expect, had perfect English. Five of us on safari and only my binoculars between us.

We were taken to the small border town of Kasane and dropped off on a main road. We sought shelter from the sunshine under a large tree and looking around. I could see a small hotel, a furniture store, a motor vehicle workshop, and a cafe where people were seated outside under smaller trees, enjoying their breakfasts. We were standing on flattened red earth. Some children passed on their way to school. They were immaculately dressed in a blue and white uniform with shiny black shoes and white socks, and happily smiled their hellos. Nowhere could I see a detective agency, nor for that matter any traditionally built women.

A teenage boy approached and asked if we would follow him, and he led us down a path behind the hotel to the riverbank and along a small wooden jetty to meet Captain Jackson, and board his small flat-bottomed boat. We knew he was the captain, his hat said so. A sign on the jetty warned against bathing and washing, and Jackson told us a teenage boy was taken by a crocodile only last week.

We began a slow meander down the Chobe river, Botswana on our left bank, Namibia on the right.

Seated on bar stools, looking out over the river, we chatted excitedly. Will we see lions, are there elephant, what will camping in the bush be like? Almost immediately we could see hippos in the water.

"Shouldn't we have a bigger boat?" I nearly asked the skipper.

We could see monkeys and baboons, and as we followed them along the riverbank, a ten foot crocodile hauled herself out of the river inches from the bow of the boat, evidently to protect her nest. On islands we could see buffalo and waterbuck, antelope and huge monitors, and an abundant variety of birdlife. Vultures surrounded a carcass, there were fish eagles, kites, stork, both black and marabou, ibis, egrets, heron, snake birds, large and small hornbills, bee eaters, kingfishers and swallows. In the distance I spotted some grey dots. I wondered if they were elephant. It was really exciting.

We slowly approached the grey dots which grew larger and larger. Suddenly we were in amongst them. There were elephant everywhere; young, old, babies, adolescents, big bull males, females fussing around their families. Elephant by the hundred, coming down out of the bush to our left, swimming in front of us, swimming behind us in lines; the youngsters who were out of their depth were snorkelling. On our right they were on the islands, pulling up and eating great clumps of grass, scratching themselves on tree trunks, wallowing in the mud and dust. It was such a mind blowing scene. Doing a 360 I could see we were in the midst of at least a thousand pachyderms.

We saw one big bull on all five legs! The Americans giggled sheepishly, the Belgians shrugged matter-of-factly, Jackson and I exchanged knowing looks.

A little past the elephant herd and Jackson beached the boat and we were met by Johnson, a powerfully built Batswana wearing safari khaki and a big smile. He welcomed us with the news that we have just experienced the greatest concentration of elephant in the world, a fact of which Botswana is justifiably proud. However in the course of conversation he admitted the sheer numbers of elephant was becoming a problem and the powers that be were considering a cull. The country could make money by selling killing rights to Japanese tourists.

I was dumbfounded. "Surely," I told him, "it has taken half a century to regain the trust of the elephant after the slaughter by the great white hunter. Introducing guns again would undo all that good." He agreed and assured me that these concerns were almost universal in the country.

Johnson was to be our driver and guide for the main part of the safari, and as we headed into the bush in our Toyota safari wagon on our first game drive we encountered more and more elephant in the shade of nearly every tree. We came across warthogs and waterbuck, sable, roan, kuku and kudu, a beautiful antelope with lyre shaped horns and huge colourful ears to complement doe eyes. There were impala galore, the MacDonald's antelope, so-named after the M shape on its hind, and as they are so common. I tend to feel frustrated seeing impala. Nothing against them themselves, but a happily grazing herd of impala is an indication that there are no cats around. To be honest, big cats are what most people really want to see.

After an hour or so happily mooching about in the bush, we came upon a beach by the river, and there, snoozing in the sunshine was a pride of lions. They were lying on the beach, two females and six adolescents. The only thing missing were their towels and loungers. I stood up in my seat for a better view and Johnson pushed me down.

"At the moment they only see a truck" he whispered. "If they knew there was food on board, one paw could drag you off for their lunch."

Speaking of lunch, we made camp at about three where macaroni cheese awaited amidst a plague of tiny black flies. Camp was in a clearing in the middle of dense bush, three dark green tents, one for the girls, one for Johnson and his crew and one for me. There was a camp fire upon which lunch had been cooked and a table and chairs set up in the middle of the clearing. A little apart was a latrine tent. After lunch I took to my tent for a siesta, but I was not alone. There were hundreds of bees, on the floor and in the corners, mostly napping and, I was assured, totally safe.

Our next game drive began at five, and before muster I took a stroll into the bush. Less than 20 yards from the camp and I was in wilderness amongst the scrub. It would have been very easy to get lost so I didn't wander too far. I took the opportunity to appreciate my surroundings. The sky was a pale duck egg blue, with a searing sun beginning to sink quite low. The trees were spindly and mostly bare, with their dry leaves crunching underfoot. The air was still and alive with insects, all of their different noises gathered into one huge monotonous hum.

Right at the beginning of the drive Johnson received a call that a leopard has been spotted. You could call it the bush telegraph, but it was mobile phones. There followed a bone-jarring 30 minute race through the scrub until we could see a veritable fleet of six Toyotas lined up together.

"That's how to find cats," I said. "Just look for the Toyotas."

Sure enough when we sneaked in and joined the throng, there she was, about 50 yards away, laying on a branch, half way up a favourite tree, all four paws and her tail hanging loosely. Once or twice she raised her head to look at us, as if to say "Have they gone yet?" Seeing we hadn't, she lay back down.

All of the trucks gradually sloped off, and we were last to leave. With the light fading we made our way back along the river bank to check out our lion family. As luck had it they chose that moment to stir and one by one they got up, stretched, yawned, snuggled their respective mum, toileted, and strolled around our truck to go down to the river to drink. Magic.

There was another magical moment when we saw a family of elephants framed by the sunset crossing the river. Such moments will last a lifetime in the memory.

We took one more look at the leopard and returned in pitch darkness to camp, encountering a family of hyenas on the way.

Camp was pleasantly cool and we sat around the fire chatting of elephant and lion, bird and river life, and home, wherever that may be. We drank from plastic beakers copiously filled with red wine, out of which we had to occasionally lift and throw giant moths.

Dinner was beef stew and potatoes, excellent fare for such sparse cooking facilities, and we repaired to bed, me with my bees, for the appointed hour. We were to rise before five, before dawn. Such are the timings on safari.

We were woken with steaming mugs of coffee placed outside our tents and bowls of warm water for washing and (in my case) shaving. The bees and I had slept well and were now buzzing to be off. After a brief breakfast of cereal and fruit, and as dawn broke, we set off for game drive number three.

For much of the drive more of the same, but highlights included the sightings of a honey badger or rattel, like a giant, ferocious weasel, jackal, giraffe and a family of warthogs.

Safari game drives consist of long periods of slowly winding through the bush endlessly looking and being as quiet as possible. All conversations are held in hushed tones, and it doesn't matter how hard you look, the trained eyes of the driver will nearly always make the "spot" first. You live for the accolade "Great spot", then you get the usual, "Can we borrow your bins?"

My Roger-the-Tiger moment (see Ranthambore), when I insisted vehemently, almost pleaded with the safari leader to wait just one minute more, remains one of my proudest spots. It is not like on television wildlife programmes. Sometimes you can go for long periods seeing no animals at all. It is the anticipation that excites.

We arrived wearily back at camp expecting lunch, only to realise it was not yet 10 o'clock. However a pasta brunch was on hand and we broke camp for our final game drive back to the river. Johnson joined us on board when we met up again with Captain Jackson who asked us what we'd seen, as he untied.

Thus we began the leisurely meander home, back up the Chobe River, past inlets and islands. Again there was game galore, with hippos and crocs surrounding our flimsy craft. Some hippo were actually grazing on the islands, very rare daytime behaviour.

We came upon a sad scene. About ten adult elephant were crowded around, almost in a huddle. They parted as we approached and there in their midst was the corpse of their matriarch. She was on her belly, feet splayed fore and aft. I imagined her great heart must have given out sometime during the night. Her sisters and daughters were in mourning, and we noted that all of the adolescents and babies had been ushered elsewhere. As we gently floated by to pay our respects, we could count a dozen or more crocs who lay partly submerged just off the beach. Evidently their intentions were much more sinister. Such is the circle of life.

I said goodbye to Captain Jackson, Johnson and the four girls. The four had become firm friends although the American girls thought that the Belgians were from Scotland. They were heading south for Gaborone, and I asked them to look out for Mma Ramotswe.

Sadly, this trip was coming to an end for me, and I was returning to Livingstone. After another two stamps in the passport Evans picked me up on the Zambia side and it was back to Jolly Boys. The next day I was flying home. I spent the evening in a bar with South Africans talking rugby, then, late on when the drink had taken hold I met a venerable lady we'll call Rose.

I wish I could remember her name, but I failed to write it down, so she'll be Rose as she reminded me of the girl from the film Titanic who led an active life in memory of Jack.

Rose was an American from New Jersey, 80 years old and apparently small and frail, although she assured me, not addicted to a cocktail of medication, like most of her peers. She had become adventurous at the age of 60 when she lost her husband.

In this time she had parachuted into the Nevada desert, bungee-jumped in New Zealand, climbed Uluru (Ayers Rock, when this was still allowed), scuba dived the Great Barrier Reef, climbed Mount Fuji, trekked the Great Wall of China, and crossed both Siberia and Canada by train. She was now on route by bus from Nairobi to Joburg, and intended when she travelled further on to the Cape, to see great white sharks in the ocean from the apparent safety of a small cage.

"But, will they allow you? Isn't there an age limit?" I asked, as delicately as I could.

"I sign lots of disclaimers," she assured and added, "The only dispensation I ever seek is a bottom bunk. Can't manage the climb these days." There was certainly a twinkle in her eye. Quite a remarkable woman.

Grace arranged for none other than Evans to take me to the airport, and there followed a short flight to Jo'burg, a tropical storm delay, and a long, long flight to Dubai. Then I had one of the strangest of experiences.

Dubai airport is wonderful, for an airport. Wide, clean, cool, pleasant architecture, well furnished and decorated, interesting shops and bars, with good food and reasonable prices. It is about as comfortable as you could wish for a long stopover. I had six hours to wait for my connection. I eventually found the departure gate, and it being the middle of the night, lay down on the floor with my hand luggage for a pillow and began to nap.

By and by I awoke and two faces were peering over me.

"Mr Leo?" asked one, "Would you like to board now?"

I rose and noticed the departure area was still empty. Nevertheless, I gathered my things and sleepily made my way with the two cabin crew, through the gate and down the ramp to the Boeing 747, capacity 467 passengers. I entered and turned right (I always turn right), and met the gaze of a sea of faces. The cabin was already full. Whilst I had slept, boarding had taken place.

As I took my seat, a little embarrassed to have made everyone wait, one or two rather strange realisations began to come to me. Firstly, every single one of those 400 plus people had had to step over my slumbering body in order to board. Secondly, no-one had thought to try to waken this sleeping tramp (as surely that was how I was viewed). Thirdly, the crew would have been aware of this human blockage at the gate to the aircraft and not one considered disturbing him. And finally, there would have been announcements all over the terminal insisting on this being a, "Last call for passenger Leo". And they would probably have been on the point of having to open the hold and remove my baggage, when it must have dawned upon one of the brighter sparks amongst the cabin crew, who might have said something like "How about waking that guy by the gate, maybe he is the mystery passenger?"

Unbelievable!

As incredible indeed, as being surrounded by hundreds of elephant on a flimsy riverboat, sleeping with a colony of bees, camping amongst prides of lion, white water rafting with five drunken Russians, meeting the real-life Rose, or even walking across and nearly falling into, the mighty Victoria Falls.

Chapter Eleven

South Africa.

Battlefields and Safari

I had two weeks planned in South Africa, but mother suffered a stroke and I had to leave after the Johannesburg leg. It would be five years before I could return to visit the Cape. Mum recovered but it had taken her right side and she never walked again. She also made the decision to never again dye her hair.

The major reason for visiting South Africa was to see the country now Nelson Mandela had been freed and made president, and to ease my conscience as I had protested so long at its apartheid stance. Post apartheid, I was keen to see the battlefields made famous in the film Zulu, Kruger National Park, snorkel in the Indian Ocean, see the Cape of Good Hope and climb Table Mountain. The latter two would have to wait, but for now I was beginning my tour with the flight into Johannesburg.

It was a three-leg journey; bus to London (four hours), flight to Dubai (six hours), flight to South Africa (seven hours). Including stopovers, virtually 24 hours from bed to bed, and my first bed in Jo'burg was in a pleasant B & B run by Dianne and Dick Elson. Their house was in a gated community, and the sign at the entrance wasn't the sort you might see in Britain, "Beware of the Dog", or even "Patrolled by Dobermans". It was a notice assuring trespassers "This community is patrolled by armed guards. We shoot first and ask questions later".

I was assured, that in Jo'burg, you never stop at traffic lights.

The house and garden of Di and Dick's B & B were very pleasant and I was greeted with a braai, a traditional barbecue. But I couldn't help notice the alarmed and locked steel gate one must negotiate to enter the yard, then another to go into the house, and finally yet another at the top of the stairs to protect the sleeping residents. Post apartheid South Africa and particularly its biggest city were apparently still very dangerous places with many unemployed black people, much perceived inequality, and a lot of unrest.

You could see the problem personified at any gas station. The cars are driven by the Boers, the white minority who, male and female, dwarf the indigenous Zulu or Xhose people. The indigents are the employees who buzz about subserviently filling the vehicles, cleaning them, checking oil and tyres and serving in the shop and the toilets. The vehicle owners stand around haughtily, occasionally firing off orders, "Boy, clean this, check that, and hurry at it."

Around the back amongst the discarded oil drums and rusted wrecks lounges a group of unemployed youths with their music blaring, smoking and drinking menacingly.

The average Boer is over six feet and naturally arrogant. The average indigenous black is only around five feet and naturally servile. Add to this the Coloureds, descendants of Dutch Boers and black wives, who are "officially" a separate race. It will need a several generations of enlightenment to bring true equality to this fascinating land.

Matters relating to race are rarely far away from the conversation around any dinner table where Brits, Americans, Antipodeans or whoever might meet and consider their own countries' lamentable race relations' histories.

I wasn't unhappy to leave Johannesburg and headed South East to Dundee, 225 miles away, from Gauteng into KwaZulu-Natal and the pleasant Royal Country Hotel. All along the roadsides as we approached the Drakensberg Mountains, bloomed colourful cosmos, a reminder I had left in Springtime and arrived in Autumn. We were now in the heart of the Anglo-Zulu battlefields.

The next day I crossed the Buffalo river, as Lord Chelmsford had inadvisedly done in 1879, to visit the splendidly named Isandlwana Hill, the scene of a terrible British massacre and the home of the great Victorian cover up which in modern times would have been called Zulugate.

Everyone knows the film Zulu with Michael Caine and Stanley Baker starring as the lieutenants who with 150 men, many hospitalised, heroically defended Rorkes's Drift from an overwhelming army of Zulu warriors. Fewer of us are aware of the prequel, Zulu Dawn which depicts the events of the previous day when the main body of King Cetshwayo's Zulu warriors had attacked and massacred 2,000 British and Colonial soldiers camped around the saddle hill of Isandlwana. And that is precisely how the expedition's commander, Lord Chelmsford and Queen Victoria's Prime Minister, Benjamin Disraeli meant it to be.

I joined up with a small group of tourists and after a brief visit to the battlefield museum we met our incomparable guide, Gordon Worthington, whose brilliant commentary brought the whole disaster to life. Imagine Lofty from It Ain't Half Hot Mum, played by Don Estelle and you have Gordon.

Chelmsford's army had crossed the Buffalo River, immediately breaking the treaty with Cetshwayo who instantly mobilised his own troops, called Impis. Chelmsford had set up camp on the apparently defensible Isandlwana Hill, then taken about half of his force off to try to engage with Cetshwayo. He left the remaining troops in the command of the inexperienced Lieutenant Colonel Henry Pulleine whose orders were to simply defend the camp. Unbeknown to either officer, the main force of Zulu Impis had totally outmanoeuvred the British and had encircled the hill, hidden in numerous valleys. Part of the Impis' motivation was the winning of a redcoat. The jackets worn by British troops were most valuable trophies.

Cetshwayo's strategy was known as "The Horns Of The Buffalo". The main body, or head, would attack with columns flanking as horns to support the attack by diverting the direction of defence.

I was awestruck by Gordon's descriptions of the protagonists and their strategies and hung on his every word. Then he described the British encampment. From the porch of the museum shack he spread his arms and pointed to the hill, the perfect shape of a saddle.

"Wherever you see cairns of white stones, that is where British soldiers fell. When Chelmsford discovered them he fled, fearing another attack. They weren't buried till many years later, their bleached skeletons picked clean."

We moved out, onto and up the hill, captivated, as Gordon brought the events of that day to stunning life.

The defences which had formed a perimeter around the hill were too wide. Groups of soldiers were too far apart to support each other, or even communicate. The enemy had been underestimated. There were instances of deplorable stupidity. Runners, sent by the vanguard requesting further ammunition from the quartermasters, were inexplicably turned away if their dockets weren't correctly signed. But also moments of last-stand heroism. Lieutenant Younghusband "shook the hands of his men then, armed only with his sabre, launched with a blood curdling howl into the advancing natives. He was never seen again."

The regiment's colours were escaping on horseback via Fugitive's Drift, but were captured by an Impi force who killed lieutenants Melvill and Coghill (awarded posthumous V.C.'s).

The end came soon after a solar eclipse and the souls of the slaughtered were set free by evisceration. This was intended as an act of mercy by the Zulus, but was seized upon by Chelmsford to illustrate their barbarism.

It was an unbloodied Impi column, held in reserve, which had decided to attack the well fortified Rorke's Drift the following day. This gave Chelmsford and Disraeli the opportunity to hide the massacre behind the heroism of what became Michael Caine's finest hour.

Following lunch Gordon took us back across the Buffalo River to Rorke's Drift, which is marvellously preserved. He told us the tale of how a handful of well disciplined men in a well constructed tight redoubt managed to fight off overwhelming forces and win eleven Victoria Crosses, still the most awarded for a single action. He took us from room to room of the improvised hospital and described how Privates Williams and Hook hacked holes in the walls to drag patients through to eventual, comparative safety as the hospital burned around them and they fought off hundreds of assailants. Marvellous stuff.

You could almost hear them belting out Men of Harlech, even though the vast majority of the defenders were actually Brummies.

I made my way back to Dundee for a quiet night's contemplation on the futility of war and drove the next day to the coast and the wetlands of St. Lucia, another 200 miles. I am much more comfortable in delighting over countryside and wildlife than considering man's inhumanity to man.

St Lucia is famous for its five precious ecosystems and I quickly got to work discovering them. There's the warm Indian Ocean, a home both to reef creatures and passing whale migrations. Joined to the ocean by a neck of water called the Narrows, I sailed through the 50 miles of fresh water, the St Lucia estuary, fed by a network of five rivers. This is a magnet for birdwatchers and hippo and croc spotters.

Behind the beach are Africa's tallest vegetated sand dunes, a system so fragile it is held together by the flimsiest of root systems. Then there was the three canopy forest. This is so different and diverse. There is the weather beaten east, facing the sea with bent over palms and pines, then the rich, high central zone of broad leafed trees, sheltered and catching both the rain and sunshine. Finally the sparser sunburnt and drought suffering west, which faces to the savannah. This itself reaches north through the Great Rift Valley all the way to Ethiopia.

The wetlands have recently been renamed Isimangaliso, meaning 'something wondrous' in Zulu, and is indeed a wonderful World Heritage Site. Thank goodness it has this protected status as mining for the rich minerals just below the surface, would ruin so many important ecosystems.

I stayed in the Namib Lodge, which provided me with an excellent dinner after my late arrival, but by 9 o'clock, I was propping up the bar by myself.

After breakfast I headed for the beach and the area I was assured was best for floating around watching fish. The snorkelling was disappointing, a group of rocks just offshore, sheltering the beach. But the water was too shallow (it could have been low tide) and the marine life sparse. So I took some of the trails around the dunes, very similar to Scottish machair, beds of low growing colourful perennials. Unfortunately, also similar to Scotland, I kept getting drenched from the tempests being blown in off the Madagascar Straight, and needed to seek shelter in the forest. At least these were warm storms.

In the afternoon I organised my activities for the following two days which meant taking on organised excursions. In order to hasten my attempt to discover an area so diverse, I decided to put myself into the hands of the experts.

With organised excursions you immediately become part of a group, thankfully in this case small. I hate following guides around with their colourful umbrellas stuck in the air. Or the Chinese thing with everyone wearing the same hats. Or having to wait around while people go to the toilet. A guide once told me that people get into sheep mode and will follow you anywhere, including into those toilets.

The group I became attached to included an Andy Parsons lookalike who was a Harry Hill talkalike, and a hilarious Dubliner, Cahir, and his wife ("Look, a tortoise, run for your lives!" sounded better from him). There were middle-aged identical twin sisters. With short hair and at only four foot six, they looked like a pair of Jimmy Krankies. We could tell them apart after the first day as one sat looking out the left window of the safari truck, and the other out of the right window, so they both had sun burn to different sides of their faces. Finally there were two handsome young couples from Cape Town who all spoke lovely English, but when they conversed among themselves in their native Afrikaans, sounded like they were spitting and snarling gutturally at each other.

We met up at dawn for the drive to the wonderfully named Hluhluwe-Umfolozi Game Reserve and had hardly entered the gates when our driver/spotter, Edward, stopped and pointed to a rhino across a valley, maybe two miles away. We all excitedly got out and trained our glasses on the huge creature, but from this distance and even with 22 times zoom, it just looked like a light grey, square rock. Edward soon ushered us back into the truck, "There is lion here, you know, and the buffalo will also charge you!"

"How much?" asked Cahir, but the attempted witticism went straight over Edward's head.

The disappointing 'spot' didn't matter because within minutes we turned a corner and were in the midst of a herd of rhinoceros, one even crossed the road immediately in front of us. Hluhluwe is famous for its programme of rhino conservation.

These were white rhino, far more common than their black cousins, which are virtually extinct in many parts of Africa. I had seen one by Lake Nakuru in Kenya, and you will know they are not in fact named for their colour. Whichever rhino you encounter, it is evident these are magnificent creatures. Every sane person's blood should boil over the thought that they are senselessly poached, and the slaughter is simply for their powdered horn, which poorly endowed Chinese men stupidly believe to be an aphrodisiac.

It was a long day of spotting, and cats were elusive, but we also saw elephant, giraffe, buffalo, zebra, kudu, nyala and impala, (It was on this safari that I learned that coming across a peacefully grazing herd of impala was never going to be good for seeing cats), there were some fantastic birds, and in all about 20 rhino.

Back in St Lucia dinner and the craique was good, I had an excellent steak with Camembert, and we were all due to meet up again at dawn.

We were again driven by Edward, this time a game drive in the wetlands and vegetated dunes. Here there were plenty of buck; water, bush and reed, plus duiker and kudu, and we had some wonderful views of both Lake St Lucia and the Indian Ocean. We swam in the ocean whilst Edward prepared our braai lunch, then took a boat out onto the lake to view Nile crocodile, hippopotamus, fish eagles, heron and kingfishers. Watching an eagle effortlessly taking fish from off the surface of the lake was an undoubted highlight.

In the late afternoon, Edward took us to view the estuary mouth with flocks of diving pelicans then returned us to the hotel. There was just enough time for another steak dinner before he picked us up in a specially adapted truck (with adjustable spotlights) for a night drive.

On a night game drive it is the eyeshine you look for, and we saw plenty more buck, grazing hippo and crocodile, but the highlights were the animals that only come out at night, the nocturnal, and we saw an eagle owl, nightjar, chameleon and three bush babies.

The following day my itinerary took me into the mountainous kingdom of Swaziland. Now known as Eswatini, it is entirely landlocked, an absolute monarchy and a little smaller than Wales. Like many African countries that have been ravaged by HIV/AIDS, the life expectancy is only 58, and the vast majority of the population are under 22. Many are orphaned and still carry HIV.

Even by the standards of sub-Saharan Africa, Swaziland is poor, the average wage being around a dollar a day. This is in contrast to the corruption said to be rife in the royally appointed government, and the excesses attributed to the royal family. King Mswati III has 15 wives and over 30 children, various mother-in-laws, his own mother and a love of luxury cars. Each of his wives command their own royal palace and household, and there are very possibly more on the way as the king often selects new wives during the annual Umhlanga Reed Dance when the country's virgins, numbering around 80,000, dance bare-breasted before him and his mother.

Putting these controversies aside (and there are many opponents to the kings lavish lifestyle, and reports of human rights violations to put down their protests. Amnesty International are on the case), I was booked into the Mlilwani Game Reserve and Lodge for two nights.

After a long, arduous but visually superb drive through the mountains, I arrived to find I shared my traditional round hut with warthogs, impala and nyala. Indeed, dinner was impala stew and I took drinks overlooking the catfish and terrapin waterhole. I could also see the eyeshine of a crocodile which could spell the end of the waterhole being called catfish and terrapin.

All of the safaris I had undertaken up to this time had been in specially adapted trucks with drivers, spotters and fellow passengers, apart from the walking safari in Zambia where I was accompanied by two rifle carrying rangers. Here was different, here I could go out into the bush alone and on foot and enjoy the scenery and the wildlife. The downside of this was that there were no leopard or lion which might mistake me for lunch, or elephant, hippo or buffalo which could decide to trample me underfoot.

The experience was wonderful. I was walking in the wild African bush and there were blesbok, snorting, grunting and shaking horns; small groups of zebra stampeding; nyala males locking horns and impala spitting. All around there were bright, colourful birds, the buzz of insects, the sun beating down, and not a road, building, pylon or vehicle in sight or earshot, pure wilderness.

I returned for lunch, a swim, a spot of sunbathing, and then I was back into the bush. In the evening some Swazi dancers entertained, and at dawn I returned to the bush. Already Swaziland with its lovely, simple, happy people was one of my all time favourite places.

That afternoon I returned to South Africa and an appointment with the Kruger National Park which, like Swaziland, is a little smaller than Wales. It is mind blowing to think of a game viewing park the size of a country, and this one also borders Zimbabwe to the north and Mozambique to the east where it joins the Great Limpopo Transfrontier Park.

Leaving Swaziland, tourists were once again treated to a dance show, this time by children dressed in leaves like little munchkins. They shook themselves so you could here the leaves rustle, whilst their mothers were seated on the floor, desperately selling trinkets.

Kruger has many gates, lodges and camps; and numerous trails for guided safaris, or even self-drive safaris. One lady I came across in a VW Polo simply got out of her car and pointed me towards a rock where she had seen a cheetah lazing in the sunshine, "...about three miles back." She had that Australian accent that raises the tone of the voice at the end of a sentence. Almost as if she were asking a question. You might read this and do the same? Needless to say by the time I reached said rock, the cheetah had been warned of my intended visit, and had walked out of sight.

I checked into the Berg En Dal lodge where there were lovely walks down to the river for spotting birdlife and saw splendid starlings, marabou storks, hornbills and another fish eagle. There were also fruit bats flying overhead.

I had booked two game drives. On the first, a sunset drive, we saw five more rhino, had some wonderful close encounters with giraffe, laughed at the yawning hippos, encountered herds of buffalo, elephant and many diverse antelope. I saw giant spiders, tortoises and a goshawk eating a snake, or trying to as it was harassed by both a mobbing eagle and its impatient squawking mate. None of them were happy about the situation, least of all the snake, which was writhing helplessly in a lost cause.

It was whilst enjoying a braai back at the lodge I had a message to phone home.

I had to cancel Cape Town and organised a flight home for the next night. I meandered back to Jo'burg after breakfast, stopping off to trek up to God's Window, wander around Bourke's Potholes and stare in wonder at Blyde River Canyon, absolutely stunning, and the largest "green" canyon in the world. Beautiful, beautiful places, but my mind was in a blur. And so, sadly and prematurely I was homeward bound.

Chapter 12

South Africa.

The Cape and Whales

Five years later I arrived back in South Africa, this time in Cape Province, hampered by my elder brother for whom my lifestyle of gallivanting is quite alien, but he was willing to give it a go. To accommodate Alan, I was willing to be organised, so I booked us a five day Garden Route tour on something called the Bokbus. But first, a 24 hour opportunity to discover Cape Town.

The Cape, is separated from the rest of South Africa by several mountain ranges and a huge inhospitable desert called the Great Karoo. Thus most of its wildlife has evolved slightly differently from elsewhere. Not as diverse as Madagascar, say, but just different enough to be classed as separate species. The same seems to be true for the towns and people of the Cape. They appear just a little more mellow than their northern counterparts. Indeed my first impressions of Cape Town were of a much safer, calmer, friendlier place than Jo-burg.

It is called the Mother City, and wherever you are in this beautiful place, always seeming to guard over you like a protective behemoth, is the iconic Table Mountain. It is everywhere you look, often covered by its cloudy tablecloth, but never foreboding or looming, it is the most welcoming of presences. I would be climbing it after the Bokbus experience.

We had arrived tired and late so spent our first evening in the Backpackers Hostel at the bar where I chatted to a school group of youngsters from Bromley in Kent. They had been awarded this holiday for achieving good GCSE results. Most kids are lucky if they get a MacDonald's as a reward. Yet these teenagers were propping up the bar half a world away, and they were delightful all the same.

How better to discover a city but with the hop-on-hop-off bus tour, and that is precisely what we hopped on, the Big Red Bus. The Victoria and Albert Waterfront complex and the Clock Tower were our first stops, and we were impressed with the quality of the infrastructure of these modern landmarks. However, these were not nearly as impressive as the group of huge Cape Seals who had hauled themselves up onto a jetty and were sunning themselves lazily whilst barking bad-temperedly at any passers-by.

We also enjoyed the views from the cable car station, taking people up and down the mountain, and then the two beach communities of Camps Bay and Bantry Bay. Situated behind Table Mountain there are lovely views of Lion's Rock, and the Twelve disciples, rocky promontories reaching down to the ocean. You can see where the beach meets the rock formation and where volcanic granite pushed through sedimentary slate millions of years ago. Also there were pretty white houses on the gentler green slopes, between the haphazardly placed boulders, before the sheer sides of the mountain itself.

Here I ascended a red and white lighthouse and inexplicably experienced severe vertigo when emerging onto the light platform. Bizarrely I had to cling to the inner wall, feeling constantly that the slope of the platform would tip me over the edge. Alan cruelly mocked my predicament.

District Six was another highlight. This had been a cosmopolitan area where Cape Malays and coloureds, blacks, whites and Indians lived harmoniously until the apartheid government decided to clear it. They claimed it was a den of iniquity, rather than the peaceful, vibrant community (a den of equality) which would have denied their apartheid philosophy. The forced removals were highly significant, and after the area was bulldozed it remained undeveloped. There have been several attempts at development and restitution of the land to the original inhabitants, but with them ageing, and lawyers profiteering, the place has become a political football.

Nearby is trendy Woodstock which nearly went the same way as District Six, but managed to survive. With much of its Victorian style architecture lovingly restored, it has become a desirable and fashionable historic suburb.

Each hop off could easily last an hour, and with so many stops, I thoroughly enjoyed the experience. So much so, that when Alan hopped off for his bed, I went around again and departed at the cable station to walk happily downhill towards the ocean and the Backpackers Hostel.

A very simple evening followed, beer then pizza washed down with a Cape Pinotage wine. This was a heavy red which I have decided is my favourite; fruity with a hint of tarmac. I chatted to Gino the barman, a strange experience. I thought all South African barmen were in London.

The next morning Dave from Bokbus picked us up. Dave was a tall suntanned tour guide who also enjoyed Cape Red and described himself as coming from a drinking village with a fishing problem. He endeared himself even more to us when he explained we could listen to any music on the bus so long as it was the Eagles. We were Dave's first pick up; we now drove around the city to collect schoolteacher Ashley, Lin-Lee, a doctor from Birmingham, Swedish twins Caterina and Christiana, and Aussie Elise.

The first leg of the tour was 300 miles East to Albertinia via Riviersonderend where we took lunch. Our first stop had been to view The False Bay, a large enclosed body of water flanked by huge mountains. It is so-called as sailors returning from the East mistook it for Table Bay, which itself is guarded by Nelson Mandela's prison, Robben Island. There is a breeding colony of Cape seals here which attract some of the hugest great white sharks. There are also large waves which attract surfers. Not a promising combination. As we looked down from the road you could see the surfers, and you would swear they were being followed by huge, menacing shadows. The western promontory of False Bay is the actual Cape of Good Hope, and sailors needed to round this to enter the sheltered Table Bay

We continued into the Little Karoo, or Klein Karoo; through mountain passes, past rugged farmland and bush, and in every direction cloud-capped mountains. It was late October, and therefore Spring, but decidedly cooler in the interior. Alan was beginning to moan about the cold when in early evening we rocked up at the Garden Route Game Lodge.

"Are we too early to check in?" enquired Dave.

"No, you can check in any time you like" replied the diminutive desk clerk.

"But you can never leave!" I responded with a grin.

"No," said the clerk checking the register. "You must go tomorrow", he looked slightly puzzled. "You wish to stay longer?"

"No, sorry, we've had it in the car all day, the Eagles," I tried to explain.

His eyes brightened. "You can see the eagles circling the rocks to the north," he was pleased to assure us.

We had to hurry and freshen up as we had a sunset game drive booked, and the light was beginning to fade. Alan, dithering, took to his bed and told me to wake him for dinner. Unbelievable, a real highlight of the trip and he would sleep through it.

"There'll be blankets," I told him, but he was having none of it.

As it happened, the game drive was unimpressive. Sure, we saw the animals; elephant, giraffe, impala, springbok, ostrich, and even lion; but they were all in their own enclosures, a little like going to a safari park at home. The Cape, I'm afraid, has been tamed and the game protected in managed game reserves. The setting though was wonderful and the sunset impressive, and back at the beautifully appointed lodge, beer, wine, a multi-course meal and the craic went down very well, around a log fire and under a moonrise equally impressive.

I loved returning to the lodge after the game drive. In the garden was a large ornamental pool and the chirping of the various insects a couple of hours previously had now been replaced by the slightly more melodious chirruping of the frogs. Cacophonous, but easy on the ears. Moths attracted by the garden lights appeared to dance to their tune.

This first day with a new group and 300 miles of travelling had been interesting. The views east from Cape Town had never been less than stunning, especially looking back at a disappearing Table Mountain. We had passed mile after mile of rich arable farmland before entering the rugged desert. But of most interest was the gelling in of the travellers, the getting-to-know-you bit. Alan was a little too forward, spouting his views on 'foreigners' in general and Muslims in particular. This didn't go down well, and too often I found myself wincing. The twins and Ashley were rather reserved, whilst Lin, our doctor was quite ebullient. The star of the show, however, was Elise. A nurse from Canberra, she was never slow to come forward, and immediately argued with Alan's views. We liked her, but being Australian, she was the target for all our jokes, and we ended up teasing her mercilessly.

This huge distance, in one day, in a cramped minibus, may seem a ball-breaker, but with Elise it literally flew by. Every subject was covered, from convicts to Kylie, cricket, rugby and Aussie rules, Crocodile Dundee, Steve Irwin, and even the inimitable Dame Edna Everage. A great laugh, and wonderful sport.

One night we had been discussing the social problems faced by Aborigines when a nosy busybody came over to our table and asked us not to use that word. "We prefer native Australians," she announced. Elise told her to piss off, then laughed uproariously.

The next day at the Garden Route Lodge we were up at dawn, and Alan consented to join us on a similar but much warmer game drive. We stopped half way to disembark and spend some time with three cheetahs; brothers who were tame enough to stroke, but not to play with.

"Those claws and teeth, even playfully, could cause serious problems," explained the guide. "Cheetahs haven't been known to attack humans, except pregnant women. Something to do with the smell of hormones," she continued. How strange, but what wonderful cats, and a special memory.

We did manage to leave the Garden Route Safari Lodge, after breakfast, and headed to Mossel Bay where we turned north and over the Outeniqua pass, back into the Klein Karoo. This, Dave told us, was Ostrich land. Sure enough we passed dozens of farms with thousands of ostrich grazing by the roadside.

Before long we pulled into a tourist ostrich location and were delighted by the huge birds craning around our necks to peck at food strategically located on our persons. Everyone had a try at riding them, but we were all too nervous to experience a gallop. The keepers showed us ostrich racing, and naturally there was the opportunity to purchase ostrich related memorabilia. I loved the hand painted ostrich eggs.

I have to admit I felt a little guilty riding birds. After all, at home Kaz won't let me ride a horse. She reckons I'm too big. Here I just looked like a demented Bernie Clifton.

Following lunch (ostrich kebabs, medium rare, with the texture of fillet steak, but a gamey taste) Dave drove us to the Cango caves where he had booked us on the Adventure Tour. How thoughtful. In the reception were some facsimiles of the cracks and holes we would have to fit into. They were tight.

Disregarding my previous vertigo I risked major claustrophobia and joined the tour. My brother was nowhere to be seen. Throughout there were lovely roof crystals, grottos and weird and wonderful shapes of stalagmites and stalactites.

After the Grand Hall, and some tricky climbs and descents. we came to Lumbago Alley. This was aptly named as it was a long, tight crawl leading to the Devil's Chimney. Then there was the Tunnel of Love, a squeeze only 12 inches wide in parts which deposited me into the Coffin. This led into the Devil's Kitchen, and the only exit was up the Chimney, 12 feet high and kinked in the middle to trap the wider girth. There was a further a crawl and finally I had to push myself through an even smaller gap to land head first onto the floor of the final chamber. This was where I got stuck.

Ashley had been ahead of me and had vanished. I suddenly hated him. Why had he left when he knew he should wait to help the next person through? Behind me I lost my shoes and could get no purchase on any wall. I was beginning to panic, lighthouse style, when suddenly I felt a petite Aussie hand on my backside, and with a heave Elise pushed me out, birthing style, and I fell unceremoniously onto the chamber floor.

"I believe these are yours," she laughed handing me my Crocs, after I had helped pull her through.

"You berk!" was all the sympathy Alan, who himself had chickened out, could muster. Ashley merely laughed, and by the time Dave drove us into the Backpacker's Hotel in Oudtshoorn, I was over it, but never allowed to forget it.

Ostrich steaks for dinner, still tender, still a touch gamey, cooked on a traditional braai, a barbecue using only wood for fuel.

We watched a game of cricket and Hans, the owner described how South African sport was inevitably, according to him, in decline due to the quota system.

"They're trying to reverse decades of lack of opportunity. And now all teams have to include blacks and coloureds into their squads, whether they're good enough or not," he complained.

"Now, those who get there on ability are doubted, and many whose ability should merit them a place are discriminated against."

There will inevitably be many false dawns and steps backward before the decades of devastating apartheid can be despatched to the annals of history.

That night Hans showed us how to spot the Southern Cross constellation. He had mellowed after his earlier rant.

From Oodsthoorn we headed back out to the coast and spent some time admiring the views from Dolphin Point. We spotted pods of dolphins in the distance including spinners. From Wilderness we hired kayaks for a paddle on the inland lagoon behind Wilderness beach, pleasant but uninspiring. Then, after a quick lunch of Gorgonzola pasta in Knysna we headed east for the Tsitsikama forest. I am sure it is a wonderful place, but with the weather closing in we only had brief windows to enjoy its highlights, one of which was the Storms Rivermouth Walk. This included a series of suspended wooden bridges joining an auditorium of granite cliffs and precipices. The area is permanently populated by baboons with fearsome jaws who exist solely to steal your food.

"Never leave the doors or windows open on the bus," warned Dave. "If you want to get back on it!"

It is possible to overuse the word stunning, but all along the Garden Route, especially this eastern end, there was stunning coastal scenery.

We overnighted in storm lashed tents and began our return as early as we could get ourselves dried off. The rain prevented us from admiring the highest bungee jump in the world, and we briefly stopped to overlook Plattenberg Bay, and then on to view the twin heads of Knysna from the eastern one, before being forced back inland into the Karoo to find some decent weather. That was the good thing about Dave, he knew how to squeeze the best out of a bum deal, and in the welcome sunshine he took us to Calitzdorp for winetasting, Ladismith for cheesetasting and Barrydale to visit the world famous Ronnie's Sex Shop, not as sleazy as it sounds.

It used to be simply Ronnie's Shop, then some of Ronnie's "friends" added the word sex on the sign for a joke and people flocked to it, so Ronnie turned his shop into a pub. Some visitors are genuinely disappointed, but most just take the photo and have a cold beer. Its popularity has never looked back.

The spot Dave brought us to for our final sleepover was different to anything we had experienced thus far. It was a bunkhouse attached to a farm in a valley surrounded by rolling, undulating green hills. The hillside meadows were populated by cows, sheep and horses, and we were welcomed by a Staffordshire Bull Terrier called Punch.

Elise and I kitted up and took two horses on a hack around the hilltops for spectacular wilderness views. We returned to find Punch greeting us as enthusiastically as if we were long lost friends.

Next to the bunkhouse was a small lake which only a few miles further north would have been home to crocodiles and hippos. Here it was calm and peaceful, and I took to a kayak accompanied by Punch to glide along and admire the most wonderful, idyllic sunset. As I drifted lazily along with my faithful dog at my feet, and a trusty steed waiting for me back at the ranch I hummed Desperado. Far from any Life In The Fast Lane, I was Taking It Easy and it was certainly a Peaceful Easy Feeling. Dave's never-ending Eagles tapes were taking their toll, and you know I've always been a dreamer.

A lovely Xhosa lady called Mthobeli arrived to cook us the most delicious chicken dinner which I demolished with a whole bottle of Pinotage as we chatted about naughty baboons, missed bungee opportunities, dolphin spotting, cage diving with great white sharks, and the wonderful birds we see all the time in the temperate land of Karoo.

"Tomorrow is whales and penguins," assured Dave, but I was Already Gone.

Mthobeli returned to cook breakfast and then we left this beautiful valley for Swellendam and Cape Agulhas beyond.

This is the most southerly point in the whole of Africa, and Dave, Alan and I sat on a bench looking south over the most beautiful, seemingly endless, blue ocean. Here was where the Indian Ocean meets the Atlantic. Alan pointed to the right. "So Australia is over there," he confidently asserts.

"No, that's to the west and South America, directly ahead is Antarctica. Australia is to our left, south-east," I corrected.

"Don't be a berk! What do you know?" Alan angrily insulted me.

"No, he's right, Al," Dave interjected, "Australia's to our left."

Alan just harrumphed and got up to walk towards the lighthouse.

"Asshole!" I thought. He hadn't even contemplated an apology.

However I wasn't about to get any satisfaction at the lighthouse, where I had another inexplicable bout of acrophobia, and my backside of a brother just laughed as I clung to the wall inexplicably unable to walk anywhere near the edge.

Back on the bus Dave took the coast road to DeKelders, at the western end of Walker bay. Out beyond the kelp we could see three, maybe four whales, then one breached far out, and the excitement was tangible, but it proved nothing compared to Hermanus.

Hermanus is a little town on the coast popular with retirees and whale watchers. Next to a car park, between the little group of shops and the sea is a grassy knoll where people sit and wait. So I did just that with Ashley and Lin, who had some fearsome camera equipment, whilst Alan and the girls went to seek out lunch and other shopping opportunities.

Directly in front of the grassy bank was a bay which, because of some trick of the light or optical illusion appears to lap at your feet, even though it must have been well over 100 yards away. We knew where to look, because everyone was looking in the same direction.

After several minutes of peering out onto a calm, tranquil vista, there was a sudden collective intake of breath as, right in the centre of the bay the hugest thing you've ever seen in the sea rose up out of it. She seemed to hold the pose, then tilted to the side, and crashed back in with a thunderous splash. Wow!

It was a southern right whale (so-called because in the bad old days of whaling this was the ideal prey), a cow, and she breached another four or five times to the gasps of the delighted onlookers. She was soon joined by an even bigger whale, a bull, and the two engaged in courtship. After a while she breached one last time, and they were both gone.

The self-styled Mayor of Hermanus, a tall, black man with white beard, colourful robes and a jester headdress can often be seen strutting through the town blowing his vuvuzela. He had done so today, and apparently blows his horn every time a whale is sighted. He is a well known, busy character.

Back at the Bokbus we related the tale of our encounter to those who had missed it. Luckily, Lin had taken a number of photographs for them to enjoy.

We travelled on to Stoney Point, the home of a huge African Penguin colony. They are actually Jackass penguins, so-called because of their braying call, and have been reclassified for the Cape. On a promontory there was a boardwalk built above and among the colony. We could see young brown fluffy birds, some in crèches, being fed by their apparently smaller parents. The adults have a very sleek black and white coat.

There were groups diving in to catch dinner, and groups re-emerging from the waves, remarkably sprightly, landing upright with their full stomachs. Naturally enough, sea lion and shark also patrol these waters. The noise from the braying colony was cacophonous, as was the stench from their fishy faeces.

It was 7:30 and already dark when Dave dropped us off, back at the Backpackers Hostel and there was a series of tearful goodbyes and an exchange of email addresses. His closing gambit was, "You better let somebody love you, before it's too late."

The next day we were due to fly home at 6pm. So I had a choice; visit Robben Island, cage dive with great whites or climb Table Mountain. Whichever I chose I'd regret missing the other two. But wherever I go, I always seem to leave a reason to return, so maybe not. The mountain got the vote.

I rose early for a breakfast of fried banana waffles, then took a taxi to Platteklip Gorge to begin my ascent. The climb was fairly arduous at first, and my heart was pumping heavily, but the uneven limestone steps were well signed, and although there was some scrambling, the views when you could rest and turn towards Cape Town, were never less than spectacular. There was the Lion's Head and Devil's Peak, False Bay and even Robben Island, out in the ocean. In the foreground were three, ugly high-rise buildings which really looked out of place. Dave had ventured they may well have been the product of a few well placed town planning bribes.

It took two hours to reach the top where it was cold and wet, and I was soaked in sweat, but the sky was blue and the vistas clear. As I had discovered on other flat top mountains, notably the tepuis of Venezuela, the terrain was anything but flat. There were ravines and rises, and sharply formed rock sculptures which could rip your skin and turn your ankles. Occasional steel chains or wooden steps had been positioned to aid ascents and descents. Everywhere the flora was magnificent and totally different to below. It is a completely new and almost unique bio-system. All around were flowering trees and shrubs of all colours in a beautifully green and rocky Shangri-La.

After a rest I took up the Jan Smuts Trail around the mountain culminating at Maclear's Beacon, the highest point at 3,563 feet above sea level. The mountain was deserted so I had to be extra careful not to lose my way or risk a fall, and eventually I made my way back to Echo Valley at the head of the gorge. Here I sat on a rock overlooking Cape Town, devoured my packed lunch, and tried to reminisce and look back at my time in South Africa, journeys separated by 5 years.

First there'd been Isandlwana and Rorke's Drift; St Lucia's five ecosystems, Umfolozi, Swaziland, Kruger and the other big five (minus cats). Here we'd seen whales and penguins and Eagles. Dave and Elise had made the trip so interesting and he had single handedly driven over 1,000 miles. We'd also had cheetahs, ostriches, fearsome lighthouses and now this incredible mountain.

In between there had been the fight to get mum well after the stroke; therapy, dressing, feeding, toileting, learning to talk or even walk again, learning to use different equipment, the conversion of her home, the caring arrangements. A stroke affects unseen aspects of a person's life, not only removing mobility, but also brain functions which shape the victim's mental strength. Mum seemed to lose her capacity for compassion and empathy. She had developed a strange sense of humour.

I had found her a gardener, Eleanor, a retired colleague. Mum had a beautiful large garden and prided herself on maintaining its upkeep through years of widowhood. Now it was becoming increasingly difficult for Alan, John and I to manage. We had our own homes and gardens. Occasionally mum had even fallen out of her mobility scooter when attempting left handed weeding, something which had amused her.

Eleanor loved gardening and for six months loved mum's garden. Then she told me she had breast cancer and would have to give up the garden whilst she undertook treatment. When I told mum, she turned her chair to the bay window overlooking the garden, pulled herself to her feet and shook her left fist at it.

"Just my luck!" she shouted, "I finally get a decent gardener and she goes and gets cancer!" She sat back heavily, totally unembarrassed and completely unashamed.

I smiled at this as I rose to begin the journey back. Progress down the mountain was good, but my knees and ankles suffered. I was descending in shadow but at about 3pm I branched left to follow the contour and had the warmth of the sun on my face again. The path now gradually zigzagged back to the cable car station where I took a taxi to the hostel. I was making some notes in the back of the taxi when the elderly, white driver asked, "You a writer?" in a heavy South African accent.

"No, not really, just like to record where I've been," I replied.

"I am a writer," he declared. Evidently when not driving a taxi, I thought. "I've written about climbing and like to climb Table Mountain at least every month," he announced proudly.

Then even more proudly, "I'm publishing my first book." His grin disappeared and he shook his head, "My children don't like it, though."

"Oh, that's a pity," I said, looking up from my notes. "Why is that?"

"It's the title, 'South African Politics From The White Man's Point Of View'"

We arrived at the hostel, I paid him and wished him luck with his publication. Then I met up with Alan and told him about my climb.

"Why didn't you use the cable car?" he asked incredulously. "You're just too tight to spend money," he then concluded, scornfully

"So what have you done today?" I asked.

"Just mooched round the hotel and went for a bit of a walk," he replied.

I showered and changed and we made the 6 o'clock flight and were back home by noon the next day.

Mum passed away peacefully in 2013. The doctor said she had had a good eight years following her stroke. Eleanor is fully recovered. I was asked would I travel with Alan again, and replied "Not Until Hell Freezes Over". We lost him anyway, four years after mum passed. Too soon. He always talked about Dave.

"So put me on a highway,
and show me a sign,
and take it to the limit,
one more time"

courtesy of The Eagles, and Dave

Epilogue

My African adventures have seen me gallivanting through eleven countries, from the most northerly to the most southerly capes of this great continent. I've experienced the steamy west coast, and the ideal climate of the east. I've tackled dense jungle and parched deserts, great mountains and the Rift valley, birthplace of our species. I've marvelled at the world's longest river, from its twin sources to the delta, and from where our most mysterious, yet accomplished and long-lived civilisations flourished.

On many safaris I've sought out the magnificent animals of the jungle and savannah, all endangered, and the diverse biospheres of flora found at a variety of altitudes and climates. I've searched the waters both above and beneath the oceans. As in all my adventures, I have met the most amazing people, both indigenous and travellers like myself. They've been knowledgable, clever, humorous, caring and always interesting.

With any level of gallivanting there is the unseen that calls you to return. There is always something you missed. The more you experience the more you realise the limitations of your knowledge. I'd never known, for example, of the ancient civilisations of Ethiopia and how Christianity had evolved there, so different to Europe and the new world. Nor was I in the slightest aware that the continent's smallest country had over 20 tribes. Or for that matter that you could sleep with bees, fall off Victoria Falls, ride ostriches, walk the ocean reef, stroke cheetahs, buy hashish off tourist police, pass for David Beckham, graze with apes, take Russians for a ride, or be amongst so many elephants in the sunset.

So I am left with a sense of unfinished business. I am keen to see the Roman town of Leptis Magna in Libya, Timbuktoo in Mali and ancient Nubian ruins in Sudan. I want to trek to the Congo rainforest waterholes, called *baïs* where live the western lowland gorilla, the miniature forest elephant, chimps and bonobos. I've been to Botswana but missed the Okavango Delta. I've been to Mauritius and sat with giant tortoises who were alive to see the last dodo, but I've not been to Madagascar to see the lemurs.

And of course, I have yet to conquer Kilimanjaro.

So much done, so much still to do. Then a worldwide epidemic makes travelling to these less developed countries too risky for them. What could I introduce, what could I bring back?

And the world mindset is changing. Great explorers are no longer admired, indeed they may well be vilified. How can you be an advocate for protection of habitats when you are constantly increasing your own carbon footprint through flights and fossil fuel consumption?

What will be the new normal, whence will we return, how will our journeys continue?

Meanwhile, I have been to many islands. Random Jaunts Around Islands, you might say.

Excerpt from book 4 of the

Random Jaunts Trilogy

WHALE WATCHING IN THE AZORES

The Azores are an archipelago of seven inhabited islands belonging to Portugal and found in the middle of the North Atlantic Ocean. For centuries their economy was based on fishing and in particular whaling. In an enlightened world whaling is now quite rightly banned, but the infrastructure of spotting towers (Vigia) and experience are deeply ingrained in the islanders' culture.

The islands lie on various cetacean migration routes, but pods of sperm whale live here and feed off the giant squid living in the depths of the channels between the islands. Absolutely perfect for whale watching.

My destination was the island of Pico, dominated by a dormant volcano of the same name, via Lisbon. I thoroughly enjoyed a night in the Portuguese capital, experiencing the custom of port drinking. You must stand, and socialise, to enjoy a glass of port for the princely sum of one euro. I flew from Lisbon to Faial, and spent a couple of hours discovering the town of Horta before taking the ferry to Pico and a taxi from Madalena to its southernmost village, Lajes Do Pico.

I was staying at the Whale Come Hotel attached to Espacotalasse whale watching base. Apart from its awful name, the hotel was very basic. No reception or lounge, just a white-tiled breakfast room with a couple of kitchen tables and hard chairs. But I wasn't here for comfort, just to see whales. However, perhaps a decent sofa or armchair might have been a good idea for the 21 hours between each whale spotting trip.

Then there was the weather to contend with. Some sunshine and warmth would have been welcome, but The Azores are washed by the Gulf Stream and aired by the Trade Winds. They are wet. And during this particular trip, cold and wet.

I arrived on a Saturday. Sunday I was inducted into safety procedures for our boats, rigid inflatables called Zodiacs, and we went out onto the ocean for three hours and many wonderful dolphin encounters. We saw common dolphins plus dusky, bottlenose and Risso's, often in large schools, so that sometimes you felt you were in the middle of a huge aquatic playground. But we had seen no whales. Neither, unsurprisingly as it happens, had we seen any seals, as these mammals, so populous around our coastlines, have never made it this far into the ocean.

Delightfully our Zodiacs were constantly accompanied by Manx Shearwaters which swoop and glide so close to the tips of the waves and I would sing to myself *"Everybody's Talking"*, especially the lines that go *"Sailing on a Summer breeze, skippin' over the ocean like a stone"*.

Monday was too wild and windy and we could not put to sea. When you are not on the sea there is precious little to do here. We couldn't even swim as the medusas were blooming. Medusas we know as the deadly jellyfish, Portuguese man o' war

Tuesday morning dawned dry with traces of blue sky. I breakfasted long and found myself at the Espacotalasse at 9:20. People were gathering. Firstly the group of 12 French elderly folk who were here on a private charter, kept themselves to themselves, and spoke to no-one else. Then there was my group which comprised a Swiss family of five whose youngest, Marilou guessed I was Un Professeur de Mathematiques, close; a German father and daughter from Sardinia, and a young Austrian couple on their honeymoon. Being pregnant she preceded everything with, "I am pregnant so..."

Typical was, "I am pregnant so we cannot eat late," or, "I am pregnant so we cannot walk to the shops."

A fresh breeze was blowing away the bad weather, but the sea was still very choppy. We togged up in waterproofs and life protectors but were told the Vigia had spotted no animals. The Vigia are islanders who have evolved the vision to spot spumes ten miles out to sea. With no sightings and rough seas, it was decided we were not going out. We stood down. Bad news.

We kicked our heels for a couple of hours, drinking coffee and staring out to sea, and taking in the few rays of sunshine which came our way, hoping for better news.

Martha, the tall blond mother of Marilou asked who would be willing to risk a trip now, or wait till the afternoon. Someone said, "I am pregnant so I will not go." I also decided to defer till the afternoon, but the Swiss family wanted to go now. While we were still debating, news filtered through that whales had been spotted ten miles east, and we re-togged.

Arriving at our twelve seater Zodiac we were told the bumpiest area would be in the bow. I suggested that therefore all the children should go in front, and everyone agreed. No way. The front seat was mine, and we set off.

Clear of the harbour we turned left and into the wind and the ten foot swell. We were bouncing and landing with a juddering thud, then hitting the next wave. Spray was soaking us so fiercely you couldn't look directly ahead. And I found I had to adopt a gallop posture to minimise the pounding on ankles, knees and hips.

We endured this switchback, fighting the elements for over an hour. More than once I was reminded of the film The Perfect Storm as at one moment you could only see sky, the next the grey swirling waters of certain doom.

Suddenly the engines stopped. We came to a halt, just bobbing on the heaving ocean. Martha announced that this was the area where blowhole spray had been seen. Ridiculous, I thought, as you could not even see land, and anyway, any self-respecting cetacean would surely be sunning themselves further south, in the Canaries.

Ten, fifteen minutes passed. Nothing. I noticed the other craft about 500 metres astern, then to my right a dorsal fin, or surely just another shadow thrown up by the waves. Then six foot in front of the dorsal fin, a plume of spray. I can't claim first spotting because everyone pointed and shouted at once "La!". We were in French. But I was the first to notice "Il y a deux", and sure enough we saw a second dorsal fin and the elongated back of the sperm whale, for which we must thank the French for the alternative, more elegant name, Cachalot.

Gradually we followed the pair of females, only glimpsing them if we all three crested waves together. Then we lost them, then we regained them, then they both came to look at us to satisfy their curiosity. We were not giant squid so they slid beneath the boat and disappeared again.

After long minutes scouring every wave and shadow we saw them again, but three, no four dorsals; then five blowhole spumes and eventually we settled on seven. This was unusual behaviour because they normally remain at the surface only to regather oxygenating strength ready for their next 45 minute dive down to the depths. Regeneration usually takes about 15 minutes, then you see the flukes, then it is bye-bye. But no, no flukes this time, this was purely socialising behaviour between females and youngsters, and eventually we left them in pcacc. Our inflatables after all were merely interlopers.

The craft almost literally flew us back to harbour. With a following wind we rode the waves in an almost windless cocoon and swept majestically back into the sheltered port, a huge arc at over 45 degrees. Exhilarating. Only then I noticed I was soaked from head to foot and had been for the best part of three hours.

I stepped onto the concrete jetty and welled up. "Un des plus belle moments de ma vie!" I choked. Grammatically correct or not, everyone agreed.

There were more encounters over the next two days, and it surely is a most spectacular sight to see the tail flukes rise resplendently into the air to flick once and disappear into the depths. I've seen whales since, off Hermanus near Cape Town (southern right) and Samana Bay, Dominican Republic (humpback), and pilot whales (big dolphins, really) in Tenerife. But nothing compares to the first spot. I suppose I should have shouted "Thar she blows!", but "La! Il-y-a deux!" seemed just as good.

If you have enjoyed reading about my gallivanting, please leave a review on Amazon. You may like to visit my website on RandomJaunts.com for news of future exploits. Should you wish to comment on my adventures or ask questions about them, I would love to hear from you on geoffleo@hotmail.co.uk

Finally, a friend once asked why I didn't accompany my chapters with maps to show the routes of my journeys. The truth is that copyright infringement prevent me from including them. But, you could take a leaf out of the book of the schoolboy me. I always read with both a dictionary and an atlas at my side. Old fashioned, I know, especially with Google to consult, but still a good habit to get into.

THE END

Printed in Great Britain
by Amazon

75980977R00159